ENVIRONMENTAL QUALITY

ENVIRONMENTAL QUALITY

Edited by

J. T. COPPOCK
and
C. B. WILSON

School of the Built Environment
University of Edinburgh

SCOTTISH ACADEMIC PRESS
EDINBURGH AND LONDON

PUBLISHED BY
SCOTTISH ACADEMIC PRESS LTD.
25 PERTH STREET, EDINBURGH 3

Distributed by
Chatto & Windus Ltd.
40 William IV Street
London WC2

First published 1974

SBN 7011 2032 0

Printed in Great Britain by R. & R. Clark Ltd., Edinburgh

Contents

Notes on contributors

F. J. C. Amos, CBE, BSc(Soc), DipArch, SPDip, ARIBA, PPRTPI

is the City Planning Officer of Liverpool, and was President of the Royal Town Planning Institute 1971/72. He is a sociologist and architect as well as a town planner and plays a major role in the corporate management structure of Liverpool Corporation. He is a member of the Planning and Transport Research Advisory Council, advising the Secretary of State for the Environment, and has recently chaired a Working Group of the Centre for Environmental Studies on 'Education for Planning'.

E. Brooks, MA, PhD

is Senior Lecturer in the Department of Geography, University of Liverpool. From 1958 to 1967 he was a Councillor in Birkenhead C.B., and Chairman of the Building Committee. He was M.P. for Bebington and a member of the Committee of Public Accounts from 1966 to 1970. He became President of the Conservation Society in 1967.

Connie Byrom, MA

is a research worker at the Architecture Research Unit, Edinburgh University, and has carried out a number of studies into the social aspects of housing. Her present interests centre on the provision, maintenance and use of shared open space in different forms of housing. Her recent publications include a study of high density low rise housing and, jointly with her husband, a review of shared open space in recent Scottish private housing.

J. T. Coppock, MA, PhD

is Ogilvie Professor of Geography, University of Edinburgh. He was elected President of the Institute of British Geographers in 1973. He has been a member of numerous government committees on natural resources, including England Committee, Nature Conservancy (1965–71); Education and the Countryside (1968–); Scottish Joint Committee on Information for Planning (1968–), and was Specialist Adviser to the Select Committee on Scottish Affairs in 1971–2. He is the author of more than seventy books and articles, mainly on land use.

Eileen Crofton, MA, BM, BCh

has worked since 1961 as Honorary Research Assistant in the Department of Respiratory Diseases, University of Edinburgh, and is now Medical Secretary of the Scottish Committee of Action on Smoking and Health. She has published papers on the epidemiology of lung cancer and chronic bronchitis, and was the co-author of a report 'The Social Effects of Chronic Bronchitis' in 1965.

A. J. Crosbie, MA, PhD

is Senior Lecturer in the Department of Geography, University of Edinburgh. He directed a small team carrying out an Air Pollution Survey of Edinburgh from 1966 to 1970 on contract to the Warren Spring Laboratory. He has particular interests in the environmental problems of urbanisation in tropical lands and the effects of natural hazards.

R. W. Gloyne, BSc, PhD

joined the Meteorological Office in 1940 and was engaged in weather forecasting (mainly with Bomber Command) during the war. From 1946–55 he was with the National Agricultural Advisory Service in SW England and since then has been concerned with the impact of weather and climate on agriculture in Scotland.

G. Hoinville, BSc

is Co-director of Social and Community Planning Research, an institute which specialises in the application of survey research methods to social research problems. During the past few years he has made a special study of the measurement of trade-off preferences with particular reference to environmental attitudes and priorities.

R. G. Hopkinson, BSc, PhD, FIEE

is Professor of Environmental Design and Engineering at University College, London, and a consultant to the Department of the Environment on problems of environmental evaluation. He has made a special study of methods for the quantification of subjective responses and is now applying these techniques to the evaluation of noise and visual intrusion in relation to urban motorways.

P. M. S. Jones, BSc, PhD, FRIC, MInstP, AMBIM

is Director of the Joint Department of Trade and Industry/UKAEA Programmes Analysis Unit, Chilton. He graduated in natural sciences and managed teams engaged on chemical and materials research until entering the field of techno-economic appraisal when the PAU was formed in 1967.

Una Maclean, MD, PhD, DPH

is a Lecturer in Social Medicine at Edinburgh University, where she is concerned with developing courses in sociology for medical undergraduates and diploma students. Her research interests stem from an interactionist approach and relate to the differing views of professionals and clients regarding various human misfortunes. She has published numerous articles and three books.

A. E. Philip, MA, PhD

is head of the Department of Psychology, Bangour Village Hospital, and an Honorary Lecturer in the Department of Psychiatry, University of Edinburgh. While on the research staff of the M.R.C., he was concerned with studying social and psychological aspects of suicidal behaviour.

W. R. D. Sewell, MA, PhD

is Professor of Geography and Economics, University of Victoria (B.C.). He has held various research posts in government and universities, and is Consultant to the United Nations on flood problems and to various government agencies in Canada and the United States. In addition he is a member of numerous committees, including the National Advisory Committee on Water Resource Research (1968–) and the National Science Foundation Task Force on the Social Consequences of Weather Modification (1971–). He is the author of more than seventy books and articles, mainly on the management of air and water resources.

R. A. Waller, MA, MInstHE

is head of a multi-disciplinary consultancy team concerned with environmental development in Atkins Research and Development, Epsom. He is Vice-President of the British Acoustical Society and a member of the Society of Environmental Engineers. He has written many technical papers and a book, and lectures to various post-graduate courses.

Acknowledgments

This book had its origin in a symposium. Its compilation has depended upon the cooperation and assistance of a number of people whose names do not appear in the text and we would like to express our thanks particularly to Mrs Dorothy Shannon (née Dick) and Miss Helen Simpson. We are also grateful for permission to use copyright material in certain instances.

J. T. COPPOCK
Ogilvie Professor of Geography

C. B. WILSON
Professor of Architectural Science

School of the Built Environment
University of Edinburgh

March 1973

CHAPTER 1

Environmental quality: an introduction

J. T. COPPOCK

Environmental quality is, in a very real sense, all things to all men, for the quality of an environment is judged by the attitudes of individual men to it, and such judgments are likely to vary with age, culture, education, experience, income and sex—in short, with life style, and with personality. The American Public Health Association has suggested four levels of concern in assessing environmental health, viz., (a) ensuring survival, (b) prevention of diseases and accidents, (c) maintenance of an environment suited to man's efficient performance, and (d) preservation of comfort and the enjoyment of living (Stead, 1960, p. 313), and these might well form the basis for an assessment of environmental quality. Whether conceived in medical, economic or psychological terms, these criteria are all assessed on a human scale, though they are progressively more difficult to measure.

This book is primarily concerned with the quality of the urban environment, in which all but a small proportion of the inhabitants of developed countries spend by far the greater part of their lives. This concentration of population in large urban agglomerations has probably been the most important single change affecting the lives of ordinary people over the past hundred years. Nowhere is this more true than in the United Kingdom, where the shift from a predominantly rural to a predominantly urban population began earlier and has gone further than anywhere else. Already by the middle of the nineteenth century as many people lived in towns as in the countryside, and although the urban population in the United Kingdom (as elsewhere) cannot be very accurately assessed from available data, the proportion is probably nearer nine-tenths than the four-fifths indicated by the population census. Similar trends are observable in other developed countries.

Such changes have undoubtedly brought great benefits, by permitting the specialisation of employment on which an industrial society depends and by providing access to a much wider range of services and facilities than would have been possible in a dispersed rural community with the resources and technology then available. Equally, however, there were disadvantages from such concentration, some so obvious in human ill-health and mortality that they quickly led to remedial action to ensure at least minimum standards, as with the Public Health Acts, and others whose seriousness is only now coming to be appreciated. Still others have emerged, as social and technological changes, especially the successive revolutions in transport, have transformed the nature of cities. In their most extreme form these are seen in the spread of urban decay in the Chicago ghetto and in the sprawl of Los Angeles, where the motor car has played a major part not only in shaping the city but also in determining the quality of life that is possible in it.

For the most part, this urban environment was like Topsy—it 'just growed'. Very few British towns and cities were ever conceived as a whole, and much of what was planned was inevitably created in ignorance both of the likely consequences of such a new environment and of the kinds of environment in which people would like to live. The same is true of other parts of Europe and, while the planned component in most cities in the New World is much more evident, the planning problems are no less acute. What has become increasingly clear is that practices which are tolerable for an individual or on a small scale are not acceptable in a large urban community. A family living in an isolated cottage can dispose of sewage through a septic tank without risk of serious pollution, a single car may not greatly affect noise levels, and an individual building may not modify the local climate to any considerable extent; but waste disposal for the population of a city becomes a major problem, the noise from an urban motorway may cause mental stress and a mass of buildings may create a substantially different urban climate. Moreover, to a degree which generally increases with technological development, those who suffer most from such modifications of the urban environment are often not those responsible for bringing the changes about. Both kinds of problems are particularly well-illustrated by air pollution. Fires in individual homes, each contributing to the well-being of a family, help to create an atmosphere which is bad for all families; and a major source of emission of pollutants, such as a factory chimney, does not generally affect people working in the organisation responsible, but only those who live down-wind, a situation which has been aggravated by increasing personal mobility and the flight to the suburbs.

A rapidly-growing concern with the problems created by man-made environments has been characteristic of the last decade and found expression in the United Kingdom in the 'Countryside in 1970' conferences, in the creation of the Natural Environment Research Council and in the appointment of a standing Royal Commission on Environmental Pollution, as well as in the enlargement and renaming of the ministry responsible for housing and planning in England and Wales, the Department of the Environment. Similar developments have taken place in other countries, notably in the United States with the creation of the Environmental Protection Agency and the obligation on public bodies to prepare environmental impact statements, while international recognition of the importance of these problems is to be found in the Stockholm Conference on the Environment, held in June 1972, and in the creation later that year of a new United Nations Environmental Programme. These developments have made people increasingly aware of some of the consequences of living in large cities; but the range of effects caused by such large concentrations of people is still only very imperfectly understood, as are the solutions of the resulting problems, both in existing towns and in those which must be built to house or rehouse a population already born, let alone the vast increases predicted by the end of this century. Moreover, the emphasis so far has been essentially negative, on preventing the harmful from happening, rather than on achieving a good environment that makes a positive contribution to the quality of life. To review the possibilities of making such an approach, the School of the Built Environment at Edinburgh University established an Environmental Standards Study Group; and it is largely as a result of the initiative of this Group that this collection of papers has been published.

Any discussion of environmental quality inevitably poses acute problems of selection and balance. In part these arise from the interdisciplinary nature of the subject-matter and from the little work that seems to have been done in many of the fields which bear upon environmental problems; but it is also a consequence of the fact that urban systems are open systems. There is no point at which it can be said that the impact of a particular city ceases, short of the global system of which it is part, and modern technology is steadily extending the range of a city's contacts with the outside world. The inhabitants of cities in developed countries draw their supplies of food and, to an increasing extent, of water, from far afield, while their waste-products may also affect a wide zone far beyond the built-up area, as is epitomised by the impact on Scandinavian countries of atmospheric pollutants originating in Great Britain. Increasingly, too, they seek their recreation in the surrounding countryside, and the motor car, which confers on each individual the freedom to go where he wishes, may collectively restrict this freedom, especially in areas within easy reach of towns. Indeed, many of the environmental problems created by urbanisation are most acute in the twilight zone between town and country.

Much of the recent discussion about environmental quality, especially in the United Kingdom, has been concerned with problems on and beyond this urban fringe, especially with the consequences for wildlife and for the visual appearance of the countryside. Countryside Commissions have been created for both England and Wales and for Scotland to conserve rural amenity, and it is only recently that a Parliamentary Committee has recommended the creation of a Commission for the Urban Environment and the establishment of Environmental Management Committees in each urban area (Select Committee on Scottish Affairs, 1972). It is true that the emphasis on the countryside was itself an attempt to redress an imbalance implicit in earlier planning legislation, that the dividing line between town and country is increasingly arbitrary, and that any solutions to environmental

problems must take account of both intra-urban and extra-urban effects;
but it is the urban environment which presents the most acute and
pressing problems and where the question posed in the title of a report
of the working party preparing for the Stockholm Conference (Dartmouth *et al.*, 1972), 'How do you want to live?', must be answered.

Yet to have considered the quality even of the urban environment
at all adequately would not have been practicable within the space
available, and discussion has therefore been restricted to aspects of three
major themes: the effects of urbanisation on the physical character of
the urban environment and on the well-being of its inhabitants; the
perceptions and preferences of these inhabitants; and the problems of
achieving environmental quality. Measurement of the changing
physical character of the urban environment is probably the easiest of
these tasks. Both the atmosphere and the hydrological cycle are substantially affected by the building of towns and cities, the former by the
shape and arrangement of buildings and by the discharge of gases and
solid pollutants, the latter by the replacement of a permeable cover of
vegetated soil by large areas of impermeable brick, concrete and
tarmac. Noise is another part of the physical system which is substantially affected by the arrangement and character of the components of
the built environment, although in itself it is largely a product of the
social and economic habits of city dwellers, especially their use of motor
vehicles. Smell, too, is a characteristic that contributes to (or more
frequently detracts from) the quality of the urban environment, a fact
that is all too obvious in those cities where there are noxious industries,
such as rubber manufacturing. Less obvious, but no less important, are
the effects of the urban environment on the mental, physical and social
well-being of the inhabitants themselves, a field of enquiry which
concerns a wide range of medical and social sciences. The ecology of
both physical and mental health and their relationship to human
living conditions are receiving increasing attention; so, too, are various
aspects of social pathology which may also be related, such as the
incidence of alcoholism, crime and vandalism. Discussion on this theme
illuminates some of the problems which must be solved in creating an
environment which will provide its inhabitants with clean air and
water, quiet and adequate space, and which will help to reduce the
likelihood of mental, physical and social ill-health.

The second theme, the perceptions and preferences of the inhabitants
of the urban environment, draws mainly on the social sciences, especially psychology and sociology. It is often said that the current concern
with environmental quality is largely confined to those from middle-
class backgrounds, and this bias is not surprising; for such people tend
to be more articulate on any subject. It may also be that, since only a
small proportion of time is spent outside the home or workplace, most
people are concerned primarily with the quality of the internal environments of their homes, and it is only when these are satisfactory that
much attention is paid to the external environment. Nevertheless, there

is abundant evidence that, even within a single country, neither perceptions of environmental quality nor environmental preferences are uniform, though the chains of causation are complex. Why, for example, had only some five per cent of those living near Heathrow airport, who were entitled to claim government grants towards the cost of reducing noise levels in their homes, done so by 1970, despite the considerable public outcry against this environmental hazard? (Hopkinson, 1970, p. 69). Was it because they could not afford the remaining fifty per cent of the cost, or because they did not regard noise levels as sufficiently high or annoying to justify such expenditure, or for some other reason? It is important that those who make policy and take decisions should know how far those in different social classes and with different life styles do differ in their perception of the environment and in the values they place upon the individual components, and how such differences, if they exist, can be measured; this is a neglected aspect of the study of urban environments in which contributors to this book have done pioneer work. How far these values and preferences should determine what, if anything, is done to improve environmental quality is a matter for debate, for entirely apart from questions of the nature of political and administrative decision taking, these preferences and values relate to past experience and cannot cover the full range of possibilities, many of which are not known to those questioned. Decisions will be needed on the weight that should be given to the creative imagination of the architect or planner who envisages new urban forms or proposes others which have never been attempted; to human needs, whether these are perceived or not; and to the conflict between urgent claims in the short run and the achievement of long-term goals. Policy makers will also need to decide how far the urban environment should be good for its inhabitants, present and future, as well as being thought good by those who live there now.

Defining long-term goals is fundamental to achieving environmental quality, the third theme, but there are many difficulties in the way. Each year for the next thirty years it will be necessary to build in Great Britain between 300,000 and 500,000 houses or their equivalent and an appropriate complement of factories, offices, schools, shops and the like (Stone, 1970a, p. 260). The actual figure will vary with the rate of population growth, but it is also dependent on the scale of replacement of older buildings. Some of these new dwellings will be built in New Towns and some on the outskirts of existing towns, but an increasing number will be replacements in the older, often decaying inner parts of cities, especially those which mushroomed in the first Industrial Revolution and so have a high proportion of substandard dwellings. Similar changes will be necessary in other countries. Answers are needed to such questions as: where shall such dwellings be built, what sort of structures shall be erected, at what density and on what layout? At present both the theoretical and the empirical foundations for such decisions are inadequate; there is no sound basis for saying whether a city is too large and so should not be permitted to grow further, or that a given density of housing is unacceptable. There is thus a need to define desirable as well as minimum standards and to base both firmly on fundamental research; it will also be necessary to recognise that they must change with rising standards of living and with technological progress. Yet even changing standards will not be easy to apply, for so rapid is the pace of technological advance that the life of buildings now being erected will greatly exceed that of the standards used in their construction. It is not improbable that present concepts of urban life will be made quite inappropriate by the electronic revolution, which may make the journey to work unnecessary for large numbers of people, and by the growth of leisure, which may give pride of place to the journey to play.

Whatever the shape of desirable future environments, there is little doubt that, despite the inadequacies of present knowledge of environmental requirements, the quality of living of most urban dwellers could be greatly improved by the wider application of present technology. Nevertheless, what can be achieved will be severely limited by non-technical constraints. These are largely administrative, economic and political, but the scope for overcoming such constraints is limited by past commitments and by present resources. Already an eighth of the gross national product of the United Kingdom is spent on extending, maintaining and servicing the built environment, and the proportion can be increased only by creating more wealth or by diverting resources used for other purposes, such as defence, education, health and welfare (Stone, 1970b, p. 38). The capital invested in the existing urban environment also acts as a constraint, in respect of both its location and its character.

An important theme which runs through the book, either explicitly or implicitly, is that of the perceptions of the professionals themselves—whether research workers, planners, technical experts or administrators. There is no comprehensive shared picture either of what the environment is or of what constitutes good quality in the environment, and this is a matter for particular concern when people take decisions or act on behalf of others. A lop-sided view of the character and relative importance of factors in the environment seems to be an almost inevitable side-effect of the development of the knowledge and skills which the specialist needs in order to work at a technically competent level (and in this sense the planning officer is as much a specialist as the academic); as a result, both the problems that are perceived and the solutions that are favoured have a professional bias. It is difficult to see how this effect can be avoided (short of a fundamental change in the nature of our society in general and of educational policy in particular), but its worst consequences can be prevented by recognising its existence and ensuring that technical skill alone is not mistaken for good judgment.

The discussion of environmental quality in this book cannot provide solutions to particular problems or to the problems of particular cities, though it is to be hoped that it will enlarge understanding of the factors involved and of the progress that has been made towards evaluating them. What must be appreciated is their interconnection and their complexity; a piece-meal approach often provides a solution that creates another problem. In the United Kingdom in the post-war period, for example, there has been such a concern to conserve agricultural land (in itself a desirable goal) that housing densities in New Towns have been increased to a point where there is a real risk of inadvertently creating the slums of tomorrow (Best, 1964); similarly, the application of daylighting regulations, again beneficial in themselves, has adversely affected levels of noise in the resulting buildings. It is not always appreciated that, even at a technical level, some compromise is necessary; for it is impossible to optimise simultaneously each of the factors involved in environmental quality. The assumption must also be avoided that the present represents some fall from grace in a pre-industrial Garden of Eden, in which everyone lived in attractive surroundings, free from the noises, smells and other assaults on the senses which characterise the present urban environment; for while the latter undoubtedly has many serious defects, many of these are a by-product of achieving standards of space, lighting and heating in homes and workplaces which would have seemed luxury itself to the peasant forefathers of members of the present generation, or even to their grandfathers.

Much of what has been written about the environment in recent years has understandably stressed what is wrong, and some critics have gone so far as to allege that these problems are the result of a conspiracy in which those responsible for environmental planning are deeply involved. There are undoubtedly weaknesses in their understanding of the problems they face and in the machinery for making decisions, but restraints of cost and of existing investment in the urban fabric cannot be wished away. It will be more productive to adopt a positive approach, recognising the great improvements that have been made in the internal environment of buildings since the Second World War (as well as the great deal that remains to be done) and considering how an external urban environment to match can be achieved. As with the problem of derelict land, the technology that creates many of the most pressing environmental problems is also capable of contributing to their solution.

REFERENCES

Best, R. H. (1964) *Land for New Towns*, Town & Country Planning Association, London.

Dartmouth, R., Lady (1972) *How Do You Want to Live?* A Report on the Human Habitat, H.M.S.O.

Hopkinson, R. G. (1970) 'The artificial environment and its implications' in *Communications and Energy in Changing Urban Environments*, D. Jones (ed.), Colston Papers No. 21, Butterworths, London, pp. 63–71.

Perloff, H. (ed.) (1969) *The Quality of the Urban Environment*, Resources for the Future, Washington.

Select Committee on Scottish Affairs (1972) *Land Resource Use in Scotland*, House of Commons Paper 511–i, 1971–2, H.M.S.O., London.

Stead, F. (1960) 'Levels in environmental health', *American Journal of Public Health*, 50, pp. 312–5.

Stone, P. A. (1970a) *Urban Development in Britain: Standards Costs and Resources 1964–2004*, Cambridge University Press, Cambridge.

Stone, P. A. (1970b) 'Some economic restraints on building and form development' in *Communications and Energy in Changing Urban Environments*, D. Jones (ed.), Colston Papers, No. 21, Butterworths, London, pp. 37–52.

CHAPTER 2

Urban climates and micro-climates

R. W. GLOYNE

The assessment and discussion of 'environmental quality' involves considerations wider and even less easy to define than those which serve to specify environments which are acceptable on purely physical and physiological grounds. Psychological and aesthetic factors are relevant and these are associated with a very wide spectrum of individual responses and preferences.

Urban climate and micro-climates are very extensive subjects—as evidenced, for example, by the voluminous proceedings of the W.N.O. and W.H.O. Symposium on Urban Climates and Building Climatology held in Brussels in 1968 (World Meteorological Organisation, 1970)—and this contribution will be limited to a brief account of those meteorological factors believed to be particularly relevant to environmental quality.

In order to make progress, it is clear that an investigator must be prepared to create a physical model based upon criteria derived from an examination of human responses. This attitude is even more necessary when dealing with psychological and aesthetic needs than when the investigation is concerned with physiological requirements. Human responses must be sought in defining the threshold values of physical variables, durations at particular levels, the acceptable combinations of different elements, sequences and the like which are necessary to develop a conceptual framework: for as expressed rather mildly by A. F. E. Wise (1970) '(as far as the wind environment is concerned) it would be a pity if aerodynamic knowledge outstripped that of human requirements'. The investigation might, for example, ask what are the threshold values of wind, temperature and sunlight, either singly or in combination, which induce holiday-makers to desert a sandy beach and move to the promenade cafes and, furthermore, to choose tables inside rather than on the pavement. Such an enquiry may appear trivial, but it might not be so regarded by a local authority considering how best to allocate resources in the development of their tourist potential. Indeed, if the meteorologist is to be enabled to assist resource managers, architects and planners, he must know a great deal more about how people react to external conditions, how they behave, how they utilise space during working time, when shopping and engaged in similar duties and, most important, during leisure activities when considerations relating to the quality of the environment might well be the dominant ones. A useful pioneer effort has been made by A. H. Paul (1971).

9

To clarify issues, it might be suggested that to achieve a desirable level of environmental quality it is necessary to highlight the following postulates.

(1) The situation must impose no more than an acceptable level of physiological stress—as expressed in terms of energy and mass (mainly water) exchange between the human and the surroundings, and of the pollution load. The level will depend upon such things as age group, sex, occupation, social and cultural groups, and, for a given individual, on the particular activity in which he is engaged.

(2) A degree of visual amenity higher than is necessary at many, if not most, places of work.

(3) Easy and safe access to, and freedom of movement and wide choice of habitats within, public places, e.g., parks, shopping centres, pedestrian precincts, sports arenas, museums, concert halls and other cultural centres.

In respect of (1), it should be noted, that a higher degree of physiological stress than is acceptable under working conditions might well be 'traded' by the individual for enhanced psychological satisfaction, as in some active pursuits, such as mountaineering, where stress is prized. The conflict between optimal physiological and psychological thresholds is clearly evident in the context of visual amenity. The desire for the maximum penetration of sunshine into rooms, and for a pleasing outlook, will certainly lead to a built environment in which the unit cost of temperature control would much exceed that required for denser and thermally more efficient structures and complexes. Similarly the desire for space and freedom of movement can lead to an apparent waste of physical resources and possibly an exposure to physiological stress requiring additional counter-methods.

If meteorological knowledge and expertise are to be mobilised in the most effective way to aid decision making by planners, categorised, codified and, as far as possible quantified, data on human responses to the quality of the environment are essential.

A useful point of departure is C. C. Wallén's (1970) categorisation of 'building climatology' as the analysis and interpretation of (a) the *macro-climate* of the overall surroundings of a building; (b) the *meso-climate* of the close surroundings of a building; (c) the *micro-climate* around a building; (d) the transport of moisture and heat through the building material; and (e) the indoor climate.

Categories (a) and (b) are the obvious concern of the meteorologist, (d) and (e) of the engineer whilst (c), dealing with the 'climatic sheath' of the building (Ryd, 1970), is a shared responsibility. Meteorologists are therefore concerned with the general (the 'regional') climate of the area; with the modifications imposed by the geometry and physical properties of the terrain; and with the interactions of the structure with this modified 'climate'.

The urban scene is one dominated by vertical or near vertical surfaces in contrast to the basically horizontal surfaces characteristic of rural areas and of sites on which the urban complex develops, and upon which meteorologists focus most of their attention. The difference in surface geometry materially influences airflow and the interception, transformation and exchange of radiant energy. Both these topics have been extensively studied in recent decades, particularly the first, but much remains to be done at all levels, not least in forging links between the controlled environment of the wind-tunnel and the real weather and climate.

Air movement and radiation balance, singly or in combination, account for most of the properties of the atmospheric environment, the most important of other inputs being that of precipitation, in all its various manifestations, and the agents of pollution. Other topics, electrical fields, for instance, will need attention at times.

The assessment of quality is peculiarly a matter of the joint action of several factors, but at this stage of knowledge there is little choice but to consider the individual meteorological factors separately.

THE WIND CLIMATE

The following must be considered:

(1) The regional wind impinging on the area. This is a matter of the global circulation and its modification by large scale geographical features.
(2) The characteristics of the general landscape upwind of the urban complex.
(3) The interaction between the incident wind and the complex of obstructions presented by the built-up area.
(4) Local circulations set up at and between individual buildings and groups of buildings.

The regional wind

At least over the more populated parts of the advanced countries, the broad features of surface wind régimes are known, although an inadequate network of continuous recording units leads to insufficient basic data on wind structure. Elsewhere uncertainties exist, even in the British Isles. For example, design data for the town centre of Cumbernauld in the Forth-Clyde valley were heavily dependent upon data from Glasgow and Edinburgh.

Information is not readily available on certain basic properties of the regional wind distribution, for instance on the incidence and duration of spells of light winds; and on other characteristics of wind important to aspects of atmospheric pollution on a regional scale such as mass transport, residence time and recirculation (mentioned for example by A. P. Altshuller (1970)). The relevant wind properties include the 'reliability', 'steadiness' or 'constancy' of wind (Singer and Nagle, 1970; Brooks, Durst, Carruthers, Sawyer and Dewar, 1950; Gloyne, 1959) and the sequential behaviour of wind. Other aspects concern gust speeds and the spectrum of turbulence generally.

Local wind circulations (meso-scale phenomena)

The regional wind is constrained in direction and altered in speed by landscape geometry (the lie of the hills and valleys) and is subjected to drag by the aerodynamic roughness of the surface.

Work on the topographic constraints to airflow is resulting in a firmer picture of the qualitative aspects of the flow pattern, for instance, that of M. E. Berljand (1970), and case studies such as those reported by J. van Eimern, R. Karschon, L. A. Razumova and G. W. Robertson (1964); and N. Rutter (1968); whilst some quantitative data for individual hill situations can be gleaned from papers by E. W. Golding and A. H. Stodhart (1952), J. R. Tagg (1957), and J. Frenkiel (1962). Over rolling country, with slopes of the order of $5°$ or less to the horizontal, the air flows preferentially around obstructions but with some increase of speed at shoulders. Otherwise it flows over them with an increase of speeds but usually without 'break-away'.

The analysis and presentation of data have been criticised. R. E. Munn (1970) notes that, whilst the 'prevailing wind' can be a useful concept, yet 'in many parts of the world . . . (it) can provide little guidance for engineering studies' but points to the 'useful solutions arising from the prestratification (of the wind data) on the basis of the problem in hand'. Whilst shortcomings in collections of official data can be admitted, it must be stressed that there is a strict limit to the amount of special processing which can be done as a routine and published for the general good. Such publication cannot even be considered unless a wide spectrum of interests can agree upon a series of categories for any contingency analysis. However, modern data processing facilities and an expanding data bank are available to meet many specific needs.

Urban wind circulations

Given the local (area) wind circulation, the impact of the wind on the complex, and the feed-back phenomena, must be examined. Two main classes of situations have emerged: (a) when the regional, and hence the local, winds are light; and (b) in all other cases.

With light winds an urban circulation can be set up, typically associated with the 'heat island' phenomenon and most marked when the vertical temperature lapse rate is small or reversed (an inversion). In brief, air at low levels moves from the periphery, radially into the urban centre (see, for example, Munn, 1970 and Georgii, 1970). The local wind speed necessary to override and destroy this circulation has been usefully related to the size of the urban complex and this is discussed later in the chapter.

With local speeds exceeding a threshold value, the interposition of an urban combination of bluff body obstruction and smaller scale roughness alters the three-dimensional character of the flow. A new field of flow (a new boundary layer) develops within and above the complex. The properties of this layer have a profound influence upon the circulation between and around structures and upon the transport and dispersal of pollutants emitted into the flow. Figure 1 (from Singer and Smith, 1970) illustrates the genesis of the new flow pattern whilst its

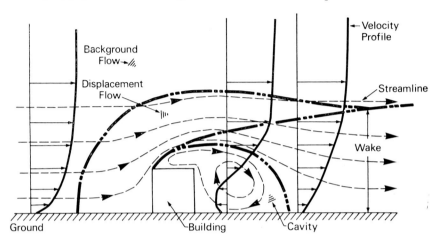

Mean Flow around a Cubical Building

FIG. 1. *The presence of a bluff structure in otherwise open terrain will produce aberrations in the wind flow generally similar to those shown. (From Singer and Smith, 1970.)*

gradual development with successive obstructions has also been studied (for example, Munn, 1970). However, the rate of growth with downwind fetch is not completely known: P. M. Jones, M. A. B. de Larrinaga and C. B. Wilson (1971) found evidence for an internal boundary layer which grows vertically at a slower rate than would be expected from observations in the open country, and recently W. Z. Sadeh, J. E. Cermak and T. Kawatani (1971) have noted similar phenomena in a wind-tunnel study of flow over a 'forest'. As a guide to the depth of this layer the ratio of the maximum speeds at varying intervals, from 5 secs to 30 secs to that over one minute, might be used as a criterion for the undisturbed flow, and on this basis N. Helliwell (1970) reports that over London (with an average roof height of 80–100 ft) the free-flow situation is reached at 200 ft: T. A. Singer and M. E. Smith (1970) suggest that, for cities in U.S.A., 'the layer extending from 150 m to 1,000 m above ground is usually free of low-level aerodynamic turbulence and building-induced down-wash'.

F. L. Ludwig's (1970) study in Dallas, Texas, draws attention to a characteristic of the structure of certain cities in which there is a central core of very tall buildings surrounded by a more regular array of mixed development of much lower average height (one might contrast, for example, the layout of Cumbernauld with its dominating town centre, with the whole central area of Edinburgh). This contrast suggests that two types of roughness could usefully be recognised: (a) that in which roughness elements of strongly differing dimensions are scattered randomly or in clusters. and (b) that in which elements of similar geometry are regularly disposed at distances of a multiple or so of their height. A. E. Perry, W. H. Schofield and P. N. Joubert (1969) have studied a somewhat analogous situation and define two types of roughness in which, in the case corresponding to (a), eddies are shed into the general stream, and to (b), roller eddies form between the elements, so partially sealing off the upper from the between-element flow. Consequently for case (a), unlike (b), the customary logarithmic law of velocity becomes valid only at some distance above, and in proportion to, the height of the roughness elements.

Wind circulation around and between building complexes

Work on flow around single and groups of building shapes, and upon the pressure or suction loads on structures, has been extensively documented, and other points will be briefly discussed here.

General level of wind-speed on or near cities

According to T. J. Chandler (1970), incident rural winds of moderate or greater strength will be reduced within towns at street level, but light winds may be increased (for London a threshold of 5 m sec^{-1} is quoted). Local gusts and acceleration of the wind along streets will, of course, occur.

A. F. E. Wise (1970) makes the helpful remark that with winds above about 5 m sec^{-1} (Force 4 or more on the Beaufort Scale) unpleasant buffetting of clothes, disturbance to hair and the raising of dust will occur. He also states that a wind of about 5 m sec^{-1} is tolerable for strolling about shopping centres, assuming normal winter clothing and an ambient temperature of 10°C. Clearly, a much lower wind speed is needed for the full enjoyment of open spaces. Merely for illustration, it may be noted that the average annual percentage frequency of winds of 12 m.p.h. (approximately 5 m sec^{-1}) or less at several stations is: Croydon 73, Kew 77, Abingdon (Oxford) 74, Birmingham (Airport) 73, Glasgow (Airport) 70, Edinburgh 62, Shoeburyness (coast) 49, Felixstowe (coast) 58. The wind speed is measured at 10 m, and at 2 m may be roughly estimated at 9–10 m.p.h.

Corresponding data for Edinburgh and Glasgow for some individual months (1957–66) are:

	Dec.	Mar.	June	Sep.
Edinburgh (Airport)	62	57	62	67
Glasgow (Airport)	66	57	64	72

The complete absence of wind, leading to no ventilation of city streets is, from a health point of view, more serious than excessive wind; fresh air must be allowed to penetrate into building spaces.

Penetration of wind into space between buildings

Obviously the use of space between buildings will be influenced by the character of the wind experienced there. A considerable volume of data and information is now available on the wind hazards associated with tall buildings, with the juxtaposition of structures of different heights and with the layout of courtyards and patios of pedestrian precincts and so forth (Wise, 1970 and *Architects' Journal*, 1968). A particular case is the air circulation between a tall slab building and an upwind one with a direction normal to the face of the structure. An eddy forms, giving rise, at ground level, to speeds equal to or exceeding that of the free air. The details of the flow depend on the ratio of the spacing between, and of the crosswind dimensions, to height. Figure 2 (from Sexton, 1970) indicates some relationships and further details are given by A. F. E. Wise (1970).

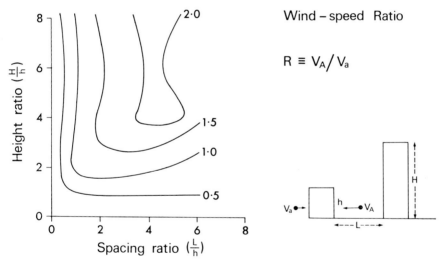

FIG. 2. *Isopleths of R(maximum) at 3 m above ground level (From Sexton, 1970)*

V. B. Torrance (1965) investigated a geometrically simple arrangement of a right prism with a symmetrically situated inner 'well' or patio with varying ratios of length and width to height for different angles of attack of the wind on the prism. With a normally incident wind across the top of the patio, an induced circulation can be set up in this space when the downwind width (corresponding to 'L' in Fig. 2) to height ratio approximates to about unity. With increasing ratio of width to height, air from the external flow begins to penetrate and a large eddy is created filling most of the space. If the width to height ratio is one-third or less, the eddy appears to be confined to the upper one-third or so of the 'well'. The penetration of the external circulation becomes more vigorous with the wind oblique to the face of the prism. Both Sexton and Torrance appear to postulate situations in which the wind speed exceeds the minimum required to set up stable circulation patterns.

For the development of an eddy within the space the speed just above the roof must exceed some low minimum value. With a space to height ratio of a few multiples, H. W. Georgii, E. Busch and E. Weber (1967) show that the circulation in a street between the buildings is weak and unorganised with a speed at roof level of less than 2 m sec^{-1}; that above 2 m sec^{-1} a circulation develops, but not until the speed exceeds 5 m sec^{-1} is there complete penetration into the street and ventilation at ground level.

The leisure use of space will clearly be influenced detrimentally by a rate of air movement lower than would inhibit its use for commerce and shopping. It would be of value and provide guidance to climatologists in assembling and assessing data if 'rule-of-thumb' speed thresholds could be suggested.

THE RADIATION ENVIRONMENT

Whilst the meteorologist's traditional interest in radiation has been in the interception, absorption, transformation and emission at a horizontal surface, of both solar ('short-wave') and terrestrial ('long-wave') radiation, architects and building scientists have given most attention to the penetration of sky light and direct sunshine into buildings through vertical surfaces and to the problem of preventing unacceptable thermal conditions developing within buildings. A preoccupation with vertical surfaces renders consideration of solar geometry and of systematic variations in sky brightness of first importance (for example, Ministry of Housing and Local Government, 1964).

There is a reasonably adequate network of stations in the southern half of Great Britain at which total solar radiation on a horizontal surface (expressed as hourly integrals) is systematically measured, and for which data are readily available. Elsewhere in Great Britain the network is sparse, whilst only some nine stations are simultaneously recording the diffuse component of solar radiation (data on which are very necessary if short period estimates are to be computed) on other than a horizontal surface under all sky conditions. Six stations systematically record the illumination integral, and routine measurements of long-wave ('thermal' or 'terrestrial') radiation and of radiation balance are confined to only five centres.

In an urban situation, much of the solar radiation reflected from a particular vertical surface is absorbed by adjacent surfaces. This, and the higher thermal capacity of building elements compared with that of the natural ground, leads to a greater storage of heat during the day and a greater heat reservoir to draw upon during the night (Ryd, 1970 and Ludwig, 1970).

Aesthetically, direct sunshine can play a much more important role than might be judged from its contribution to the total radiant income, and most certainly to that delivered to unit area of horizontal surface. Low angle sunshine is a most important feature of the natural scene, particularly in high latitudes; and the illumination of façades, including north-facing surfaces, and the 'high-lighting' of landscape detail, especially in hilly and mountainous areas, are definite environmental assets.

Some meteorologists argue that the recording of bright sunshine will become obsolescent as soon as a satisfactory network of solarimeters becomes fully operational. Certainly for daily aggregates, averaged over at least ten days, a useful correlation exists between hours of bright sunshine and total solar radiation (and, incidentally, the closely correlated illumination integral) on unit horizontal surface. However, on a shorter time-scale, and in relation to variation within the day, such statistical linkages fail.

To examine this last point, the hourly illumination integral (kilolux hours per square centimetre of horizontal surface) for selected hours was set against the proportion of the hour during which bright sunshine was recorded at Eskdalemuir Observatory in south Scotland for the month of June 1970. Attention was confined to entries for sixty minutes commencing at 0600, 1200, 1800 local apparent time (L.A.T.). During June the change in solar attitude for any stated hour can be neglected. Some very rough comparisons of range are indicated below.

Duration of sunshine per hour	Nil	60 minutes
Period of 60 minutes beginning at (L.A.T.)	Illumination integral	
0600	5–25	30–45
1200	10–40	80–110
1800	3–15	20–30

At intermediate sunshine amounts the envelopes embracing the extremes of the range were very roughly linear. One comment will suffice. For a proportion of cases in the 60 minutes category the measured illumination on a horizontal surface at hours beginning 0600 and 1800 L.A.T., for clear skies, is less than for 'nil' sunshine at 1200 L.A.T. The plot suggests that the clear sky value at 1800 L.A.T. will always be exceeded at 1200 L.A.T. if there is at that time more than about thirty minutes of the hour with bright sunshine. Should it then be argued, from the standpoint of visual amenity, that bright sunshine in the morning and evening are less desirable than a cloudy or overcast sky at noon? It would seem worthwhile to underline the individual and important place that bright sunshine plays in the hierarchy of observations of natural radiation.

TABLE 1. *Percentage frequency distribution of daily sunshine amounts at Edinburgh (Airport) 1951–67 (from Plant, 1958)*

(Duration in hours and tenths)

Month	0	0·1– 1·0	1·1– 2·0	2·1– 3·0	3·1– 4·0	4·1– 5·0	5·1– 6·0	6·1– 7·0	7·1– 8·0	8·1– 9·0	9·1– 10·0	10·1– 11·0	11·1– 12·0	12·1– 13·0	13·1– 14·0	14·1– 15·0	15·1– 16·0
December	38	22	10	10	10	7	3										
April	8	12	8	10	9	9	6	7	8	7	7	3	5	1			
June	11	9	9	8	7	6	7	6	7	4	7	4	4	5	3	3	

TABLE 2. *Percentage frequency distribution of hours within the indicated periods (L.A.T.) when stated proportion of the hour experienced bright sunshine. Averages for December and June at Edinburgh, 1966–70 (incl.).*

Proportion of hour	December (a)			June (b)					
	0900– 1200	1200– 1500	0900– 1500	0500– 1200 (c)	0400– 1200 (d)	1300– 1900 (c)	1300– 2000 (d)	0500– 1900 (c)	0400– 2000 (d)
0·0	58	62	60	41	45	43	46	42	45
0·1	8	8	8	9	9	10	10	9	9
0·2	3	4	4	5	5	4	3	4	4
0·3	4	4	4	3	2	3	3	3	3
0·4	3	3	3	4	3	3	4	3	4
0·5	3	2	2	4	4	3	3	4	3
0·6	2	2	2	4	4	2	2	3	3
0·7	4	3	3	4	4	3	3	4	3
0·8	3	3	3	3	3	3	3	3	3
0·9	3	3	3	5	3	3	4	3	4
1·0	9	6	8	18	16	22	19	20	18

(a) Data for incomplete hours of daylight at each end of the day have been ignored.
(b) Data for incomplete hours of daylight at each end of the day have been ignored in column (c) but included in column (d).

A few comments on the statistical properties of bright sunshine data are now necessary, for which purpose some data for Edinburgh will be employed. Table 1 illustrates clearly that, particularly in winter, the frequency distribution of total daily duration of sunshine is strongly of the 'reversed J' pattern: the arithmetic mean value of 0·9 hours is clearly of little physical significance. In summer (as for June) there is much flatter reversed-J pattern with a long span (from the '2·1–3·0 hour' to the '12·1–13·0 hour' classes) of approximately uniform frequency. The intermediate distribution of April resembles that for June if allowance is made for the difference in the length of the day.

In Table 2 the distribution of hourly durations is illustrated. Clearly, in any selected sixty-minute period, the most likely amount of bright sunshine is nil, particularly if cases having 0·1 hour (which takes in 'traces' due to momentary glimpses of the sun) are included. The next most likely category is a full sixty minutes of sunshine, and for the month of June in the particular sample being examined, full sunshine hours are about half as frequent as completely sunless ones. That this is a general tendency is illustrated by some roughly comparable results for July 1890–1904 at Greenwich (Pearse, 1928), which gave 39 per cent of overcast hours and 19 per cent occasions of clear skies.

For most outdoor activities, a sufficiency of sunshine sometime during the pre-noon and sometime during the post-noon period will be acceptable, and the data indicate no marked differences in the expectation of sunshine between these two periods. For any designated hourly interval in the month of June at Edinburgh the cases of no sunshine and of complete sunshine together account for the entries on some twenty of the thirty possible days. An increase in sunny hours will be at the expense of the sunless ones, the outstanding ten or so entries being fairly evenly spread between the categories 0·1 to 0·9 hours with a definite bias towards the extreme class intervals of this range.

For architectural purposes, however, the fixed geometrical relationship at any moment between the orientation of a building and the position of the sun renders data on sunshine within each particular sixty-minute period of importance. Recourse to the detailed data shows that the ratio of completely sunny to completely overcast hours during June is about 1:2 or better between the hours of about 0900 hours to 1600 L.A.T., but that outside this range the ratio falls to about 1:3 or 1:4, giving obvious advantages to a southerly aspect.

THE THERMAL ENVIRONMENT

This is a subject in which physiological criteria play the major role. There is, however, one aspect of the urban thermal environment, the 'heat island' which, through its association with pollution, has a strong influence upon 'quality'.

It is generally agreed that ambient temperature within built-up areas tends to reach a slightly higher maximum by day than in rural areas

and falls more slowly during the night, giving a measurable temperature excess ranging from about 1 °C to 5 °C or more (Chandler, 1965).
The differences are largest in clear, calm weather. Some reasons for
this temperature excess have been outlined earlier and to these may
be added the influence of atmospheric pollutants in reducing the net
outflow of long-wave radiation and the production of substantial,
additional heat energy by industrial processes (Fuggle and Oke, 1970).

In a town having a cluster of very tall buildings at its centre, ambient
day-time temperatures can be lower than some distance away, producing a cool core within the generally warmer central area.

The heat island phenomenon is a three-dimensional one, the upper
boundary being defined by the height of the temperature inversion.
Order of magnitude estimates of the height of this heat island are
quoted as three to five times the average height of the buildings
(Sekiguti, 1970) which for Tokyo gives estimates ranging between 100
and 150 m. Chandler (1967) suggests 50–150 m for London, whilst T. F.
Clarke is quoted by H. W. Georgii (1970) as stating that over Cincinnati
the 'nocturnal boundary layer' may extend to 300 m or even to 400 m.

The magnitude of the temperature excess (DT) at night depends
jointly upon the size of the built-up area and the vertical lapse rate (γ)
of temperature in the surrounding rural areas. For Edinburgh, a
'medium sized' city, F. L. Ludwig (1970) suggests:

$$DT = 1 \cdot 7 - 7 \cdot 2\gamma$$

(where DT is in °C, γ is in °C per mb and is negative for an inversion).
Unfortunately the data for γ which are required to test this relation are
not available.

Wind tends to destroy the temperature difference, and an empirical
equation (using population, P, as a measure of the size of the urban
area) has been proposed by T. R. Oke and F. G. Hannell (1970):

$$V = 3 \cdot 4 \log P - 11 \cdot 6$$

(where V is the critical speed in sec^{-1} and $V = 0$ when the population is
approximately 2,000).

However, in practice, it appears that a 'heat island' can be created with
a much smaller aggregation and H. E. Landsberg (1970) notes an
urban heat island emerging with only a small complex of buildings;
whilst Chandler (1970) states that a relationship can be detected
between the temperature excess at a point and the density of urban
development 'within a circle of as little as 500 m radius from the
(reporting) station'.

The critical speed for Edinburgh (population 5×10^5) would be about
8 m sec^{-1} and equal or greater speeds occur on rather less than 20 per
cent of occasions at Turnhouse Airport.

PRECIPITATION

There appear to be few contrasts in precipitation between urban and
rural areas. Some authorities (for example, Changnon, 1970, and

Atkinson, 1970) present evidence that the amount and frequency of rainfall are increased by the existence of an urban complex, but the differences appear to be small.

The disposal of precipitation (both liquid and as snow) raises particular problems in towns, but these, being largely hydrological and engineering matters, are outwith the scope of this chapter. There are, however, a few topics on which comment is appropriate.

Extensive information on amounts of rainfall is readily available, as well as much detailed data on 'rain-days' and 'wet-days' (24-hour periods when amounts of, or exceeding, 0·01 in. or 0·04 in. respectively were reported). Less readily available is information upon the duration of rainfall and upon 'driving-rain', both of which directly affect the use of space and the choice between a range of possible activities.

J. A. Plant (1968) has analysed hourly rainfall records for Edinburgh in an attempt to assess the probable amount of time which might be lost on outdoor building work owing to interruption by rain. A few comments will illustrate the type of information which can be derived and which, given appropriate postulated 'threshold' values, might enable rational judgments to be made on the planning and provision of facilities for other activities.

Averaged over ten years, there were ten days (range six to fifteen) in June at Edinburgh Airport on which 0·1 mm of rain or more fell during the 'working day' (the period 0700 to 1700 G.M.T.). A total fall of the order of 0·1 mm is a very small amount, and can well include a brief passing shower which constitutes a very minor interruption to summer-time activities. The average number of separate hours in June in which a rainfall of an intensity of 0·1 mm per hour occurred was 25·0 (range 12 to 41) which represents 8 per cent of the working hours. The month of June is the driest summer month in Edinburgh, the wettest being August with 43·5 hours (range 3 to 63).

Taking as a higher threshold of falling rain the rate of 0·5 mm or more per hour (which includes all 'moderate' or 'heavy rain'), Plant found that the number of days in June on which falls of these intensities occurred averaged nine (range 6–13), and an average of some twenty-one separate sixty minute periods (range 11–35) within which falls of these intensities were reported. The total time occupied by such rain averaged 10·6 hours (range 4·7 to 21·1). It should be noted that if 'moderate' or 'heavy' rain falls for part of an hour it may well be followed or preceded or both by others of a less intensity, perhaps resulting in the complete hour being wet.

The importance of 'driving rain' to building science and practice is receiving increasing attention, and it is a matter of everyday experience that it constitutes one of the most inhibiting manifestations of weather especially in relation to outdoor leisure activity. R. E. Lacy (1971) gives a map of an annual index of 'driving rain'. Obviously it will bear a relationship to a rainfall map; the lowest values are in central England increasing by about 33 per cent in eastern Scotland, to over double in west central Scotland (including the Glasgow area) to a seven-fold maximum in the western Highlands. A further map shows the wind directions associated with a particular value of the index and a point of immediate interest is that, in the Forth–Clyde gap, winds from the northeast feature as strongly as do those from the southwest. Data are not readily available on a monthly basis, but Lacy's Table 1 incorporates details of the maximum hourly driving rain index for some twenty-three stations in Great Britain and it is significant that, of the cases listed, none occurred in spring but *thirteen in summer*, six in autumn and only four in the winter (in December and January). A further point of interest is that at four of the eight Scottish stations quoted (Kinross, Edinburgh, Glasgow and Prestwick) this maximum value was associated with wind directions of 030° or 060° (that is directions lying between north and east.)

The effect of the wind around a structure on the trajectory of rain drops (and snow flakes) has been documented (Architects' Journal, 1968a) and has clear implications for the design, layout and utilisation of the space between buildings.

CONCLUSION

The consideration of environmental quality directs attention away from the preoccupation by architects with extreme conditions (high winds, excessively high or low temperatures, heavy snowfall, rain storms and so on). Limits and thresholds of meteorological elements within their whole range assume importance, as does 'mean-value' climatology. Furthermore, contingency analysis, taking account of several meteorological elements and tied to various time-scales, plays a vital role. Techniques are required for expressing acceptable ambient conditions in a multidimensional frequency format, and one so designed to respond to increasingly unacceptable threshold values of any one element. Empirical expressions such as 'wind-chill' become useful aids.

Two main groups of topics have received particular attention: the importance of the climate of the open spaces within an urban environment; and visual amenity and direct sunshine. In temperate latitudes, the spacing between buildings which is required for the penetration of light and sunshine is usually greater than that needed if the between-building circulation is to be decoupled from the stronger external wind. For the latter, a width to height ratio of not more than about unity is required, although a degree of decoupling can be achieved with a wider spacing provided the buildings are all of approximately the same height. The hazards arising from buildings of different heights (the 'tall slab' problem) are now well known, but it should also be noted that an irregular skyline has the advantage of inducing greater turbulence and so ensuring the all-important ventilation at street level in conditions of light winds.

On the question of wind régimes in the British Isles, gaps do exist in present knowledge; but equally there is a mass of data, as yet only partially analysed, which could be exploited. On the macro-scale there are gaps in the network, especially in certain hilly regions; and more generally an insufficiency of stations with continuous recording of wind speed and direction. However, much information of the vectorial, persistence and sequential characteristics of wind merely awaits analysis. On the meso-scale, there is inadequate information on the effect of landscape features and topography on air-flow. Apart from the output from a necessarily limited extension of the general network, studies are required (which may well be of limited duration, say, two to three years or less) of wind flow in areas where topography can be defined in simple geometrical terms. Case studies, supplemented by wind-tunnel work, will lead to an expanding 'library' of knowledge and experience. Once again, however, it must be stated that existing data have not been fully utilised. On the micro-scale (within the urban complex) the responsibility is pre-eminently one for the architect and building scientist; however, the examination of the vertical structure of the wind, and the properties of the urban boundary layer are of joint concern with the meteorologist.

The importance of visual amenity has been mentioned, and it remains to emphasise the value of direct sunshine. Much information contained in the existing data is inadequately used, and the implications of the statistical properties of the distribution of hourly and daily sunshine amounts, of sequences and so forth, are not fully appreciated.

The problems of pollution and the 'urban heat island' are being vigorously tackled and point to the need for better data on the radiation balance and the vertical gradient of temperature (especially, of course, in relation to inversions). A slow but steady improvement in the network of stations measuring elements of the radiation balance is taking place. It is, however, a matter for discussion, in the context of necessarily limited resources, whether it is better to increase the number of stations measuring only the primary element (total radiation on a horizontal surface), or to concentrate on a smaller number at which diffuse radiation and the radiation balance are also measured—and all on an hourly basis.

ACKNOWLEDGMENTS

This chapter has been approved for publication in the United Kingdom by the Director-General of the Meteorological Office.

Thanks are due to the respective authors for permission to reproduce their diagrams as Figures 1 and 2.

REFERENCES

Many of the papers referred to below occur in two volumes containing contributions to the symposium on 'Urban Climates and Building Climatology' jointly organised by the World Meteorological Organisation and the World Health Organisation in

Brussels in October 1968. These are referred to as *Technical Note 108* and *Technical Note 109* and a full reference is given under World Meteorological Organisation (1970).

Altshuller, A. P. (1970) 'Composition and reactions of pollutants in community atmospheres', *Technical Note 108*, pp. 177–93.

Architects' Journal (1968 a, b, c) *Handbook of Building Environment*, Section 3, 27 November, pp. 1283–98, 4 December, pp. 1345–64, and 11 December, pp.1413–1430, London.

Atkinson, B. W. (1970) 'The reality of the urban effect on precipitation—a case-study approach', *Technical Note 108*, pp. 342–60.

Berljand, M. E. (1970) 'Meteorological factors determining the dispersion of atmospheric pollutants under urban conditions', *Technical Note 108*, pp. 196–213.

Brooks, C. E. P., C. S. Durst, N. Carruthers, D. Dewar and J. S. Sawyer (1950) *Upper Winds Over the World*, Geophysical Memoirs No. 85, Meteorological Office, London.

Chandler, T. J. (1965) *The Climate of London*, Hutchinson, London.

—— (1967) 'Night-time temperatures in relation to Leicester's urban form', *Meteorological Magazine*, 96, p. 244.

—— (1970) 'Urban climatology—inventory and prospect', *Technical Note 108*, pp. 1–14.

Changnon, S. A. (1970) 'Recent studies of urban effects on precipitation in the United States, *Technical Note 108*, pp. 325–41.

van Eimern, J., R. Karschon, L. A. Razumova and G. W. Robertson (1964) *Windbreaks and Shelter Belts*, *Technical Note 59*, World Meteorological Organisation, Geneva.

Frenkiel, J. (1962) 'Wind profiles over hills (in relation to wind-power generation)', *Quarterly Journal of the Royal Meteorological Society*, 88, pp. 156–69.

Fuggle, R. F. and T. R. Oke (1970) 'Infra-red divergence and the urban heat island,' *Technical Note 108*, pp. 70–8.

Georgii, H. W. (1970) 'The effects of air pollution on urban climates', *Technical Note 108*, pp. 214–37.

Georgii, H. W., E. Busch and E. Weber (1967) 'Untersuchung uber die zeitliche und raumliche Verteilung der Immissionskonzentratum des Kohlenmonoxid in Frankfurt/Main', No. 11, Bericht des Instituts für Meteorologie und Geophysik, University of Frankfurt.

Gloyne, R. W. (1959) *Studies Relating to the Influence of Topographical Features upon Surface Airflow and Incident Radiation*, unpublished Ph.D. thesis, University of Edinburgh.

Golding, E. W. and A. H. Stodhart (1952) *The Selection and Characteristics of Windpower Sites*, Technical Report C/T 108, Electrical Research Association, London.

Hass, W. A., W. H. Hoeker, D. H. Pack and J. K. Angell (1967) 'Analysis of low-level, constant volume balloon (tetroon) flights over New York City', *Quarterly Journal of the Royal Meteorological Society*, 93, pp. 483–93.

Helliwell, N. (1970) 'Some open-scale measurements of wind over Central London', *Technical Note No. 108*, pp. 46–8.

Jones, P. M., M. A. B. de Larrinaga and C. B. Wilson (1971) 'The urban wind velocity profile', *Atmospheric Environment*, 5, pp. 89–102.

Lacy, R. E. (1971) *An Index of Exposure to Driving Rain*, Building Research Station, Digest 127, H.M.S.O., London.

Landsberg, H. E. (1970) 'Micrometeorological temperature differentiation through urbanisation', *Technical Note 108*, pp. 129–37.

Ludwig, F. L. (1970) 'Urban temperature fields', *Technical Note 108*, pp. 80–107.

Ministry of Housing & Local Government (1964) *Planning for Daylight and Sunlight*, Planning Bulletin No. 5, H.M.S.O., London.

Munn, R. E. (1970) 'Airflow in urban areas', *Technical Note 108*, pp. 15–39.

Oke, T. R. and F. G. Hannell (1970) 'The form of the urban heat island in Hamilton, Canada', *Technical Note 108*, pp. 113–26.

Paul, A. H. (1971) 'Weather and the daily use of outdoor recreation areas in Canada', Paper presented at Symposium No. XIV, *Weather Forecasting for Agriculture and Industry*, University College of Wales, Aberystwyth, March 17/18.

Pearse, G. E. (1928) 'Frequency of estimated intensities of cloudiness at Greenwich 1890–1904 for the month of July', *Biometrika*, 20A, p. 336.

Perry, A. E., W. H. Schofield and P. N. Joubert (1969) 'Rough wall turbulent boundary layers', *Journal of Fluid Mechanics*, 37(2), pp. 383–413.

Plant, J. A. (1968) *The Climate of Edinburgh*, Climatological Memorandum No. 54A, Meteorological Office, Edinburgh.

Rutter, N. (1968) 'Geomorphic and tree shelter in relation to surface wind conditions, weather, time of day and season', *Agricultural Meteorology* 5(5), p. 319.

Ryd, H. (1970) 'The importance of meteorology in building', *Technical Note 109*, pp. 23–36.

Sadeh, W. Z., J. E. Cermak and T. Kawatani (1971) 'Flow over high roughness elements', *Boundary-layer Meteorology* 1(3), pp. 321–44.

Sekiguti, T. (1970) 'Thermal situations of urban areas, horizontally and vertically, *Technical Note 108*, pp. 137–40.

Sexton, D. (1970) 'Wind deflection by buildings', *Technical Note 109*, pp. 57–9.

Singer, I. A. and C. M. Nagle, (1970) 'Studies of the wind within the United States', *Technical Note 109*, pp. 61–71.

Singer, T. A. and M. E. Smith (1970) 'A summary of the recommended guide for the prediction of the dispersion of airborne effluents', *Technical Note 108*, pp. 306–24.

Tagg, J. R. (1957) *Wind Data Related to the Generation of Electricity by Wind-power*, Technical Report C/T 115, Electrical Research Association, London.

Torrance, V. B. (1965) *A Critical Investigation of Shelter and Wind-effects on Buildings with Patios*, Unpublished M.Sc. thesis, Heriot-Watt University, Edinburgh.

Wallén, C. C. (1970) 'Organisational aspects and future activities', *Technical Note 108*, pp. 387–90.

Wise, A. F. E. (1970) *Wind-effects Due to Groups of Buildings*, Building Research Station, Current Paper 23/70, H.M.S.O., London.

World Meteorological Organisation (1970) *Urban Climates*, Technical Note 108, and *Building Climatology*, Technical Note 109, The Organisation, Geneva.

CHAPTER 3

Air pollution and the built environment

A. J. CROSBIE

Air is a natural resource which should be used, within its capacity, for the technical and economic advantage of mankind. In the past, the ability of the atmosphere to disperse most contaminants without harmful effects has been adequate, but it is not limitless and the quantity of pollutants added, directly or indirectly, has increased rapidly since 1945. The dynamic characteristics of the atmosphere also mean that the volume and mobility of the air masses overlying an area vary seasonally or even daily. Consequently, the dilution rate for pollutants in the lower atmosphere may be viewed as a function of time and space.

Large urban centres, with their concentration of human activities, represent both the most frequent sources of air pollution and the areas of greatest concern about its detrimental effects. Since cities differ, however, in their geographic setting and in the nature of their industry and function, so their air pollution problems vary with the quantity and type of emission, air movements and topography. Each area is to some extent unique, although, as neighbouring urban areas expand, so their waste products may affect each other.

Pollution must eventually either be removed from the atmosphere by various natural processes, as yet little understood, or accumulate indefinitely on a global scale. The latter alternative, because of the implications for climate, is critical for the human race. By comparison, local problems are of minor significance although they may be complex in origin, expensive in effect and solution, and relevant to a relatively large population.

Three factors require consideration before environmental quality may be evaluated.

(1) What are the characteristic features of the principal emission sources?
(2) What are the variations in the speed and extent of dispersal?
(3) What are the effects of pollution?

SOURCES OF POLLUTION

Air pollution is not peculiar to the built environment. Natural pollution, derived in the main from volcanoes, deserts and vegetation, is beyond Man's control and far exceeds in weight and volume emissions derived from human activity.

Volcanic eruptions merit primary consideration both in terms of the quantities involved and the effect on human life. In the 1883 Plinian eruption of Krakatoa (Royal Society, 1888) an estimated 3.6×10^{10} kg of dust and vapour (Astopowitsch, 1934) were violently ejected to an altitude of at least 20 km. The total amount of volcanic matter involved (6–18 km³) pales, however, before the estimated 100–300 km³ discharged in the 1815 eruption of Tamboro in Indonesia. Vast quantities of gases are also emitted with volcanic activity. The hydrochloric and hydrofluoric acid liberated into the atmosphere by the Katmai volcano in Alaska in 1912 tarnished brass in Victoria, Vancouver Island, and damaged washing on lines as far away as Chicago; while the associated fumaroles which gave rise to The Valley of Ten Thousand Smokes annually discharged 1·25 million and 0·2 million tons respectively of these gases between 1919 and 1921.

The velocity and temperature of the dust clouds and gases aggravate their hazard potential, and catastrophic events are not infrequent. In 1902, St. Pierre at the foot of Mount Pelée in Martinique was destroyed within seconds and only 30 survived out of the 30,000 population. With the possible exception of nuclear disasters, pollution episodes due to urban or industrial sources are unlikely to match loss of life at this scale. Fortunately, volcanic activity represents isolated and intermittent point sources of pollution widely distributed around the globe. In contrast, human sources are continuous and increasingly concentrated in low level, low velocity emissions within large areas which may be of the order of 10,000 square miles.

Dust from the oceans, estimated at two billion tons of salt annually, forms another major component of the atmosphere. Arid areas also provide enormous quantities of dust which may be lifted into the atmosphere by convection, although the general circulation may be too weak to blow it away to other regions. In northwest India during the hot season, the dust blanket extends over a wide area, attains depths of 10,000 metres and may give ground level concentrations of about 5–800 micrograms per cubic metre, which are three to four times greater than dust concentrations in western cities.

Dust of natural origin is hardly ever a problem in the United Kingdom. Over the United States, however, some 43 million tons of dust settle annually, of which approximately 31 million tons are derived from natural sources, including one million tons of pollen, while the balance is caused by human activities. Although pollen is the smallest quantity, the suffering resulting from these aeroallergens may be considerable and widespread. In this respect, the presence of pollen sources within urban areas is worth attention.

Factors in emission

The fundamental cause of atmospheric pollution is the conversion of energy. All forms of energy conversion have some material by-products and the degree of atmospheric pollution depends, in the main, on the relative proportions of the various by-products which are airborne. With advanced technology, pollution may occur with other processes, and new substances have entered the balance.

The energy explosion (Reid, 1970) of postwar years is the prime contributor to global atmosphere pollution. The combination of a rapidly increasing population and an ever growing use of energy per capita has led to an unprecedented demand on energy resources. Early estimates of world energy consumption are largely surmise but data are available from 1937 onwards. These indicate a growth rate of about 3 per cent per annum and projections for the future are based on a growth of 3·8 per cent per capita per annum (Table 1). Energy projections, such as the fuel policy outlined in the 1967 White Paper, are characteristically unreliable and usually underestimate demand. There is no doubt that general industrial development and urbanisation will continue and that developing countries will convert to an energy-rich economy. No nation, therefore, unless it wishes to be described as a purely agricultural economy, can afford to be ignorant about air pollution. Concentrations may be low at present but there is no hope that they will remain at this level.

TABLE 1. *Projected total energy demands*

Year	Population, millions		Annual average energy demand per capita, $10^4\,kWh$		Projected total energy demand, $10^{12}\,kWh$	
	United States	World	United States	World	United States	World
1970	210	3,700	8·2	1·9	17	70
1980	250	4,500	9·1	2·8	23	130
1990	300	5,400	10·1	4·0	30	220
2000	360	6,600	11·2	5·9	40	390
2025	450	11,000	14·6	14·9	66	1,600
2050	490	18,000	19·0	37·9	93	6,800

SOURCE: Reid, 1970

The pattern of energy consumption is geographically varied, reflecting the uneven distribution of raw energy resources, climate and stage of economic development. Where the choice of fuel is limited but supplies are abundant, for example, lignite in Czechoslovakia, then economics demands that it be used irrespective of its pollution potential; where the choice of fuel is unrestricted, as in the United States, there has been a marked change in preference. Fuel wood became insignificant as a source of energy after 1955; coal declined between 1930 and 1960 but demand has increased since then, largely for pulverised coal-fired thermal power stations; oil has steadily increased in use with the rapid growth of private and public transport; residual oil has also become a major component in electricity generation; natural gas continues to grow in popularity especially for domestic use; hydro-electricity power has increased in total power generated, but as a percentage of the total energy consumed, has decreased from 4·6 per cent (1950) to 3·4 per cent (1970); nuclear power will develop, but the technical difficulties have proved greater than expected.

At different scales these patterns influence the intensity and type of pollution. The average annual smoke concentrations for the United Kingdom decreased by one-third to one-half from north to south reflecting, in large measure, the regional distribution of domestic coal consumption per head of population. Within cities, the fuel consumption varies with different types of housing, for example, in Edinburgh (Table 2), where coal is the principal fuel used in those areas where cost is the main factor.

Sources of urban pollution are usually categorised as multiple or single. Multiple sources include domestic and car emissions and the spatial and temporal variations range from dense tenements, with a concentration of chimneys, and traffic jams, to low density housing areas with infrequent traffic. They are of major importance in ground level concentrations, irrespective of the type or quantity of pollution emitted, because the dispersion is poor, the emission rate is high for a given rate of energy conversion owing to inefficient combustion, and they occur where people live and at levels where people breathe. Single sources are identifiable as point sources of emission, usually by the presence of tall chimneys. Their effect on ground level concentrations depends on the age and type of installation, the method of operation and the human factor in terms of the boilerman's efficiency.

Temporal variations are highly significant. Seasonal patterns are related to climate, while weekly sequences are distinct in response to surrounding land use. Diurnal profiles of pollution are influenced by meteorological factors and land-use function with the latter resulting in differences for each day of the week. Exposure to air pollution is therefore markedly irregular in dose, frequency and duration within an urban area even without the further complications arising from travel, working environment and social habits.

Types of pollutants

A useful classification of pollutants is: (1) grit and dust—particles which fall out of the air more or less rapidly; (2) aerosols—particles in more or less permanent suspension; (3) gases. The distinction between the first two is not clear cut. It lies in the terminal velocity for gravitational settling which, in turn, depends on the size, shape and density of the materials. Generally, a diameter of about 10 microns divides suspended material from the large particles. Grit and dust fall is derived in the main from power stations and industrial processes such as cement manufacturing. It is a common nuisance in urban areas and the cause of many complaints, but it is not a health hazard.

TABLE 2. *Energy sources for space heating in Edinburgh*

House type:	Bungalows		Villas		Terraces		Tenements		Corporation *	
Single source	177	(39·6)	110	(25·9)	189	(33·7)	2,142	(55·0)	639	(57·6)
Multiple source	264	(59·1)	296	(69·8)	336	(60·0)	1,506	(38·7)	435	(39·2)
No reply	6	(1·3)	18	(4·3)	35	(6·3)	247	(6·3)	36	(3·2)
Sample total	447	(100·0)	424	(100·0)	560	(100·0)	3,895	(100·0)	1,110	(100·0)

Single source

Nil	0	(0)	1	(0·9)	0	(0)	3	(0·2)	0	(0)
Coal	14	(7·9)	7	(6·4)	21	(11·1)	372	(17·4)	215	(33·6)
Coke	12	(6·8)	3	(2·7)	1	(0·5)	9	(0·4)	0	(0)
Oil	4	(2·3)	5	(4·6)	2	(1·1)	0	(0)	0	(0)
Paraffin	0	(0)	0	(0)	0	(0)	7	(0·3)	0	(0)
Gas	28	(15·8)	35	(31·8)	44	(23·3)	437	(20·4)	203	(31·8)
Electricity	119	(67·2)	59	(53·6)	121	(64·0)	1,314	(61·3)	221	(34·6)
Total	177	(100·0)	110	(100·0)	189	(100·0)	2,142	(100·0)	639	(100·0)

Multiple sources
(A) *Principal source*

None †	11	(4·2)	32	(10·8)	22	(6·5)	154	(10·2)	25	(5·7)
Coal	106	(40·2)	54	(18·2)	95	(28·3)	715	(47·5)	334	(76·8)
Coke	7	(2·7)	13	(4·4)	12	(3·6)	16	(1·1)	0	(0)
Oil	2	(0·8)	17	(5·7)	3	(0·9)	0	(0)	0	(0)
Paraffin	1	(0·4)	2	(0·7)	2	(0·6)	20	(1·3)	0	(0)
Gas	80	(30·3)	73	(24·7)	103	(30·7)	273	(18·1)	41	(9·4)
Electricity	54	(20·4)	86	(29·1)	78	(23·2)	236	(15·7)	24	(5·6)
Equal ‡	3	(1·2)	19	(6·4)	21	(6·2)	92	(6·1)	11	(2·5)
Total	264	(100·0)	296	(100·0)	336	(100·0)	1,506	(100·0)	435	(100·0)

(B) *Alternative forms used*

Coal	153	(58·0)	177	(59·8)	170	(50·6)	986	(65·5)	376	(86·4)
Coke	14	(5·3)	51	(17·2)	34	(10·1)	29	(19·3)	0	(0)
Oil	2	(0·8)	27	(9·1)	3	(0·9)	0	(0)	0	(0)
Paraffin	10	(3·8)	28	(9·5)	63	(18·7)	163	(10·8)	62	(14·3)
Gas	121	(45·8)	175	(59·1)	205	(61·0)	633	(42·0)	133	(30·6)
Electricity	244	(92·4)	255	(86·1)	315	(93·7)	1,359	(90·2)	353	(81·1)

* Sample taken from Corporation houses built before 1955; information on type of space heating in houses built post 1955 is available from the City Architect.
† None refers to houses where no one source of energy is preferred.
‡ Where two or more sources are regularly used.
Percentages are given in brackets.

Aerosols comprise the non-viable particles with a range of radius between 6×10^{-3} and 10 microns. The number of particles increases very rapidly with decrease in radius but those smaller than 0·1 micron are not important in pollution studies. Particles in the range 0·1—10 microns include smoke, which is not a definite chemical species, and these are important in air chemistry. A size distribution form is established partly by the mode of production and partly by the changes which aerosol distributions undergo with time as a result of coagulation of small particles, sedimentation of large particles and a condensation-evaporation cycle in cloud, fog or rain, and thereafter remains unchanged with time. In the United Kingdom, smoke is predominantly from domestic sources.

Gases are emitted into the atmosphere by many sources. Table 3 gives a summary of the observed concentrations in both polluted and unpolluted atmospheres of the major primary pollutants. Sulphur, carbon monoxide and carbon dioxide occur in the greatest concentrations. The common sulphur compounds in the atmosphere are sulphur dioxide, hydrogen sulphide and sulphates. SO_2 is emitted almost entirely from pollution sources, in contrast to H_2S which is derived from decaying organic matter and volcanic areas. Sulphate particles are produced by oxidation of SO_2 and from sea spray. There is no evidence of sulphur accumulation in the atmosphere (Robinson and Robbins, 1968) but there is an accumulation each year in the oceans. As an air pollution problem, sulphur is of local significance.

TABLE 3. *Concentrations of gaseous pollutants*

Pollutant	Conversion factor (μgm^{-3}/ppm)	Background concentration (ppm)	Concentrations in polluted atmospheres (ppm)
SO_2	2860	0.2×10^{-3}	$0.02-1$
H_2S	1520	0.2×10^{-3}	$(0.5-1) \times 10^{-3}$
CO	1260	0.15	$1-30$
CO_2	1960	320	500
$NO + NO_2$	1340, 2050	10^{-3}	25
NH_3	760	$(6-20) \times 10^{-3}$	2
CH_4	712	1.5	1.5
Other hydrocarbons	—	$< 10^{-3}$	$10-50 \times 10^{-2}$

SOURCE: Barrett, 1970

Carbon monoxide from petrol engines has produced a nearly linear increase of 7.4 per cent annually in global emission since 1945 (Barrett, 1970). There are few natural sources other than forest fires and the ocean. No mechanism for the destruction or removal of carbon monoxide in the atmosphere has been discovered and there is no method of predicting ambient concentrations in the future. Because of its toxic properties, local problems may be severe. In British cities, however, it is unlikely that carbon monoxide will attain levels above 30 ppm except on very rare, brief occasions; within the present urban layout traffic congestion has already reached the maximum possible.

Carbon dioxide is by far the most common pollutant in the atmosphere and it has been increasing at about 0.7 ppm per year since 1958 (President's Science Advisory Committee, 1965). This is usually attributed to the burning of fossil fuel although different sources have been considered. There seems little doubt, however, that with increased

energy consumption the CO_2 concentration in the atmosphere will
increase, possibly to a degree which will cause changes in the environment either in the rate of photosynthesis or in world climate.

DISPERSAL OF POLLUTION

The ability of the atmosphere to disperse most contaminants without
harmful effects depends on three factors: first, the degree of ventilation
or air movement; second, the scale, rate and duration of the discharge;
third, the form of pollutant and the chemical history after discharge.

Ventilation is the product of the mixing depth, that is, the layer
characterised by neutral stability or instability and the average wind
speed through it. It depends on large-scale atmospheric conditions, it
varies diurnally, it is modified by topographic features, and it deter-
mines the rate of horizontal dilution and vertical dispersion. Much
depends on the quantity of emission to be dispersed. Under stagnant air
masses, pollution may accumulate from one day to the next; no stagnation of consequence will occur however, if the ventilation during the
afternoon hours exceeds 6,000 m³/s or if the average wind speed is
greater than 4 m/s (about 15 km/h). In the United States, air pollution
warnings are issued if inadequate ventilation is forecast for an area of at
least 135,000 km² and appears likely to persist for a minimum of 36
hours.

The atmosphere is a vast chemical retort and the primary emissions
may be radically altered during their subsequent history. Secondary
pollutants are the products of reactions in the atmosphere. Photo-
chemical smog is particularly important, e.g., in southern California.
The raw materials are principally nitrous oxide, alkenes and a few
other organic compounds which are derived from automobile emissions.
Both long and short reaction chains occur and these give rise to a
variety of products including alkyl nitrates, peroxyacl nitrates, alcohols,
ethers, acids and peroxy-acids. Many free radicals act as intermediates
and these, because of the great dilution, have lifetimes of minutes or
hours.

Climate, as a description of the general atmospheric circulation, is
pre-eminent in dispersal mechanisms and therefore marked geographical relationships are evident. Seasonal variations which aid or inhibit
pollution dispersal are beyond human control and they may also
influence patterns of emission. Low temperature air pollution, for
example, is associated with settlements in high northern latitudes such
as Alaska or Siberia (Benson, 1970). Ice fog is formed when the output
of water vapour from the urban area meets an air mass which is too
cold to dissolve it and pollution is trapped within this layer. On the west
coast of continents, subsiding high pressure cells with their sluggish
horizontal movement and reduced vertical exchange give rise to dense
pollution over cities such as Los Angeles or Lima. In contrast, maritime
climates are not conducive to the accumulation of pollution although

due account must be given to short-term variations and local climates.

Modifications in the regional climate by geographical location and topography are also significant in pollution studies. Land and water interfaces create air movements which may influence dispersion, while valley locations are acknowledged problem sites. Within an urban area, the micro-climatic conditions are affected by city plan, the density and height of buildings, the location of roads and the density of traffic, the location and extent of parks and open spaces and the height and type of vegetation. Dilution of the pollution is achieved either by features which maximise ventilation or by the presence of emission-free areas.

Two meteorological factors which are commonly misunderstood are the prevailing wind and inversions. The location of industrial plants to the lee of a settlement with respect to the prevailing wind direction was a rule of thumb practice. Unfortunately, it is the periods of calm or near stagnation conditions which favour the accumulation of pollution and on these occasions such air movement as there is may be opposite to the prevailing wind. Inversions exist when warm air overlies cold and buoyancy forces inhibit vertical air movement. Such stable layers occur frequently and may be at any level in the atmosphere. Cities often have a stable layer at night overlying a well-stirred layer in which pollution will be retained. The difference between stable and unstable conditions is one of degree rather than of kind, and usually there is a daily cycle from stability to instability and back again. Serious accumulation of pollution is possible when the cycle is interrupted by prolonged stable conditions. Most pollution is of local origin, however, and, given sufficient emission, there is no region for which the self-cleansing properties of the atmosphere cannot be overwhelmed.

On a larger scale, the global circulation of pollutants is complex (Newell, 1971). Mixing within a hemisphere may be measured in weeks whereas the exchange between hemispheres is slower. The tropopause is a permanent inversion and consequently exchange between the troposphere and the stratosphere is difficult, with most of the movement into the stratosphere occurring at the high tropical tropopause. Much depends on the type of pollutant and there is also a marked seasonal cycle.

THE EFFECTS OF POLLUTION

The vulnerability of Man as a creature with limited environmental tolerance living within a thin atmospheric envelope around a finite planet, is appreciated more today than ever before. At the same time, the biological revolution is altering attitudes to disease, the human life-span may be extended, and leisure time is increasingly abundant. Concern with air pollution, therefore, ranges from the hazard potential at various scales to a desire for an optimum environment for different objectives.

Climate

The possibility that the global atmosphere may be saturated with pollution, possibly irreversible, is of major importance. There is added concern about the presence of specific toxic substances and, in particular, radioactive pollution.

Trace elements and constituents play a subtle and complex role in the atmosphere. In particular, terrestrial radiation is strongly absorbed by H_2O, CO_2 and O_3, although the last is important only in the stratosphere. The earth's surface radiates as a black body of about $288°K$ with maximum wavelength of radiation of 10 μ. The water vapour absorption extends over a wide region of wavelength, but the main CO_2 absorption is around 15 μ where H_2O absorption is small. The net result of all this absorption is to keep the earth warmer than it would be otherwise. Any change in the quantities of the trace constituents would have an effect on climate.

CO_2 has received most publicity in terms of this, the so-called greenhouse effect. Observed temperatures are, however, influenced by air movements in that convection distributes heat vertically while the general circulation redistributes it globally. Doubling the CO_2 concentration would produce an estimated increase in temperature of $2°C$; by the year 2000 the CO_2 concentration could well be 25 per cent above the 1950 level and significant warming may be expected. In calculating the effects of increasing CO_2, it has been possible to take into account convection but not, as yet, atmospheric circulation, and the treatment of the water vapour, which will increase with temperature, is a further difficulty.

Other factors also require consideration. The increasing turbidity (a measure of the optical effects of aerosols) of the atmosphere during this century is due partly to natural causes and partly to human activity. Recent measurements (Peterson and Bryson, 1968) appear to show an increase of 30 per cent within a decade, while calculations suggest that a turbidity change of three to four per cent, averaged over the whole world, would produce a reduction in temperature of $0.4°C$. Another feature which would operate as a counterbalance to CO_2 effects is the introduction of water vapour into the stratosphere by supersonic aircraft. The main effect therefrom would probably be to increase cloudiness wherever there is rising motion and this would diminish solar radiation reaching the earth, with a consequent cooling effect.

Above all, any changes must be evaluated against long-term climatic change due to natural causes. There is ample evidence of such changes in the past, including changes in the CO_2 concentrations, which were entirely independent of human activity. In recent years the temperature over the earth's surface rose by an estimated $0.4°C$ from the 1880s to the 1940s, followed by a fall of about $0.2°C$ in the succeeding quarter century. The case that present trends in pollution will produce significant changes in the radiation balance cannot be dismissed but it remains not proven.

Urban climates are undoubtedly altered by pollution, however. Airborne pollutants aggravate the heat island effect of cities and also alter the vertical temperature profile in a way that hinders their dispersion. The upward directed thermal radiation emitted at the surface is absorbed by the pollution pall: part of this is re-emitted downward and retained at the surface, but part warms the ambient air and hence tends to increase low level stability and enhance the possibility of higher concentration of pollution.

Precipitation may be affected by pollution. Sources of combustion certainly add to the quantity of water vapour in the atmosphere, but it is a moot point whether pollution increases urban precipitation. Condensation nuclei certainly increase and there are many studies stemming from the classic work of John Aitken (1923) at Falkirk.

Dust particles are much greater in urban environments. Smoke and combustion products are, on average, ten times greater over the city than over the rural surroundings, although the general shape of the size distribution curves is similar in both areas. In consequence, visibilities are usually lower in the former and fog may be more frequent. With the introduction of smoke control areas there is evidence of a resultant increase of visibility in many British cities. Little work has been undertaken on the effect of sulphur dioxide on visibility, except by Georgii and Hoffman (1966).

The combined effects of pollutants and some of the meteorological variables have yet to be unravelled, and this fact bedevils many attempts to evaluate the influence of pollution. Such influence may be beneficial as well as harmful, however, and it would be wrong to neglect the positive aspects of pollution over cities. Soils within urban areas are contaminated (Purves, 1966), but there are marked seasonal variations; vegetation is influenced but selectively; airborne bacteria harmful to Man may be inhibited. Health is a major consideration but the mechanism whereby pollution operates is as yet imperfectly understood (Lawther, et al., 1968).

PROBLEMS IN AIR POLLUTION RESEARCH

The preceding review is not intended to be either thorough or comprehensive. Many aspects of air pollution are ignored, such as indoor pollution, radioactive pollution, or viable particles such as spores and bacteria. The aim is to illustrate the range of spatial and temporal variations, to indicate the relative importance of these factors, and to hint at the subsequent history of pollutants after emission. Although air pollution is a subject which appears, at first sight, to be simple, it has been found to be increasingly complex in all its manifestations. While it is fairly easy, therefore, to obtain generalised information about air pollution, the cost involved in taking a further step towards the heart of the problem will rise out of all proportion to the amount of information which may be obtained.

A basic problem is simply choosing which pollutant to investigate. There are many pollutants and some selection is necessary either on the grounds of toxicity or on facilities to measure the substance.

Ambient air varies in three dimensions and time. The problems of sampling an unconfined, constantly changing medium are particularly difficult but they are compounded by ignorance of the atmospheric composition. There are many substances about which little is known either of their properties or characteristics. In such conditions, it is virtually impossible to isolate one substance for analysis. Titration, conductivity or chromatography are the three principal methods employed in measuring sulphur dioxide on the assumption that a particular reaction or response has brought about its presence in the atmosphere. There are difficulties in calibration, techniques and comparability, for not only do different methods often give incomparable assessments, but two adjacent instruments using the same method may differ in response.

The local nature of pollution has been noted. The spatial distribution of samplers which will give representative areal patterns is therefore complex and some knowledge of the general distribution is required before specific sites are selected. Associated with this problem is the difficulty of obtaining convenient sites at approximately equal heights in an urban environment. In practice, samples are situated some three to four metres above ground level, but the diurnal sequence of fumigagation is very important. Little is known of the vertical distribution of pollution over the city. Cost is also a factor and instruments are limited by supply and price. In urban patterns there is a need for a network of stations; if cheap instruments are utilised then the data are crude and a large number of man hours is required for maintenance; if an expensive system of communication is required, is it justified as a permanent feature?

CONCLUSION

The variations in the sources of atmospheric pollution, the contributory factors and the mechanisms for dispersal, mean that the significance of the problem differs in various countries and localities. Prediction, remedy and control will vary with each situation and it must be recognised that no one form of preventive measures will meet all needs everywhere.

Air conservation programmes, therefore, may be of local importance only and consequently cost/benefit ratios must be carefully calculated in each case. There is frequently a danger of blindly copying practices from other countries without a clear understanding of the applicability to the local area.

The implication of air pollution for society in the spheres of health, amenity, comfort and cost are only slowly being appreciated. There is a need to evaluate cost by other than economic criteria, but again it must be borne in mind that economic and cultural norms vary geographically. In particular, the criteria for assessing quality must be clearly defined.

Legislation is not very effective in air pollution because comprehension of the processes involved is limited; consequently measures tend to lack precision. The changing nature of pollution and the development of industrial processes also require that modifications in legislation and methods of enforcement will be required from time to time. The international significance is now recognised, for pollution knows no political boundaries; but the recent United Nations Stockholm Conference illustrated the difficulties involved in achieving acceptable international co-operation.

In many areas, air pollution problems have diminished in recent years. Techniques of abatement are improving but they must be used with caution. The essential factor in overall pollution control is to reduce the number of sources.

REFERENCES

Aitken, John (1923) *Collected Scientific Papers of John Aitken*, Cambridge University Press, Cambridge.

Astapowitsch, I. S. (1934) 'Air waves caused by the fall of the meteorite on 30th June, 1908, in Central Siberia', *Quarterly Journal of the Royal Meteorological Society*, 60 (257), pp. 493–504.

Barrett, C. A. (1970) 'Air pollution', *Royal Institute of Chemistry Reviews*, 3 (2), pp. 119–134.

Benson, Carl S. (1970) 'Ice fog', *Weather*, 25 (1), pp. 11–18.

Crosbie, A. J., N. J. Crosbie and J. H. A. Dick (1971) *Air Pollution in Edinburgh, Part III*, MSS.

Georgii, H. W. and L. Hoffman (1966) 'Assessing SO_2 enrichment as dependent on meteorological factors', *Staub*, 26 (12), pp. 1–4.

Lawther, P. J., J. McK. Ellison and R. E. Waller (1968) 'Some medical aspects of aerosol research', *Proceedings of the Royal Society*, A, 307, pp. 223–34.

Newell, R. A. (1971) 'The global circulation of atmospheric pollution', *Scientific American*, 224 (1), pp. 32–42.

Peterson, J. T. and R. A. Bryson (1968) 'Atmospheric aerosols: increased concentrations during the last decade', *Science* 162, pp. 120–1.

President's Science Advisory Committee (1965) *Restoring the Quality of our Environment*, Report of the Environmental Pollution Panel, The White House, Washington.

Purves, D. (1966) 'Contaminations of urban garden soils with copper, boron and lead', *Plant and Soil*, 26 (2), pp. 380–1.

Reid, William T. (1970) 'The Melchett Lecture, 1969—the energy explosion', *Journal of the Institute of Fuel*, February, pp. 43–51.

Robinson, E. and R. C. Robbins (1968) *Sources, Abundance and Fate of Gaseous Atmospheric Pollutants*, (Final Report S.R.I. Project PR-6755), American Petroleum Institute, New York.

Royal Society (1888) *The Eruption of Krakatoa and Subsequent Phenomena*, Report of the Krakatoa Committee, edited by G. J. Symons, London.

CHAPTER 4

Urban environment and physical health

EILEEN C. CROFTON

The concept of the urban environment is a complex one and comprises many factors which may exert independent effects on various aspects of physical health. Many of these factors interact. In some cases they may have a cumulative effect, so that the relative responsibility of different factors may be difficult to disentangle. Even if this were possible the exercise might prove a profitless one when it is the improvement of the total urban environment that should be the aim and not one or another particular aspect.

The urban environment comprises physical factors such as standards of housing, domestic overcrowding, density of population and atmospheric pollution. These are relatively simple to assess, and are susceptible to some form of measurement. But 'environment' also includes the services available such as health, educational and recreational facilities. The effect of these on the inhabitants depends partly on their ability to make use of them; this in turn is conditioned by cultural background and educational attainment. These factors may impose a lag between achieving physical improvements in the environment and its reflection in statistically demonstrable benefit to the inhabitants.

It is also necessary to consider all that is involved in the concept of 'social class': income levels, size of family, nutrition and occupation or the lack of it. The relationships are never simple and it may be difficult to separate the effect of one factor from another. The unskilled manual worker tends to have a larger family than the professional man. He lives in the most crowded and most polluted parts of the town. He is less able to mitigate the effects of a poor environment owing to limitations resulting from his own deprived childhood. Because of his overcrowding he is more exposed to infection at all ages.

The unskilled manual worker is also at more risk in an urban environment than in a rural one. Although domestic overcrowding may be as great for the poor rural worker as for the urban one, there is less risk of infection because of the lower population density. Though the rural worker's income may be equally low he may have facilities for supplementing his family's nutrition, his wife may have greater domestic skill, and he certainly breathes cleaner air. He is likely to smoke rather less heavily than his counterpart in the town, though the differences in this respect are probably less than they were.

Finally, in any consideration of physical health in a community, the effect of mental health cannot be ignored. The higher sickness rate in mothers and young children living in flats may be a reflection of the greater strains of flat life, including isolation and loneliness, rather than anything inherently unhealthy in the flats themselves. The subject is enormously complex and much of what follows may seem to be an over-simplification of the problems; but it is an attempt to identify some fields in which planning action could most usefully be concentrated to produce the greatest effect on improvement of physical health in an urban environment.

MORTALITY

That towns on the whole are less healthy places than rural areas can be shown by an examination of the death rates. Table 1 shows the death rates from all causes at the ages of 45–64 according to the degree of urbanisation, and it shows that death in middle age follows an urban/rural gradient. If the urban areas are regrouped in terms of their levels of atmospheric pollution (smoke and SO_2), as in Table 2, the gradient

TABLE 1. *Death rate at ages 45–64 from all causes:
England and Wales 1950–3*

Rate per 1,000 (all areas)	Urban areas				Rural areas
	Conurbations	>100,000	50–100,000	<50,000	
Males 14·4≡100	107	108	101	98	81
Females 8·4≡100	101	104	98	102	93

Reproduced by permission of E. and S. Livingstone, Edinburgh and London (Morris, 1964) and H.M.S.O., London (Registrar General for England and Wales, 1951b).

TABLE 2. *Death rate at ages 45–64 from all causes
related to atmospheric pollution: England and Wales 1950–3*

All areas	County Boroughs			Rural	
	'Dirty'	Intermediate	'Clean'	Industrial	Agricultural
Males 100	124	112	97	94	73
Females 100	114	108	94	104	89

Reproduced by permission of the Editor and the *British Journal of Preventive and Social Medicine* (Daly, 1959).

becomes more marked. Table 3 is confined to deaths from respiratory disease, and Table 4 to bronchitis which, in fact, is the cause of the biggest difference in urban and rural rates. These figures all relate to

TABLE 3. *Death rate at ages 45–64 from respiratory disease related to atmospheric pollution: England and Wales 1950–3*

All areas	County Boroughs			Rural
	'Dirty'	Intermediate	'Clean'	
Males 100	153	116	93	62
Females 100	141	118	84	76

Reproduced by permission of the Editor and the *British Journal of Preventive and Social Medicine.*

TABLE 4. *Death rate at ages 45–64 from bronchitis related to atmospheric pollution: England and Wales 1950–3*

All areas	County Boroughs			Rural
	'Dirty'	Intermediate	'Clean'	
Males 100	176	126	80	52
Females 100	186	132	71	59

From Morris (1964) and Keys (1963).

1950–3 (Morris, 1964). The most recent figures available relate to 1968 (Registrar-General, 1951 and 1968) and in Table 5 are placed alongside those of 1951. Death rates per 100,000 are shown (not mortality ratios as in Tables 1–4). Owing to a change in the mode of classifying bronchitis as a cause of death the rates in 1951 and 1968 cannot be compared directly. The table should be used only to compare the urban/rural gradients in each year, and shows that the gradient is less marked than formerly. There were 2½ times as many deaths in the conurbations as in the rural areas in 1951 for males and

TABLE 5. *Urban/rural gradient in bronchitis mortality in England and Wales at ages 45–64 in 1951 and 1968 (rates per 100,000)*

	Conurbations	Urban areas			Rural areas
		>100,000	50–100,000	<50,000	
1951					
Males	176·3	154·9	127·7	121·1	71·1
Females	43·2	37·9	31·6	32·5	20·1
1968 *					
Males	118·3	107·8	101·0	91·7	77·7
Females	23·3	23·6	27·3	19·3	14·8

* A change in the method of coding deaths from bronchitis in 1968 does not allow a direct comparison of the rates shown here. The table should be used only to demonstrate the decrease in the urban/rural gradient.

in 1968, $1\frac{1}{2}$ times as many. In females the ratio has fallen from 2·1 to 1·6. There are two possible explanations for this. One is that the decrease in the amount of pollution in the larger towns that has occurred since the introduction of the Clean Air Act in 1956 has reduced the number of deaths in this age group; the other is that there has now been a longer experience of cigarettte smoking in the rural areas and this is resulting in more bronchitis. Possibly both these factors are important. In the country as a whole these trends tend to cancel each other out. There has been little change in overall mortality.

Pneumonia

The urban/rural differences in pneumonia are small, much less than they are for lung cancer or bronchitis. For this reason and because there is some possibility of overlap in diagnosis with bronchitis, pneumonia will not be considered separately.

Lung Cancer

The role of atmospheric pollution

Although lung cancer death rates show a marked urban/rural gradient there are good reasons for considering that only a very small part of this is due to atmospheric pollution in urban areas. In the absence of cigarette smoking the chance of developing lung cancer in an urban environment is small, though slightly higher than it is for a non-smoker in the country. At each level of smoking the risk is higher in the towns, and increases with increasing population density. It seems likely that there is some factor in the urban environment, possibly atmospheric pollution, which acts synergistically with cigarette smoking to increase the chances of developing lung cancer in cigarette smokers. But there is another factor to be taken into account. Town dwellers have been smoking cigarettes for longer than have country dwellers and they still smoke more heavily, although the differences are less great than they were. It takes many years of smoking to produce lung cancer and the rates we are seeing now are the result of past cigarette smoking and can certainly account for some of the urban/rural differences.

The role of cigarette smoking

The increase in lung cancer in this century has paralleled the rise in cigarette consumption. It has occurred while coal consumption (the most important cause of atmospheric pollution in this country) has been falling, and was extremely rare in the nineteenth century when atmospheric pollution was far higher than it is now or has been for many years. Diesel oil consumption followed the rise in lung cancer and must therefore be exonerated. Petrol consumption increased as lung cancer increased, but lung cancer deaths rose in men before they began to rise in women (Royal College of Physicians, 1971). These rises followed their respective increases in cigarette smoking. In men, cigarette smoking began to be really widespread in the First World War. Women began smoking later (Todd, 1969). Lung cancer death rates are very much higher in men than in women, just as cigarette smoking is still heavier in men. There is no such difference in the sexes in exposure to petrol fumes, and occupations that involve an exposure to such fumes carry no added risk of lung cancer (Doll, 1953; and Royal College of Physicians, 1971). The overwhelming role of the cigarette in causing lung cancer has now been thoroughly established in many countries in long-term prospective studies covering many years. There can be no further room for doubt.

Urban planning and lung cancer

The corollary of this for the urban planner is that his efforts to improve the quality of air are unlikely to produce a great effect on the lung cancer death rate unless this is accompanied by a major reduction in cigarette smoking. To achieve this his responsibility is as great as that of any other member of the informed public in helping to generate a climate of opinion in which cigarette smoking is unacceptable. But he can make an extra contribution in promoting the reduction of smoking in public places to safeguard the rights of non-smokers. Smoking should be banned in theatres, cinemas, restaurants and public transport. Though it is not susceptible of proof, it is quite possible that some of the differences between urban and rural rates is due to a greater exposure in the towns to smoke from other people's cigarettes.

In spite of the overriding importance of the cigarette it is likely that atmospheric pollution makes some extra contribution to the risk run by the cigarette smoker in developing lung cancer and that this contribution is greater in the areas of higher pollution and higher population density (Royal College of Physicians, 1970). It follows that a reduction of pollution is likely to result in some decrease in lung cancer rates, and that this reduction could be greatly increased if cigarette smoking were tackled at the same time. Theoretically, this is an almost totally preventable disease.

Bronchitis

This disease has a higher urban/rural gradient than any other, and because of its great importance in this country it demands particular attention.

International comparisons

The United Kingdom has the highest death rate in the world from bronchitis, and has probably done so for a very long time (World Health Organisation, 1964). It has sometimes been called 'The English Disease' and the density of our urban air has been the subject of comment by visitors to this country for several hundred years.

It could be argued that our high mortality is due to different diagnostic habits, and that other countries have as much 'bronchitis' but call it something else. This has been checked by comparing case notes and death certificates in this country and the United States, and suggests that the British excess of chronic lung disease is a true one. The excess is also shown in a number of international surveys where similar occupational groups have been compared by similar methods. Men of similar age and smoking habits living in London had more bronchitis, and more severe bronchitis, than men in Norway or the United States (Royal College of Physicians, 1970).

The size of the bronchitis problem

Bronchitis causes about 30,000 deaths every year in the United Kingdom. About 7,000 of these are in men aged 35–64, so that it is a very important cause of death in middle-aged men. It is a disease which runs a long course and causes a great deal of disability. It is the greatest single cause of loss of working days: over 39 million days are lost every year owing to bronchitis (Office of Health Economics, 1965). It is the most expensive disease in terms of sickness benefit: in 1965 it cost the country £28 million (Office of Health Economics, 1964). It is the greatest cause of long-term absence from work. In 1965, 14,000 men had drawn sickness benefit continuously for over two years. In 1961 the costs to the National Health Service were £21 million, and are certainly much higher now. In 1961 a survey undertaken by the College of General Practitioners (College of General Practitioners, 1961) estimated that almost half a million men suffered from a disabling degree of breathlessness, almost all of which was attributable to bronchitis. Nor is the disease decreasing. The overall mortality in England and Wales has remained steady for some years, but that in Scotland has been rising, particularly in middle-aged men (McKinley, 1960; and Crofton, 1970). In spite of more awareness of the disease and improved (though still very imperfect) methods of treatment it remains one of our greatest problems.

The problem of bronchitis for the patient

The onset of chronic bronchitis is usually very insidious so that the patient is often unable to say when it began. He may have had a productive cough for years but experienced little inconvenience from it. This may be followed by periods of increased cough and phlegm in the winter months, interspersed with bouts of chest infection which take progressively longer to clear up. Later, cough and sputum may persist all the year round. Along with this there is a gradual increase in breathlessness caused by destructive changes in his lungs. Frequently the patient has to change to a lighter job and finally is unable to work at all. His social activities become more and more limited, and he may ultimately become completely housebound. He is now a respiratory cripple until his death from an exacerbation of his infection or from heart failure due to his disease. In a severe case such as is described here he usually dies before the age of 65, often earlier. Not all patients are as severely affected as this, but the condition is sufficiently common to fill chest clinics and hospitals and to result in many demands on the social services. A few years ago when an enquiry was being carried out in Edinburgh and Glasgow into the social effects of the disease (Neilson and Crofton, 1965) no difficulty was experienced in finding 500 patients who were progressing along this path.

Bronchitis in urban areas

Bronchitis mortality is higher in towns than in the country (British Medical Journal, 1971), and in Britain is particularly high in the more polluted industrial towns and in London. A country-wide survey of postmen (Fairbairn and Reid, 1958a), a uniform occupational group, showed that their absence from work on account of bronchitis was related to the amount of fog in the area in which they lived. In this study thick fog was used as an index of pollution. In another study in London (Ministry of Pensions and National Insurance, 1965) absence from work due to bronchitis for men in all occupations was related to the measured smoke pollution to which they were exposed. Patients suffering from chronic bronchitis experience an increase in their symptoms when there is a peak in the smoke pollution to which they are exposed, provided that it is above a certain level. This was demonstrated some years ago by patients recording their own symptoms every day in the London area. More recently repetition of the investigation failed to show this association, but smoke pollution was a great deal lower, and it would appear that London air is now much healthier for bronchitics (Lawther *et al.*, 1970).

Bronchitis and social class

There is a social class gradient in mortality from bronchitis so that six times as much occurs in social class V—the unskilled manual labourer—as in social class I—the professional class (British Medical Journal, 1971). The precise factors involved are not clearly identified. Some of the differences will be due to the greater exposure to atmospheric pollution of the members of social class V and their greater exposure to infection associated with domestic overcrowding, but the subject will be considered again in connection with the health of children. The social class gradient has changed little in the last 50 years.

Bronchitis and cigarette smoking

The role of cigarette smoking in bronchitis is extremely important and may be increasing. Unlike lung cancer, however, in which abolition of cigarette smoking would in time practically abolish the disease, the same cannot be said of bronchitis which was an extremely common and fatal disease in the nineteenth century when cigarette smoking was unimportant. Much of the mortality then was probably associated with infection. This element has tended to come under control with modern treatment, but smoking has become a far more important factor. In the nineteenth century the mortality from bronchitis was only slightly higher in men than in women. It is now over five times as high in men dying at the ages of 45–64 as it is in women, and this change is probably a reflection of the greater part now played by cigarette smoking in causing the disease and the much higher smoking rate in men. Bronchitis is commoner in smokers than in non-smokers, and it increases in prevalence with the amount smoked. In a very important prospective study on the mortality of doctors (Doll and Hill, 1964) it was found that they died from bronchitis in proportion to the level of smoking which they had recorded many years before they died.

Air pollution and cigarette smoking acting together

A recent survey (Lambert and Reid, 1970) in different parts of Great Britain has correlated smoking habits of people in middle age with their area of residence classified by four different air pollution levels. At each level of pollution there was about three times as much bronchitis found in smokers as in non-smokers. There was about twice the amount of bronchitis in the most polluted areas as there was in the cleanest areas both for the smokers and the non-smokers. Smokers in the dirtiest areas had five times as much as non-smokers in the cleanest areas. This shows that both factors are of major importance and they act together.

AIR POLLUTION AND THE HEALTH OF CHILDREN

A good deal of recent work has been carried out on children in an attempt to find out if air pollution has any effect at early ages and, if so, whether the origin of the bronchitis seen in middle life can be traced back to early childhood experience.

A long-term follow-up study has been made on the health of children born in one particular week in 1946 (Douglas and Waller, 1966) in the United Kingdom. The children have been examined at intervals since and have been reported on up to the age of fifteen years. They were analysed according to the level of pollution to which they were exposed. There was no difference in the amount of upper respiratory tract infections (colds and sore throats), but the amount of chest illness (bronchitis or pneumonia) was closely related to the amount of pollution to which they were exposed. This correlation was found as early as the age of two and was still present at the age of fifteen.

A more precise survey (Colley and Reid, 1970) has been made recently on over 10,000 schoolchildren aged 6–10 years (an age when it was hoped there would be no cigarette smoking). Three levels of pollution were compared and the results supported the earlier survey in finding no difference in colds and sore throats. There was an urban/rural gradient in chest illness, but only in social classes IV and V. There was a social class gradient in chronic ear infections (which may result from repeated and prolonged colds and sore throats). More children had chronic ear infections in the most polluted area whatever their social class, but the gradient between town and country was not consistent.

Another large survey of schoolchildren in Kent (Holland *et al.*, 1969) measured lung function. This was impaired in those who had had a previous chest illness. It was also lower in the more polluted areas, in the lower social classes and in those who came from larger families. Although all these factors were important and exerted an independent effect, an analysis of variance suggested that the area of residence might be the most important.

In the days of National Service it was found that chronic ear infections were commoner in recruits who came from homes where pollution levels were high (Lee, 1957). They were also more liable to chest infections during their service (Rosenbaum, 1961). This suggested that their early experience and/or the physical environment to which they had been exposed was still affecting their health.

A study of the medical records of postmen who had died from bronchitis (Fairbairn and Reid, 1958b), or who had become so severely disabled from it that they had had to retire prematurely, showed that they had had significantly more chest illnesses in early adult life than had their contemporaries. The records threw no light on childhood experience, but a survey of transport workers in London (Fletcher, 1965) has suggested strongly that, in the absence of cigarette smoking (which is such a potent factor of itself in causing the disease), men who suffer from bronchitis after the age of 30 have had significantly more chest illness as children than had non-smokers without bronchitis.

Chest illnesses and chronic ear infections

The evidence suggests that children in highly polluted areas experience more chest illness and chronic ear infections than do those in less polluted areas. For chest illness the effect of pollution has been demonstrated in children of the lower social classes. It seems that pollution is only one factor in a generally adverse environment, but the evidence from the Kent survey indicates it may be at least as important as the other factors which relate to social conditions.

Bronchitis

It is less clear whether the bronchitis seen so often in adult life has its origins in childhood or is a result of childhood exposure to pollution and adverse social circumstances. The evidence from non-smokers is suggestive that the damage begins early. The evidence from National Service recruits suggests that an increased liability to respiratory illness results from earlier exposure to pollution. Cigarette smoking is so often involved and is such an overwhelming factor in producing bronchitis in middle age that it has not yet been found possible precisely to define the roles of other less powerful influences originating in early childhood.

Is atmospheric pollution important now?

Although atmospheric pollution is now much less in many areas than it was even a few years ago the differences are not such that the evidence produced here can be ignored. It is probably true that in the past National Service recruits from the most polluted areas experienced levels of pollution higher than any to which children are now exposed, but the large Kent survey (published in 1969) detected differences in children who were exposed to the kind of pollution levels which are still very common, and which are exceeded in many towns. It seems that one should aim at a level of atmospheric pollution in all towns at which a survey of children—of any social class—fails to reveal any pollution gradient in chest illness, chronic cough or chronic ear infections. It is not yet known what level is 'safe', but it is known that it has not yet been reached. Surveys of children have the advantage of being relatively easy to carry out, they can provide an answer in a relatively short time, and they could be used as a monitoring system to check our progress in reducing atmospheric pollution over the country as a whole as well as in selected areas.

INFANT MORTALITY

Infant mortality rates are considered to be sensitive indices of the health of a community and as such should be considered in the present context. They refer to deaths occurring in the first year of life and are expressed in terms of a rate per 1,000 live births. They have fallen in England and Wales from about 150 in 1900 to 18 in 1968. This decrease has occurred at all ages within the first year, but in recent years the decrease has been mainly in the neonatal period, that is, in the first four weeks of life. The post-neonatal mortality rate (deaths occurring between four weeks and one year) fell steadily until 1957 in England and Wales and has thereafter remained steady.

The neonatal mortality rate includes a considerable number of deaths due to congenital malformations, some cases of immaturity and deaths resulting from birth injury, that is, many deaths are due to natal and pre-natal causes. Post-neonatal death rates, on the other hand, reflect the standards of care received by the child and the nature of its physical environment, and infections are more prominent among the causes of death. Table 6 (which refers to Scotland) shows that there is an urban/rural gradient for all three infant mortality rates, and Table 7 shows a social class gradient which is much greater than the urban/rural gradient (Registrar-General for Scotland, 1967). Table 7 also shows that the social class gradient is most marked for the post-neonatal deaths, confirming the important role of social and environmental factors at this age.

The post-neonatal death rate is almost four times higher in social class V as it is in social class I. (The neonatal mortality rate is less than

TABLE 6. *Infant mortality and urbanisation: Scotland 1967*

Area	Infant mortality rate per 1,000 live births 0–1 year	Neonatal mortality rate per 1,000 live births 0–4 weeks	Post-neonatal mortality rate per 1,000 live births 4 weeks–1 year
Cities	23·1	15·0	8·1
Large Burghs	21·6	14·1	7·5
Counties (exclusive of above)	19·3	12·9	6·4

Adapted from Table T57 (Registrar-General for Scotland, 1968) by permission of the Controller of H.M.S.O., Edinburgh.

TABLE 7. *Infant mortality and social class: Scotland 1967*

Social class	Infant mortality rate per 1,000 live births 0–1 year	Neonatal mortality rate per 1,000 live births 0–4 weeks	Post-neonatal mortality rate per 1,000 live births 4 weeks–1 year
I	14·0	10·2	3·8
II	16·1	12·4	3·7
III	19·4	13·2	6·2
IV	22·4	13·9	8·5
V	33·6	18·9	14·7

Adapted from Table T57 (Registrar-General for Scotland) by permission of the Controller of H.M.S.O., Edinburgh.

twice as high.) From 1939 there has been some reduction in the ratio of social class V to social class I, as Table 8 shows, but the trend is not consistent. Table 9 shows that the social class difference is greater in the four Scottish cities than in the larger towns and other areas of Scotland.

Because of the concern felt at the lack of improvement in the post-neonatal mortality rate in recent years an enquiry was made in a few selected areas of England and Wales in 1964 to 1966 to find out what factors might be involved (Department of Health and Social Security, 1970). A total of 679 deaths were investigated. Respiratory infection was involved in almost half the cases. Congenital malformations accounted for about one quarter, and the remainder were chiefly due to gastro-enteritis, and accidents or violence. There were more deaths than would be expected in social class V and fewer in social class I. The proportion of deaths due to respiratory infection was higher in social classes IV and V than in the other social classes.

An attempt was made to find 'avoidable factors' which were classified as 'social', 'parental', and others connected with medical and welfare services. Sixteen per cent of the deaths due to respiratory infection and twenty per cent of the deaths due to gastro-intestinal

TABLE 8. *Social class and post-neonatal mortality: Scotland 1939–67*

Year	Ratio of social class V to social class I
1939	5·9
1949	6·3
1959	6·7
1964	4·7
1965	4·4
1966	6·7
1967	3·9

TABLE 9. *Post-neonatal mortality, social class and urbanisation: Scotland 1967*

Area	Ratio of social class V to social class I
Cities	4·7
Large Burghs	2·46
Counties (exclusive of above)	3·90

infection had 'avoidable' social factors. These were in most cases un-satisfactory housing, with or without overcrowding. The size of the family intensifies any inadequacy of the housing, and overcrowding is a source of respiratory and intestinal cross-infection. There were 'frequent' cases of five individuals sleeping in one room, but there was one case of two parents with five children under six years of age living in two rooms, and one of two parents with nine children in three rooms. It was not unnaturally concluded that children born into such circum-stances were at risk whatever the supporting medical and social services. One might also add that such children were at risk whatever standard of personal care the mother was in a position to provide.

CONCLUSION

In spite of the difficulties of isolating different factors in the urban environment it is possible to draw some practical conclusions. We are still a very long way from achieving the reduction of atmospheric pollution to which our technical knowledge should entitle us. If an all-out attack were made on this, an improvement could reasonably be expected in the health of young children in the short term, a reduction in adult bronchitis, particularly of the more severe and disabling forms of the diseases in the long term, and perhaps a slight effect on the lung cancer death rate.

Housing standards are still very unsatisfactory and overcrowding is all too common. Improvements in housing and the elimination of overcrowding could lead to an immediate saving of infant lives. A considerable improvement could reasonably be expected in the health of children of all ages, particularly in chest illness. One could expect fewer damaged ears and less deafness resulting from chronic ear infections and, as with pollution, one would hope to achieve a reduction in the dreadful—and disgraceful—toll of bronchitis in the United Kingdom.

ACKNOWLEDGMENT

The author wishes to thank Professor J. O. Forfar of the Department of Child Life and Health, University of Edinburgh, for his advice.

REFERENCES

British Medical Journal (1971) (Answer in Parliament), the Journal, 1, p. 616.

College of General Practitioners (1961) 'Chronic bronchitis in Great Britain. A national survey carried out by the respiratory diseases study group of the College of General Practitioners', *British Medical Journal*, 2, p. 973.

Colley, J. R. T. and D. D. Reid (1970) 'Urban and social origins of childhood bronchitis in England and Wales', *British Medical Journal*, 2, p. 213.

Crofton, E. C. (1970) 'Recent trends in the mortality from bronchitis in Scotland', Health Bulletin, C.M.O., Scotland, XXVIII, 12.

Daly, C. (1959) 'Air Pollution and Causes of Death' *British Journal of Preventive and Social Medicine*, 13, p. 14.

Department of Health and Social Security (1970), '*Confidential Enquiry into Post-neonatal Deaths* 1964–66', Report on Public Health and Medical Subjects, No. 125. London, 1970.

Doll, R. (1953) 'Bronchial carcinoma: incidence and aetiology', *British Medical Journal*, 2, pp. 521 and 585.

Doll, R. and A. B. Hill (1964) 'Mortality in relation to smoking: ten years' observations of British doctors', *British Medical Journal*, 1, p. 1399.

Douglas, J. W. B. and R. E. Waller (1966) 'Air pollution and respiratory infection in children', *British Journal of Preventive and Social Medicine*, 21, p. 1.

Fairbairn, A. S. and D. D. Reid (1958a) 'Air pollution and other local factors in respiratory disease', *British Journal of Preventive and Social Medicine*, 12, p. 94.

Fairbairn, A. S. and D. D. Reid (1958b) 'The natural history of chronic bronchitis', *Lancet*, 1, p. 1147.

Fletcher, C. M. (1965) 'Some recent advances in the prevention and treatment of chronic bronchitis and related disorders', *Proceedings of the Royal Society of Medicine*, 58, p. 980.

Holland, W. W., T. Halil, A. E. Bennett and A. Elliott (1969) 'Factors influencing the onset of chronic respiratory disease', *British Medical Journal*, 2, p. 205.

Keys, A. (1963) In *Atherosclerosis and its Origin* ed. M. Sandler, and G. H. Bourne, New York.

Lambert, P. M. and D. D. Reid (1970) 'Smoking, air pollution and bronchitis in Britain', *Lancet*, 1, p. 853.

Lawther, P. J., R. E. Waller and M. Henderson (1970) 'Air pollution and exacerbations of bronchitis', *Thorax*, 25, p. 525.

Lee, J. A. H. (1957) 'Chronic otitis media among a sample of young men', *Journal of Laryngology and Otology*, 71, p. 398.

McKinley, P. L. (1960) 'A note on bronchitis', *Health Bulletin*, C.M.O., Scotland, XVIII, 25.

Mork, T. (1962) 'A comparative study of respiratory disease in England and Wales and Norway', *Acta Medica Scandinavica*, 172, Supplement 384.

Morris, J. N. (1964) *Uses of Epidemiology*, Livingstone, Edinburgh and London.

Ministry of Pensions and National Insurance (1965) *Report on an Enquiry into the Incidence of Incapacity for Work*, Part II, H.M.S.O., London.

Neilson, Mary G. C. and Eileen Crofton (1965) *The Social Effects of Chronic Bronchitis*, Chest and Heart Association, Edinburgh.

Office of Health Economics (1964) *The Costs of Medical Care*, The Office, London.

Office of Health Economics (1965) *Work Lost Through Sickness*, the Office, London.

Registrar-General for England and Wales (1951(a)) *Statistical Review of England and Wales for the Year 1951*, Part 1, Tables Medical, H.M.S.O., London.

Registrar-General for England and Wales (1951(b)) *Statistical Review of England and Wales for the Year 1951*, Area Mortality, H.M.S.O., London.

Registrar-General for England and Wales (1968) *Statistical Review of England and Wales for the Year 1968*, H.M.S.O., London.

Registrar-General for Scotland (1967) *Annual Report, 1967*, H.M.S.O., London.

Rosenbaum, S. (1961) 'Home localities of national servicemen with respiratory disease', *British Medical Journal*, 15, p. 61.

Royal College of Physicians (1970) *Air Pollution and Health*, Pitman, London.

Royal College of Physicians (1971) *Smoking and Health Now*, Pitman, London.

Todd, G. F. (1969) *Statistics of Smoking in the United Kingdom*, Tobacco Research Council Research Paper No. 1, 5th edition.

World Health Organisation (1964) *Epidemiological and Vital Statistics Report*, 17, p. 366.

CHAPTER 5

The evaluation of
visual intrusion
in transport situations[1]

R. G. HOPKINSON

In a recent series of broadcast talks, Lord Annan commented that, as a result of our concern for the preservation and the improvement of the environment, we would be forced to measure things which we had never measured before. Such things as amenity, aesthetic content and intrusion are almost always related in some way to economic factors. A more pleasing building is quite often a more expensive building, if only because it has to use materials and methods of construction which are more costly. There is no inherent law of nature which decrees that this should be so, but hard experience demonstrates that it usually is.

In the field of transport design, economic factors are playing an increasingly greater role. The population generally has woken up to the fact that the cost of providing the transport system which it has demanded, following its revolt against the overcrowding which the post-war car-ownership explosion has caused on Britain's road system, is barely within our present means, and so every unnecessary expense has to be looked at two or three times on a national scale just as it has on a domestic scale. The home owner who settles for an oleograph of The Laughing Cavalier costing £5 rather than an original by a young unknown artist costing £50 makes an aesthetic judgment in relation to an economic judgment exactly comparable to the judgment of a Planning Committee which decides to put an urban motorway on bare concrete stilts at the least possible cost, rather than commissioning a design in which materials are used with thought and taste appropriate to their environmental context. In each case the money saved may be put to good use, such as taking the family for a holiday or putting up an old people's home. Amenity has to be costed in relation to other requirements. The more pressing these other requirements, the more precise must be the costing of amenity.

If this argument is extended, amenity can rarely if ever be afforded. The money spent on Versailles could have saved the lives of thousands of starving Frenchmen who would now be dead and gone and we would have no Versailles to admire.

[1] Reproduced, with due acknowledgment, from the December 1972 issue of *Traffic Engineering & Control*.

These are the kind of arguments which the transport engineer has to face when questions of amenity, over and above the cost of bare functional necessity, are brought up. The answers on either side are rarely convincing to the other.

In recent years, however, the need to give priority to operating efficiency rather than environmental amenity in the design of transport systems has produced a sharp reaction from the populations most affected and a sympathetic response from the rest of the population— motivated, perhaps, by a feeling of 'there but for the grace of God go we'—and these people, organised by professionals, have become a powerful lobby whose voice must be heard in all questions of environmental design. This is as it should be, provided that the balance of amenity and necessity is not too disturbed the other way.

Certain aspects of amenity lend themselves more readily to quantification than do others. Chemical pollution, for example, can, to a very large extent be quantified. Certain pollutants are known, in precisely measurable terms, to affect the functioning of the human body, and so levels of these pollutants can be specified for a given environment and the degree of pollution controlled.

In other aspects of environmental pollution our knowledge is not so precise, and we are less able to be objective. During the past few years a great deal has been learned about the effects of noise levels on human hearing, in the long term as well as in the short term. Tolerable levels of noise so far as they have physiological effects are beginning to be understood, and so lend themselves to quantification. The psychological effects of noise are less well understood, although here again knowledge is improving under the pressure of events and there are now tentative standards of permissible noise levels which are based entirely upon subjective factors (Wilson Committee, 1963). A further stage in the control of noise is planned by the intention to create 'noise abatement areas' (Noise Advisory Council, 1971) on an analogy with the smoke abatement areas already on the statute book. Real progress can therefore be claimed in the quantification of noise abatement and control, in spite of the fact that many of the standards have to be based upon purely subjective rather than objective factors.

As the problems of chemical pollution and noise pollution move towards some form of solution, other aspects of environmental pollution achieve prominence. Attention is now being turned belatedly to the loss of visual amenity and the demand has arisen for some method of quantifying visual intrusion comparable with the methods which already exist for the specification of tolerable noise limits.

Certain aspects of visual intrusion lend themselves readily to quantification. If an elevated urban motorway, or even a traffic direction sign, is erected in such a way that sunlight or natural daylight is excluded from a living room, there is a valid claim under existing law. For example, the owner may be able to obtain some reduction in his rates by virtue of loss of quantifiable natural light. However, it happens more often that a large transport artefact is built in such a way that the reduction in natural light or sunlight penetration is minimal, but nevertheless the landscape is so drastically changed that clearly there has been a loss of visual amenity in the sense that something less pleasant has been substituted for what was there before. What is required is to put numbers on the terms 'clearly' and 'less pleasant' in the previous sentence. The difficulties are obvious. What is 'clearly' a loss to one group of people in one environment, say middle-class home owners in a garden suburb, is less of a loss to factory workers in a busy industrial community. What is 'less pleasant' to an artist or architect with trained aesthetic perception may be perfectly acceptable to someone whose interest is in stereo record-players, rather than his visual environment.

If the problem is put in this way it becomes essentially insoluble, and unfortunately it has been put in this way all too often in the past. As a consequence, relatively little has been done to quantify visual intrusion, and even now, after possible techniques have been put forward, many planners have withdrawn from the possibilities so offered because they feel that a partial solution is worse than no solution at all.

ASPECTS OF VISUAL INTRUSION

When a transport artefact is introduced into an existing visual environment, there results a change of view which may or may not affect the quality of the visual environment. This change of view is related to the point from which the observation is made, and so it becomes immediately clear that one has to consider a change of view as seen by a householder from a viewing point inside his house (Fig. 1a), and the change of view which occurs in the neighbourhood generally (Fig. 1b). An elevated urban motorway could be driven through a community in such a way that relatively few people would be affected directly by the change in view from their living room or bedrooms, while a great number would be affected by the pervading presence of the motorway as they walked to the shops or the railway station. For a start in this quantification process, the following definitions have been put forward: *Change of view* occurs when an artefact is visible from an observation point. *Change of visual amenity* occurs when the change of view is judged to be more or less pleasing than it was before. Whereas *change of view* is assessed purely quantitatively, *change of visual amenity* involves a subjective aesthetic judgment.

First steps in the solution of the problem can therefore be made in terms of assessing the change of view. Once this aspect of the problem is better understood, attention can be turned to the problem of assessing change of amenity.

SOME CHARACTERISTICS OF HUMAN VISION

Much attention has been given recently to the mechanism of human vision as a result of a widening of the horizons of understanding which

FIG. 1a. *'Household intrusion' results from a loss of visual amenity caused by a transport artefact seen directly from inside the house.*

FIG. 1b. *'Neighbourhood intrusion' occurs when the artefact is seen prominently from the street or parks, etc., even though it may not be seen from individual houses.*

have come from an assimilation of the operational principles of the digital computer. For many years the photographic camera was the well-understood analogy of human vision, and a great many of the aspects of the visual process could be explained satisfactorily in these terms. Nevertheless, the camera analogy left a great many important aspects of vision unexplained and it is only recently, when it has been realised that the eye embodies in itself a complex information-processing mechanism which makes it effectively an extension of the brain, that some, though not all, of these camera anomalies can be explained. It has been well known for decades that the human visual process is profoundly determined by the fact that the retina of the eye is very different from the film in the camera by virtue of the system of retinal light receptors, which are of two basic different characteristics, called the 'rods' and the 'cones' from their shape, and which have a different response to light and a different distribution over the retinal surface. The cones are closely packed at the centre of the eye and become progressively less dense towards the periphery, where the rods occur most frequently, but never with the same density as the cones at the centre. The cones govern colour vision in bright light, whereas the rods evoke no sensation of colour but only of light and shade. Colour vision is therefore minimal at the periphery of the eye. Rods, however, are much more sensitive to light than the cones, and so at night the periphery of the eye evokes the greater response. Furthermore, the cones, particularly at the centre of the eye, are linked to the information-processing centres of the brain by a direct line, whereas the rods are interlinked in the retina before joining a link to the brain. This results in the central part of the eye having a very much higher acuity than the periphery, but being much less sensitive to movement changes, particularly at night.

The human eye, of course, evolved when man was a predator and a hunter, as well as being hunted himself. His peripheral sensitivity to movement alerted him to the onset of a predator off his line of sight, and he could then turn his centre of acute vision and see the precise detail necessary in order to take appropriate action.

So far as visual intrusion is concerned, these properties of the human eye, which have been barely sketched above, point to the fact that objects which are seen centrally convey more 'information' in terms of detail than objects which are seen peripherally, while moving objects which are seen peripherally will cause more distraction than those which are seen centrally. These and other aspects of human vision need to be taken into account in any assessment of visual intrusion.

The central part of the visual field is therefore more meaningful in assessing the intrusive effect of, for example, an elevated urban motorway or a large traffic direction sign. If such a large artefact is seen through a householder's living room window directly opposite, it will have a far greater intrusive effect, and make a far greater change in his visual amenity, than if it is seen peripherally.

A VISUAL INTRUSION INDEX

The proposal was therefore put forward that visual intrusion should be quantified as a function of the solid angular subtense of the intruding artefact, modified by a 'Position Factor' based upon the position of the artefact in the visual field, a greater weighting being given to an object seen centrally than to an object seen peripherally, on a sliding scale.

This proposal was initially made in the context of the evaluation of the intrusion caused by elevated urban motorways, in work undertaken by the consultancy of Ralph Hopkinson and Newton Watson for the Urban Motorways Committee of the Department of the Environment (Burns Committee, 1972; Hopkinson, 1971). It was an extension of an earlier suggestion made by Bowers that visual intrusion should be assessed as a direct function of the apparent size of the intruding object (Lassiere and Bowers, 1972).

DETERMINATION OF THE POSITION FACTOR

This proposal for a visual intrusion index was tested in the field on an empirical basis before time permitted a more systematic investigation under controlled conditions in the laboratory. This was because of the urgency of the programme of the Department of the Environment's Urban Motorways Project.

The laboratory investigation, which was done later, consisted of an experiment in which a uniform visual field (a white matt hemisphere of two metres diameter with the observing position at the centre) was presented to an observer together with one or two black targets seen against the white background. The observer was asked to make either paired comparison judgments of the relative intrusiveness of the one target as compared with the other, or he was asked to make direct subjective judgments on a 0-100 scale. A large number of judgments was obtained from a group of observers, mostly in the younger age group (students and postgraduates) and from the analysis of these judgments a map of the relative sensitivity of the visual field to intrusion was determined (Fig. 2). This experiment confirmed that the central part of the visual field is indeed much more sensitive to the intrusive effects of an object seen statically than is the peripheral field, although it also showed that the field is not symmetrical, a more rapid falling-off in intrusiveness occurring vertically upwards than in vertically downwards or horizontally to the left and right.

Previous to this laboratory experiment, an empirical judgment had been made of the magnitude of the Position Factor, and tested in the field. This judgment had been based partly on the previously known fact from one of the author's earlier research studies (on discomfort glare) that the sensitivity of the eye to the glaring effects of bright sources of light falls off towards the periphery approximately as the square of the angle between the direction of the source and the direction of view. On this basis, the visual field was divided into three basic

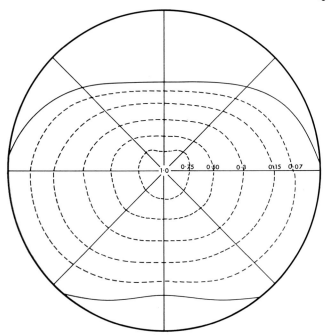

FIG. 2. *Relative sensitivity of the visual field to intrusion.*

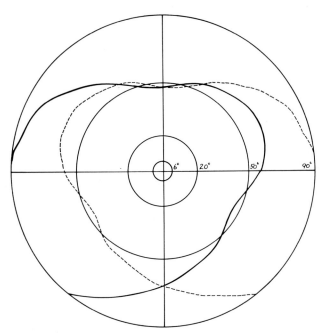

FIG. 3. *Circular zones of radius 6°, 20°, 50° and 90° from the centre of vision, together with the fields of the two individual eyes. (The 50° circle is seen to correspond approximately to the limits of the binocular limits of the field.)*

zones: (i) from the centre to 20° radius; (ii) from 20° to 50° radius (which is the approximate limit of the combined binocular field, where both eyes are functioning equally); and (iii) from 50° radius to the extreme periphery (approximately 90° radius) of the visual field (Fig. 3). It was argued empirically that the weighting of these three zones should be equal, and that therefore their position weighting should be in inverse proportion to their area. This weighting was found to be approximately in conformity with the inverse square angle function derived from the glare investigation.

This empirical weighting function was tested in the field by comparing direct subjective estimates of visual intrusion, made by a team of skilled observers, with predicted values based on the subtended solid angle modified by the empirical position factor. Good correlation was obtained, considerably better than with solid angle unmodified for position.

Comparison was subsequently made, when the laboratory studies were completed, between the empirical position factors and a comparable function derived from the laboratory studies. Good agreement was obtained, within the variance of the judgments involved.

There is every reason to believe, therefore, that the subjective magnitude of the intrusion of an artefact in the visual field can be adequately represented by an index based on the solid angular subtense of the artefact at the observing point and a position factor following approximately an inverse square angle relationship, that is: V.I. Index $= k\Sigma(W_1 P_1 + W_2 P_2 + \ldots W_n P_n)$ where W and P are respectively the solid angular subtenses and position factors for each individual element of the artefact or artefacts causing the intrusion.

This is the first step, and although it does not take us all the way towards a total quantitative evaluation of visual amenity, it is a useful tool comparable to the derivation of the dBA scale of noise measurement. The dBA scale was shown empirically to accord well with subjective assessments of traffic noise magnitude, and was therefore adopted as a useful objective measure in the field of noise evaluation, even though it could not be claimed to make any useful assessment of the degree of annoyance or intrusiveness of the noise, which depended upon environmental and demographic factors in addition.

The situation is now exactly the same for visual intrusion. An objective measure has been derived which puts a meaningful number on a limited aspect of the visual intrusion. On the noise analogy, visual intrusion now has its dBA scale. It now awaits its Wilson Committee.

Unfortunately the value of what has been done so far has tended to be submerged in the realisation of what still remains to be done. The proposed visual intrusion index has been criticised on the basis that it does not assess visual amenity, the factor which is wanted. This is true, and if, at a comparable stage of the development of the assessment of noise, the dBA scale had been rejected because it did not quantify annoyance, a great deal of valuable work would have been lost and the

Wilson Committee on Noise could not have done its work. Fortunately, however, in spite of the obvious limitations, the development work continues.

The important immediate value of the visual intrusion index is that it can be used for comparing like with like. Without the missing aesthetic component, it is not possible yet to use such an index to compare the amenity value of one design of elevated motorway with another but it is possible to use the index to put firm figures on the relative visual intrusion caused by one siting of an urban motorway with another, and this is often the information which is wanted in making planning decisions.

CHANGE OF VISUAL AMENITY

In order to employ the visual intrusion index to assess change in visual amenity, it is necessary to introduce a further factor which involves the quantitative assessment of aesthetic quality. This is a problem of a different and greater order and it is almost certain that it will have to be solved on a basis of consensus of current opinion. Many attempts have been made over the years to find some objective factors which correlate with aesthetic judgment, but they have been of limited value and have received limited acceptance and this situation is likely to remain.

There are several approaches to the problem which have been considered and are being examined at the moment in the course of the present development work. First, there is the obvious one of the social survey, of asking people what they think and subjecting the information to a statistical analysis in the hope that something of consensus value will emerge. Opinions about the aesthetic quality of human artefacts tend to change with what is called 'aesthetic fashion', but it remains sufficiently stable over a period of years to justify certain limited planning decisions. Consequently the social survey procedure is not unacceptable, in that it should reveal the kind of design which is at present acceptable and which is likely to remain acceptable for a number of years.

The second procedure is to employ a group of eminent specialists, along the lines of the Royal Fine Arts Commission, to decide on behalf of the rest of us what is aesthetically acceptable and what is not. The advantage of this procedure is that it can be relatively speedy, and, if the members of the Commission are well chosen, their judgments may often be in advance of their time, so that decisions based on their recommendations may have somewhat more lasting value than those based upon a social survey of the opinions of the laymen now.

The third is a more indirect approach making use of inductive arguments. The proposal is put forward that a visual amenity index can be expressed as a function of the solid angular subtense, the position factor, and a 'hedonic' index for each component of the visual field. The procedure then is as follows. A representative population of observers is asked to assess, on a numerical scale, the degree of visual amenity offered by a large number of different scenes. These scenes should consist of one constant element, or as nearly constant as possible, such as a rural landscape, together with a variable element whose hedonic factor is to be assessed. Then in the hypothetical equation, substitutions can be made, that is, the visual amenity value is assessed directly, the solid angular subtense and the position factor of the elements can be measured, leaving the hedonic index to be deduced. This indirect approach has a certain procedural advantage in that direct judgments of the aesthetic quality of the artefactural elements are not required. The aesthetic quality is assessed only indirectly, in terms of visual amenity in the context in which the artefact is seen.

Finally, there is the analytical approach. This has not yet been able to make much progress, but should not be discounted because of this. The analytical approach is based upon a study of the objective content in terms of, for example, visual information theory (Moles, 1966).

APPLICATION OF A VISUAL INTRUSION INDEX

Considerable progress has been made in the last two years in the application of these ideas on the quantitative assessment of visual intrusion, while recognising that much remains to be done before the subject will have advanced as far as has that of the assessment of noise intrusion. The latter has, after all, had 15 years' start and a massive research and development programme behind it. Most of the work on visual intrusion has, up to the moment, been concerned with the evaluation of existing situations. The techniques, however, are equally applicable to the prediction of proposed situations and the opportunity will come for predictive work of this kind.

A technique for the determination of a visual intrusion index, based upon the measurement of the solid angle subtended by an artefact at an observing point, and the position factor based upon the zone of the visual field occupied by the image of the artefact, requires methods which will enable this solid angle and this position factor to be assessed with speed and accuracy, preferably by technician rather than professional labour. Such methods have been devised.

The methods are based upon the use of suitable transparent angular overlays placed over photographs taken from the observing point, such that by a simple procedure of 'counting squares' or the use of a planimeter tool, the solid angular subtense and the position factor can be either evaluated separately or the product function obtained directly. The methodology permits the simple solid angular subtense to be obtained independent of the position factor, or the visual intrusion function, i.e., the combination of solid angular subtense and position factor can be obtained directly in one process.

Transparent angular overlays have been prepared for different cameras. Three types of camera are useful for the purpose. First, cameras of the usual format, e.g. 35 mm or 90 × 90 mm, can be used, but they must be fitted with a wide-angle lens. They can then be used, with the appropriate overlays (Fig. 4a), for assessing the solid angle and the position factor of artefacts near or just off the centre of the visual field. As a considerable number of visual intrusion problems arise with situations of this kind, the lack of the peripheral field is therefore little handicap, and it is a great advantage to be able to use normal photographic equipment.

FIG. 4a. *Solid angle network superimposed on a wide-angle photograph taken with an ordinary camera. Only a small part of the visual field is recorded, but this is the important central part of the field, and a quick assessment of the solid angle subtended by the artefact at the viewing point can be obtained.*

Second, there are available special wide-angle lenses which cover a very wide angle (up to 120°) along the horizontal in a 35-mm format (and therefore less in the vertical) which are able to cater for the great majority of visual intrusion problems. The use of these very wide-angle lenses requires certain refinements in the photographic technique which can, however, be acquired by a skilled photographic technician.

Finally, there is available a full-field camera (the Robin Hill camera) which covers the entire visual field (180°), but which is a specialised piece of photographic equipment, not readily obtainable, and requiring special technical skills in its operation. It is, however, the only apparatus available for obtaining in one photographic image the whole visual field and is therefore essential for research, development and planning work where the full methodology needs to be employed.

In an evaluation situation, wide-angle or full-field photographs are taken of the intruding artefact from the relevant viewing position. The photographs are processed and enlarged to a scale of the same equivalent focal length as that of the relevant transparent overlays. In order to obtain the solid angular subtense of artefacts in the visual field, the solid angular overlay is placed on the photograph (Fig. 4b) and the number of elements of the reticulation (each element being of one millisteradian) covering the extent of the image of the artefact is counted, thus giving the solid angular subtense.

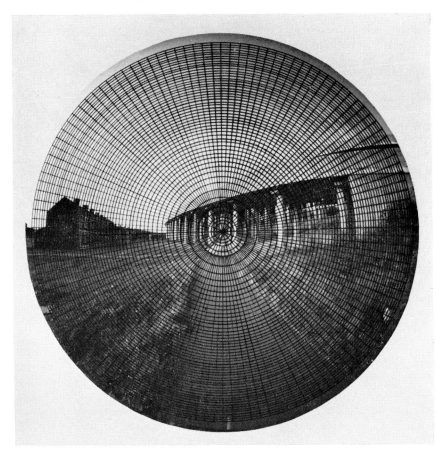

FIG. 4b. *Solid angle transparent overlay laid over a full field photograph. Each division on the solid angle overlay covers one millisteradian. Procedure is to count the divisions covered by the image of the motorway. The total gives the solid angular subtense at the particular viewing position.*

The position factor can be obtained by one of several different methods. The simplest method divides the visual field into a series of zones about the centre, each zone being given a multiplication factor derived from the empirical formula. If the whole image of the artefact lies within one of these zones, then the position factor is that appropriate for that zone. If, on the other hand, the image extends over more than one zone, then the solid angular subtense within each given zone is multiplied by the appropriate position factor for that zone. The sum of the products of solid angular subtense and position factor gives the visual intrusion index.

The alternative procedure is to employ a transparent overlay in which the values of solid angle have been modified for their distance from the centre of the visual field by a continuous function. The unmodified solid angular overlay gives the total solid angle subtended at the observing point by the artefact, and the modified overlay gives the visual intrusion index direct. The mean position factor, if it is required, can of course be obtained from these two values.

THE VISUAL INTRUSION INDEX IN A PREDICTIVE SITUATION

Techniques have been devised for the application of the methods to predictive situations, and these operate as follows. Profile angle diagrams have been prepared upon which the outline of a proposed artefact, such as an urban motorway as seen from a given observing point, can be plotted on the same co-ordinates as the relevant solid angular overlay (Fig. 5). The configuration of a proposed motorway route can, for example, be plotted on a profile angle diagram and superimposed on the relevant modified or unmodified solid angle diagram, and the solid angular subtense, the position factor or the visual intrusion index deduced for that observing point. The solid angular subtense or the visual intrusion index can then be compared with that obtained from the same observing point for an alternative route and, by performing this operation for a number of points along a proposed track, the degree of visual intrusion likely to be obtained at significant points by one or other of alternative routes can be summated.

THE USE OF THE VISUAL INTRUSION INDEX

Whether in an evaluation or a predictive situation, the numbers obtained for the visual intrusion index are of only limited value unless they can be related to their relevant social or economic context. They are the equivalent of dBA sound level values without the appropriate Wilson Committee recommendations. If it is known that one type of aircraft creates 110 dBA and another creates 105 dBA at the same observing point, something also needs to be known of the relative impact on householders of these two figures. The figures alone are not valueless, of course. They enable like to be compared with like. It is of value to know that one aircraft gives 5 dBA less than another under comparable conditions, and by itself it may give sufficient information to justify the choice of the aircraft which gives the lower figure. In the same way it is of value to know that one proposed route of an elevated urban motorway gives a visual intrusion index from a significant observing point of 45 whereas another route gives only 25, but it is of even greater value if it is known that the figure of 45 is likely to lead to

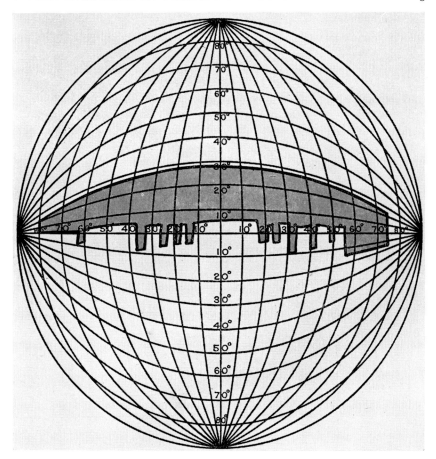

FIG. 5. *The visual intrusion index in a predictive situation. The profile angle overlay is used to delineate on the same equidistant projection as the other overlays, the proposed line or lines of the new motorway. The profile angle diagram, with the motorway placed upon it, is laid over the appropriate zonal diagram and the Visual Intrusion Index is evaluated for the alternative proposed routes.*

community action whereas a figure of 25 is likely to be tolerated. This is the missing information at the moment.

Subjective estimates by a team of skilled observers (comparable to a team of tea tasters or whisky blenders) have led to tentative estimates for the relative degree of household annoyance and community annoyance in relation to the scale of visual intrusion. Further work at the moment is being undertaken to supplement or replace these 'skilled team assessments' by judgments based upon an analysis of lay opinion derived from social surveys. When this work is completed, the way will be clear to relating values of visual intrusion index to social and economic factors. This need not await the complete solution of the problem of aesthetic satisfaction. 'Wilson Committee' standards of visual intrusion index, both on a household and neighbourhood basis, can be set without reference to the hedonic content, provided these standards are acceptable both to the environmental planning authorities and the relevant communities. The hedonic factor, when it is available, can then be introduced perhaps as a modifying or mitigating sub-index. This, however, is for the future. Just as it may well be possible to demonstrate eventually that one type of aircraft engine makes a less unpleasant noise than another, and may therefore be permitted a slightly higher dBA level, so it may be possible in due course to demonstrate that certain designs of elevated motorway are aesthetically more acceptable than others, and that therefore a slightly higher level of visual intrusion index may be permitted. This, however, is likely to be a second-order effect and progress should not be held up while we await its investigation.

This chapter gives only a very brief summary of the experimental work and the evaluation and prediction techniques upon which these new concepts of visual intrusion are based. The techniques are in course of further development for specialised use, and of simplification for purposes of, for example, public demonstration (Fig. 6). Meanwhile,

FIG. 6. *The visual intrusion in a predictive situation. The proposed elevated motorway is plotted on a profile angle diagram of the correct equivalent focal length, and superimposed on a photograph of the site, either in the form of a transparent overlay or by 'double projection' by two matched projectors. The degree of visual intrusion of alternative routes or designs can be assessed subjectively, e.g., by a planning committee or at a public enquiry. The photograph plus superimposed profile can also be laid under a solid angle overlay for the quantitative assessment of the visual intrusion index.*

there is a strong case for tentative standards of limiting visual intrusion in urban motorway situations. Such standards would inevitably lead to a conscious attempt to improve the visual environment.

REFERENCES

Burns Committee (1972) *New Roads in Towns*, Report of the Urban Motorways Committee to the Secretary of State for the Environment (Chairman, W. Burns), H.M.S.O., London.

Hopkinson, R. G. (1971) 'The quantitative assessment of visual intrusion', *Royal Town Planning Institute*, 57 (10), pp. 445–9.

Lassiere, A. and P. H. Bowers (1972) *The Social Costs of Urban Road Transport*, European Conference of Ministers of Transport, April 1972. Paper for the Round Table No. 18.

Moles, A. (1966) *Information Theory and Aesthetic Perception* (trans. J. E. Cohen), University of Illinois Press.

Noise Advisory Council (1971) *Neighbourhood Noise*, Report by the Working Group on the Noise Abatement Act (Chairman, Sir Hilary Scott), H.M.S.O., London.

Wilson Committee (1963) *Noise*, Final Report of the Committee on the Problem of Noise (Chairman, Sir Alan Wilson, F.R.S.), H.M.S.O., (Cmnd 2056), London.

CHAPTER 6

Evaluating community preferences[1]

G. HOINVILLE

It is becoming increasingly clear that public enquiries, such as the Roskill Commission on the third London airport or the Greater London Development Plan enquiry, are primarily battlegrounds for technicians and expert witnesses. They may act as a kind of safety valve in the general public's interest, but they do not provide an effective platform for general public participation of the kind encouraged by the Skeffington Report (1969).

As a general rule, the planning process seems most effectively geared to learning about the views and wants of pressure groups, either via public enquiries or, in extreme cases, from public demonstrations. It has not yet managed to extend much beyond this to learn more about the complex preference structure of the community at large. Research evidence suggests that public participation in its present form is still limited to small—and generally middle class—sections of the community. For example, a study of residents around London Airport (McKennel, 1963) showed that differences between those who complained and those who did not were much less a function of noise level experienced than of socio-economic differences between the residents. Complainants were much more likely to be middle-class, with longer education and with higher incomes. Not surprisingly, public meetings and enquiries are used to better advantage by the more articulate and informed.

The view is sometimes expressed that those who remain silent do not have preferences or are indifferent to the alternatives, but again this assumption does not stand up to careful scrutiny: different sections of the community feel powerless to influence events to varying degrees. Similarly there are differences between groups of people in the extent to which they feel they should interfere; some sections simply accept their lot more readily than others. A person's background, training and confidence still plays a large part in the way he will react. Consequently, if the planning process relies solely on the voluntary expression of

[1] This chapter has been adapted from an article by the author in *Environment and Planning*, 1971, volume 3, pages 33–50 (Pion, London). *Note by the author:* That paper was prepared for publication in the autumn of 1970. A number of the ideas for further developments suggested towards the end of the paper have in fact been undertaken and the Priority Evaluator method has been substantially developed during the past two years. In particular the analysis methods have been very considerably extended and modified as a result of larger scale studies which have now been completed.

attitudes, it will be introducing inequalities into the system: some sections of the community will be able to exert more influence than others.

In any case, the way in which people react in specific situations will often conceal underlying attitudes towards certain features of their environment. In the case of the London Motorway Box, for example, the neighbourhood environmental quality for the majority of London residents will not be affected. Moreover, many will gain from the concentration of traffic onto the motorway and away from residential streets, and large numbers will benefit from the increased speed of travel which the motorway will initially provide. In this situation, only the minority of people is likely to oppose the plan. These will consist mainly of those disturbed by the physical construction of the motorway, together with small numbers whose opposition to the general principle of urban motorways (or the London plan in particular) outweighs any benefits which they may receive. But a great many people, if presented with a real choice between, say, increased freedom of travel or increased pedestrian safety, might opt for the latter. Conversely, some of those who object to the motorway on their own doorstep might support—in principle—investment to improve travel speeds. Those who express opposition views are likely to be biased towards those personally affected. Some may be quite content to see the motorway moved to an adjoining Borough rather than abandoned altogether. So, here again, we have to be very careful about inferring general community preferences and values from the way people react in specific circumstances. Voluntary participation of this kind is obviously an important feature of the planning process, but it does not provide anything like the complete solution.

Of course, it can be argued that, in any case, community attitudes are not very meaningful as a basis for long-range planning, but the logic behind such arguments must surely be at fault. In evaluating alternative investments, we try, via a cost/benefit approach, to understand the way in which the community will react to, and be affected by, the alternatives. Since both their reactions and the way they will be affected are governed by community preferences and attitudes, it makes sense to try to understand these underlying motivations. Naturally, the attempts to include community preferences in the planning process raise many new questions. There is the problem of attaching relative weights to community preferences: social policies may require investments to be geared to minority rather than majority needs. Or again a person's preference in one direction (for example, free use of the motor car) may conflict directly with his preference in another direction (such as intrusion of traffic noise, fumes and dangers). Individual members of the community may often lack the knowledge and foresight to reach a satisfactory compromise. But these are really questions which concern the application of the information after it has been obtained—they do not really lessen the need to learn more about the nature of preferences.

Understanding the values of the people living in the city is as much a part of planning as acquiring knowledge of how the city functions. It cannot adequately be achieved by simply listening to the raised voices.

BEHAVIOUR AS A GUIDE TO PREFERENCES

Some indications of what people like and dislike can obviously be deduced from the way people actually behave in alternative situations: the choices which travellers make between public and private transport, for example, provide information about these preferences. Inferring underlying preferences from existing behaviour patterns, however, can be misleading, if this is the sole source of information. The market place is a confused situation in which to try and separate particular influences on behaviour from the whole range of motivating forces affecting demand. In addition, actual behaviour does not arise only in response to the few factors that we wish to study and evaluate. For example, people who choose between public and private transport may do so because of real differences in speed, comfort and other factors of direct concern to planners: but they may also be influenced by any or all of the following:

1. *Differences in perception*

For some factors, of course, those choosing may have insufficient knowledge of real differences between the alternatives. They may act on wrong or outdated information, or they may be influenced by a whole range of other intangible qualities, for example image differences between the products.

2. *Subsidiary and complementary choice situations*

Some choices are really subsidiary to other more important considerations and some may be made in association with other choices. For example, a traveller may choose to use a car on a long-distance journey (for example, on holiday) merely to be able to use the car at the destination, or he may choose a car for a local trip in order to combine other needs (such as taking a passenger elsewhere). In both cases he may appear to place comfort over speed but this need not reflect his preference.

3. *Availability and the buying situation*

A third factor is the psychological and physical ease with which the alternatives can be chosen. In the one case a traveller may have a car available at his point of departure; in the other he may have a twenty minute walk to the boarding point. In the second case, he may also have to go through a complex process of buying a ticket or queuing in order to undertake his journey.

4. *Loyalty and habit*

This factor may in some situations cause people to behave in an (apparently) irrational manner: a commuter may have made his decision long ago and have remained ignorant of subsequent changes, or simply not bothered to incur the trouble of changing an existing behaviour pattern.

Needless to say, the relative importance of these different factors will vary from situation to situation and from person to person. In some cases travellers may be guided mainly by real differences between alternatives or, in others, these differences may be of minor importance, and there may be even occasions where choices are simply made at random and without any really well reasoned intention.

The use of mathematical models to describe and summarise a complex pattern of travel behaviour assists in the identification of relative weights of importance to attach to the factors which determine that behaviour. But a model which can reproduce today's behaviour patterns will not necessarily provide an understanding of unfulfilled preferences. Moreover, these convenient mathematical summaries can only go a certain way towards representing the full complexities of choice. It is much easier to describe the aggregate behaviour of the community with these models than it is to explain the individual preferences which contribute to that behaviour.

Travel patterns form only one aspect of behaviour from which community values can be inferred; a much wider coverage of amenity and environmental preferences is possible from a study of house buying and residential mobility. Again, however, this is a choice situation which is subject to the same range of motivating forces that relate to travel behaviour. In this case the 'loyalty' factor is likely to be paramount: residents remain in houses long after the property and the environment fail to meet their requirements. Perceptions can also play an important role in the house purchase context; whether the house portrays the right kind of status image is an illustration of this. Similarly, the 'availability' factor and the general difficulties of house purchase will confuse the relationship between demand and community preferences. This suggests that the difference in price between houses of a similar kind, but located in different environments, will not simply be a reflection of the values attached to the environments. In areas where the amenity standard is falling, for example, the 'loyalty' aspect will help to maintain prices at an artificially high level.

There are other obstacles to the use of house price differentials as a measure of community values. The mix of environmental variables is so complex that it is almost impossible to find 'matched' houses which differ only in particular respects. This makes it difficult to associate price variations with specific environmental preferences. Moreover, house prices in cases of limited supply and excess demand can create artificially inflated prices which bear little relationship to average values. The following over-simplified example is an illustration of the type of situation when house prices would be a totally inadequate basis from which to infer community values.

Suppose that 250 identical houses were for sale (in a perfect market) amongst 250 buyers, each of whom was prepared to pay the £5,000 basic selling price of the house. We can then list the 250 buyers, according to the additional premium which they would be prepared to pay in order to live in a corner house. In Table 1 the first person would pay a £750 premium; the tenth person a £500 premium, and so on.

Clearly, if there were only two corner houses they would sell at £5,700 each (£700 above the basic price). If, on the other hand, there were ten corner houses they would then sell at £5,500 each. And if every fifth house was a corner house, each one would sell at £5,300. In these circumstances, if we use the house price differentials, we can derive a whole series of 'values', none of which correspond to the average sum the community attaches to living in a corner house.

Another difficulty in the use of house prices is that the price people pay for an amenity is the combination of both their preference and their wealth. In the example above, all 250 people may attach the same weight to living in a corner house; the premiums could simply reflect the varying ability to pay for such preferences. For many evaluation decisions 'sensitivity' values need to be isolated from 'purchasing power' in order that equal monetary weight can be given to the former, between different communities.

An alternative to the global examination of the housing stock would be, as in the case of travel patterns, to develop a model of purchasing behaviour. The population, or at least a reasonably large part of it, is relatively mobile; the factors which influence choice are not difficult to assess. A behavioural model of residential mobility, assuming it included the main motivating forces, would certainly be a major step forward in the understanding of community values, but the same limitations would apply here as elsewhere: complex and confused behaviour, on its own, is a weak basis from which to deduce preferences.

TABLE 1. *Premium which would be paid for corner house.*

Buyer No. 1	Buyer No. 2	Buyer No. 10	Buyer No. 50	Buyer No. 100	Buyer No. 250
£750	£700	£500	£300	£100	Nil

(Average 'value' attached to corner house = £350).

In any case, the range of opportunities for developing behavioural models is limited. Often people do not have effective alternatives between which to choose, and where choices exist, there may not be an alternative which combines the wants of the community. As the sole source of information, existing behaviour patterns will inevitably provide an oversimplified view of preferences; they may also provide a very misleading view. To achieve a depth of understanding of preferences and values, a specific probing of attitudes by direct interviewing methods is required.

BEHAVIOUR AND ATTITUDES MERGED

It is difficult to extend the role of the social survey investigation beyond measurements of facts and behaviour. Hypothetically phrased questions will yield answers which bear little relationship to reality; preference questions posed to those without knowledge and experience of the alternatives will not provide useful answers. A critical factor in this type of research is that the measurement of attitudes and preferences requires a depth of approach not relevant to factual measurements. The ambivalent nature of attitudes implies that simple questioning techniques are of no value. For example, to determine the relationship between racial prejudice and intelligence, the questioning approach would not simply be to ask people: 'How racially prejudiced are you?' and 'How intelligent are you?'

Instead, a series of questioning scales would need to be developed, which correlated with prejudice and intelligence, and which could be applied discreetly as part of an interview survey. The results of some fairly naive and often absurd attempts to determine attitudes have hindered the development of the basic approach. Such questions as: 'What do you think of Britain joining the Common Market?' or 'How much do you value your leisure time?' are examples of ill-conceived attempts to understand attitudes by direct questioning.

It is important, moreover, that attitude questions should not be used as a direct measurement of actual behaviour. If further evidence were needed, the 1970 parliamentary elections in Britain strongly reinforced the point that a direct intention question does not in itself provide an accurate prediction of actual behaviour. Unless one can first demonstrate that respondents have already arrived at their decision—by weighing all the pros and cons—the kind of question: 'What would you do if . . .?' or 'How much would I have to pay you if . . .?' cannot be expected to provide realistic information. To be useful as a means of determining likely behaviour, attitude research must avoid seeking the respondents' own rationalisations, fantasies or conjectures. Indeed, even if measurements of attitude could be found which provided good predictors of behaviour, it is doubtful whether they would be useful in determining preferences. Actual behaviour, as discussed earlier, is only partly (and in some circumstances not at all) governed by product preferences; the only virtue of attitude research in this context is the removal of the imperfections and confusion which occur in the market place.

The main limitation of attitude research is that respondents are not forced, as they are in a behavioural situation, to trade-off some of their preferences against others. In an environmental context, for example, it is known that, in general, people prefer quiet areas to noisy ones, safe roads to unsafe ones, shorter journeys to longer ones, and so on. A house purchaser with limited wealth has to identify his own priority preference structure and decide for which factors he will accept some element of sacrifice in order to gain in others. A second limitation is that one cannot portray in an interview the long-term effects of increased noise or faster journey speeds. Unless respondents have some experience of the alternatives, they may not be able to indicate a meaningful preference in response to attitude questions.

These two weaknesses have a common theme: can people behave in a serious and responsible way when removed from the pressure of a real behavioural decision? Since one cannot be sure that they will, the solution would seem to be to interrelate attitude measurement with studies of behaviour. For example, in a study of commuter trips we could determine, by direct questioning, what travellers think of each of the alternative modes open to them in terms of cost, time and so on. At the same time, we do know which of the modes the commuter regularly uses. So, by comparing actual behaviour with the commuter's attitudes towards the alternatives, we can begin to see how he has traded off the advantages of one mode against the different advantages of another. The same basic approach could be used to look at house purchasers (immediately after the event) to see how their choice related to their attitudes towards the alternative houses which they looked at. What factor did they, in practice, trade off against their major preferences?

An alternative way of interrelating attitude measurements with actual behaviour is to ask people first how satisfied they are with, for example, their commuter journey. Then they are asked to give a score to indicate how pleased they are with the speed of the journey, its reliability, its comfort and so on. If people who were generally satisfied with their mode were also very satisfied with its reliability (and vice versa) but not particularly satisfied with its comfort, this would also provide an indication of the weighting placed on different components of their choice. Something similar to this was carried out by the Building Research Station (Metcalf, 1968) in relation to housing preferences. The then Ministry of Housing and Local Government also used measures of satisfaction in a study of housing layout (Reynolds and Nicholson, 1970).

An alternative method of combining behaviour and attitude is to see how people describe their existing situation and then to go on to establish the direction in which they would prefer changes to occur. We could, for example, offer residents the opportunity of improving their existing situation in terms of noise level, improved amenities, faster journey times, improved safety and so on. By forcing them to choose only a limited number of the possible improvements we could determine a pattern of trade-off preference, i.e., they would implicitly have traded off the improvements which they did not choose against those which they did choose. Similarly, commuters could be asked to choose a limited number of journey improvements from a range of alternatives as a means of determining the trade-offs which occur between savings of cost, time, walking and so on.

In practice, this method can be developed further to look at the way people would trade off some of the existing merits of their journey, or their home environment, in order to gain some benefits which they do not possess at the moment. The principle on which this approach is based is similar to that of the economist's indifference curve. By seeing which different 'mixes' of a number of variables provide equal satisfaction we can see how one aspect, such as reduction in noise, is valued higher or lower than others. It was a principle first applied in an environmental context by The Institute for Research in Social Science, University of North Carolina; it is this basic principle (Wilson, 1962) which Social and Community Planning Research has since extended and developed into a research method.

THE METHOD DEVELOPED BY S.C.P.R.

The starting point for this research approach was the need to understand trade-off preferences. The general direction of preferences is already known: less noise, increased safety, faster travel, better comfort and so on. The major problem lies both in the reconciliation of conflicting preferences and, given limited investment resources, in the identification of relative priorities.

The central feature of 'relative priorities' is the basis on which this research was founded. The method is to ask people to choose a 'mix' of variables from a range of competing alternatives. The way in which respondents choose between them provides an indication of the trade-off values associated with individual items.

A simplified analogy can be found in an everyday purchasing situation. Respondents could, for example, be offered a basket of groceries, with each item carefully labelled and priced. At the same time, they could be offered enough money to buy, say half of the items in the basket. The way in which respondents allocate their limited wealth can be used to deduce the relative priorities between the items.

In an environmental context certain adaptations to the basic approach can be made. First, respondents can be presented with a range of standards for each variable (for example, high noise level down to low noise level); then they can also be asked to identify the standard which best corresponds to their existing situation; and thirdly, they can be asked, by means of the 'grocery' priority preference approach, to choose the standard which they would find acceptable for each variable in the optimum mix of variables.

For example, in a modal choice situation there might be a respondent with an existing commuter journey of '50 minutes/18p fare/and two changes of mode'. His priority preference pattern using the enforced trade-off approach could be '45 minutes/23p fare/one change of mode'. In other words, he has decided to trade off a 5p fare increment against a 5 minute improvement in journey time and the reduction from two changes of mode to one.

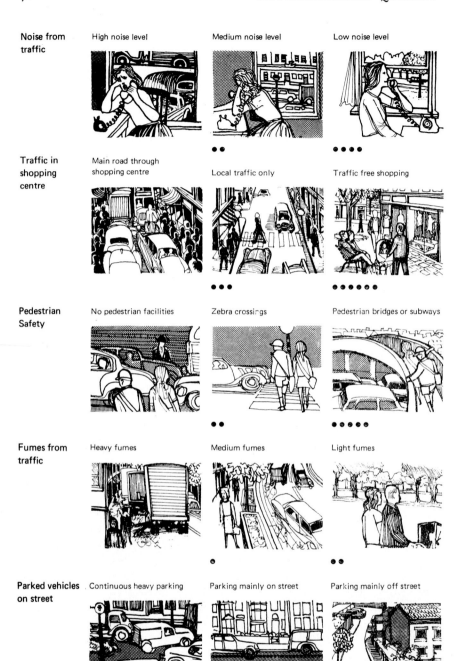

FIG. 1. *Environmental variables* (● = 1 peg).

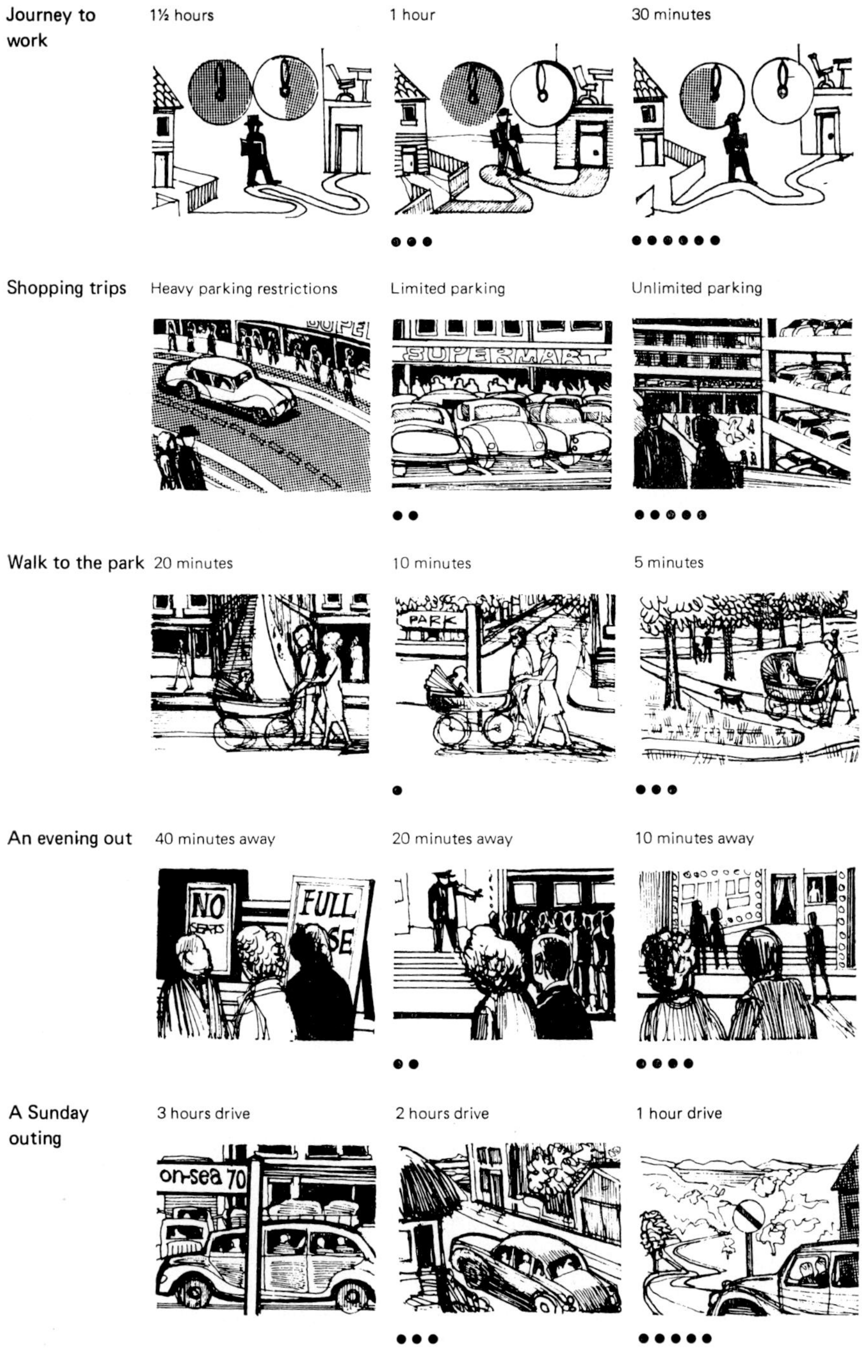

Journey to work

1½ hours	1 hour	30 minutes
	● ● ●	● ● ● ● ● ●

Shopping trips

Heavy parking restrictions	Limited parking	Unlimited parking
	● ●	● ● ● ● ●

Walk to the park

20 minutes	10 minutes	5 minutes
	●	● ● ●

An evening out

40 minutes away	20 minutes away	10 minutes away
	● ●	● ● ● ●

A Sunday outing

3 hours drive	2 hours drive	1 hour drive
	● ● ●	● ● ● ● ●

FIG. 1. (*continued*)

In respect of data collection, a whole range of practical problems had to be overcome. The main difficulty was the need to maintain simplicity for respondents and yet to approach the complex reality of a multi-choice situation. First, the range of choices offered to respondents was illustrated pictorially. The choices were then presented on a board, like that shown in Figure 1, in which each row represents a particular environmental variable, such as noise or pedestrian safety, and each position in a row represents a different standard for that variable, from 'poor' on the left hand side to 'good' on the right (for example, high noise on the left, low noise on the right).

The drawings were tested for comprehension, by traditional inter-view methods, before they were adopted. The perceived rank order of the pictures was also made to correspond to the order in which they were priced. Some of the variables are, of course, extremely complex to represent pictorially. In the case of noise, for example, the drawings were reinforced with a tape-recording incorporating three different noise levels. (Even so, there are difficulties in playing a tape-recording of the 'low noise' level to respondents in their home if it happens to be situated on a busy main road!)

Because of the composite nature of any picture, it was not possible to determine precisely how each drawing would be interpreted; certainly it was impossible to be sure that all respondents would attach the same meaning to each illustration (or even to each verbal description). One method of assessing the interpretations was to ask respondents to classify their existing environment in terms of the range of variables illustrated. Insofar as the analysis is largely a function of the relation-ship between preferences and the existing situation, the need for absolute definition of the illustrations is not of paramount importance.

The second step was to attach a price tag to each standard within each variable. In this development work the prices adopted were not chosen very rigorously. For one project they were based on the values derived from early experimental work; in the other project they were chosen to represent crude supply costs of arriving at each standard. The pricing is important, and is discussed again later, but again both the relative nature of the preferences sought and the method of analysis used suggest that general conclusions about trade-offs can be deduced from the use of specific price ratios.

Of course, a further practical problem arises with the need for respondents to allocate monetary resources between the range of alternative choices. To eliminate the need for respondents to juggle with the mental arithmetic involved in calculating the alternatives which they could buy, they were actually given money in the form of pegs, each one worth £100. When they 'bought' a picture, they inserted the required number of pegs alongside that picture. In this way, it was made clear to respondents when they had used up all their wealth.

An equally important practical consideration was the need for respondents to be made aware easily of what they had bought for a particular allocation of their wealth. To increase the degree of reality, it was necessary to maximise the flexibility of choice in a way which allowed respondents to move gradually towards their ideal, rather than force them to indicate an optimum solution in one attempt. Respondents were allowed to modify their choices after studying the outcome or 'payoff' resulting from those choices. Thus, the 'payoff' arising from any given set of choices had to be instantly apparent. This was achieved by electrifying the board and using priority switching. As respondents inserted the pegs required to 'buy' a particular picture, that picture became illuminated; if they removed the pegs, the light beneath that picture went out. The use of priority switching was introduced so that only one position in each row could be illuminated at any time.

In this way, the choices made could easily be seen from the illuminated pictures; respondents were free to modify their choices until they concluded that the illuminated squares represented the optimum payoff from the allocation of their limited wealth. In effect, therefore, the mechanism used for the research took the form of an electrified questionnaire which could be used almost as a game. It had many attractive features: husband and wife could deliberate together and indicate their combined preferences; it was fairly easy for people to use; it avoided a lot of mental arithmetic; it provided flexibility; and it presented respondents with quite a wide range of combinations from which they could choose. (For one of the projects a 10×3 matrix was used: respondents were then, unknown to themselves, faced with a range of over 3,700 possible combinations from which to choose.)

The features of the method discussed so far were all designed to assist respondents in their *choices*. What was still needed, however, was a method of forcing them to consider, equally carefully, the items which they *rejected*.

It was necessary for people to accept (either by choice or by default) one of the standards for each variable. This required the inclusion of a 'free' base-line standard which would automatically result if respondents chose to spend no money at all on that variable. There was a danger that respondents would merely allocate their wealth to a few items which attracted them, thus ignoring the fact that their position on other items would be poor as a result. To simulate reality, it was essential that the negative side (the losses) of their trade-off was reinforced to the same extent as the positive side (the gains).

The end result was that respondents were asked to play an environmental or modal choice 'game'. At the start of the game, all the left hand (base-line) positions for the range of variables were illuminated. As respondents 'bought' an improved standard for any one variable the light switched to the new chosen position.

The respondents were told, by way of introduction, to consider themselves in the position of moving to another house. An estate agent had selected a range of properties for them to see; the cheapest house was described by the pictures on the left-hand side of the board (that is, the free choice positions); but they had decided to spend £1,500 more than the price of that cheapest house. How would they spend that £1,500 to indicate the sort of place in which they would prefer to live?

The rules of the game were:

1. The respondent was provided with a fixed sum of money (in this case £1,500).
2. He must accept one 'standard' for each variable, either the free base-line position or another position which he 'bought'.
3. He must spend all the money available (except in special circumstances which arise as a result of the discrete nature of choices), and he could not buy more than his wealth allows.
4. He could amend his choices by re-allocating the money between the range of alternatives until he arrived at his final 'optimum' mix.

SOME PRELIMINARY RESULTS

In the development programme two main projects were undertaken with the 'Priority Evaluator' device. One consisted of interviews with 121 home owners in the London Borough of Brent, in which trade-off preferences between ten variables were examined:

Amenity variables
Noise from traffic
Traffic in shopping centre
Pedestrian safety
Fumes from traffic
Parked vehicles on street

Accessibility variables
Journey time to work
Parking restrictions at shops
Walking time to local park
Travel time on evening out
Travel time on weekend outing

The second project consisted of interviews with 120 Ministry of Transport employees, in which trade-off choices in relation to the journey to work (all were public transport users with a journey of around 45–50 minutes) were examined. The variables were:

Journey time
Frequency of getting a seat
Walking distance to the station
Number of changes of mode
Journey fare

In both cases the projects were primarily designed to further the practical and analytical methods of the basic approach. They were not designed to yield usable data, although they were formulated to test the viability of the responses obtained.

One of the tests was a repeat on the same sample (after an interval of around three weeks) with the identical game. The overall patterns of responses which emerged from this consistency check were virtually identical on the two occasions, as shown in Table 2.

In fact, there was compensating switching of choices amongst a minority of respondents. However, about seventy-five per cent of the sample could be classified as reasonably consistent, a higher proportion (of the same sample) than that obtained from a simple rank order consistency check.

Other tests showed that respondents behaved in a rational way regarding prices: when the price of a variable was increased, a lower average standard was chosen; as the price was lowered, the average preference for that variable improved. Respondents were also asked to

TABLE 2.

| % of total wealth spent on: | Respondents' allocation of total wealth | |
	1st occasion %	2nd occasion %
Time	18	19
Seats	23	23
Walk to station	12	11
Number of changes	25	26
Fare	22	21
	100	100

consider their allocation in a way designed to reflect the optimum budgeting of a local authority. The results suggested slightly different attitudes towards the decision-taking, which supports the view that the game was being tackled seriously. Those acting as the local authority felt slightly less responsible for reductions in traffic fumes but were more concerned with pedestrian safety.

At this stage the analysis side of the approach was less well-developed than the practical task of data collection. Already, however, it is clear that a range of analytical methods can be used to examine the data in a variety of ways. The first task of respondents is to describe their existing situation according to the range of standards and variables used for the subsequent preference trade-off. Table 3 shows, for the

TABLE 3. *Distribution of existing situation*

| | Existing situation | | | Mean position |
	Worst position	Middle position	Best position	
Journey time to work	2	29	69%	1·3
Noise from traffic	5	28	67%	1·4
Fumes from traffic	5	50	45%	1·6
Walking time to local park	12	39	49%	1·6
Travel time on weekend outing	24	26	50%	1·7
Parked vehicles on street	19	45	36%	1·8
Parking restrictions at shops	21	53	26%	2·0
Travel time on evening out	40	28	32%	2·1
Pedestrian safety	22	76	2%	2·2
Traffic in shopping centre	80	18	2%	2·8

environmental study, the distribution of the existing situation for each variable together with a 'mean' position for each one. The mean value has been calculated by giving a score of 3 to the worst position, 2 to the middle position and 1 to the best position, so that low values indicate a favourable position.

On the basis of the prices which were initially attached to each position, it is possible to compute the total 'value' of each respondent's existing situation as described by him. The next step is to ask respondents to re-allocate that wealth level as they would like it distributed, in order to indicate the 'optimum' balance between all of the variables.

The mean position in the existing situation can now be compared with the mean position in the optimum situation, in order to see the overall direction in which respondents would like their situation to change. Table 4 compares all the existing and optimum positions chosen by

TABLE 4. *Comparison of existing and optimum positions chosen by Brent residents for each variable*

	Existing mean value	Optimum mean value
Journey time to work	1·3	1·8
Noise from traffic	1·4	1·6
Fumes from traffic	1·6	1·9
Walking time to local park	1·6	2·3
Travel time on weekend outing	1·7	2·5
Parked vehicles on street	1·8	2·2
Parking restrictions at shops	2·0	2·0
Travel time on evening out	2·1	2·5
Pedestrian safety	2·2	1·9
Traffic in shopping centre	2·8	2·2

Brent residents for each variable. In this particular example, the wealth given to respondents for optimum allocation was about twenty per cent below the average value of the existing situation, so that an overall drop in standards was enforced upon them. Even so, it is clear that very pronounced trade-offs occurred amongst this group. Respondents sought much better standards regarding pedestrian/vehicle conflict both in the shopping centre and for pedestrian safety generally. In return, they would sacrifice some of the ease with which they could travel to open spaces on long and short trips and, to a lesser extent, to their place of work.

Of course, this kind of trade-off pattern results both from the particular circumstances in which these residents now find themselves and in the rates of exchange (that is, the prices) which were offered for trade-off purposes.

The relationship between the existing situation and preferences was not constant, but in general it pointed to the not unexpected hypothesis, that those in the worst situations were prepared to allocate more of their budget for what might be described as the 'essentials' than those people in more favourable situations. Conversely, for the 'luxury' recreational travel items, those already in the more favourable situations were prepared to spend a higher proportion of their total wealth on these items than other people.

In respect of the rates of exchange, it is clear that if a different set of prices is attached to the various positions on the board, this will generate a different set of trade-offs. The relative priorities derived from the analysis are only relevant to the price structure which was used. These trade-offs can, however, be viewed in another way and it may be concluded that where respondents chose *to improve* their existing situation, the price ratio used for that variable understated the relative value which respondents attached to it. Conversely, when a respondent chose to sacrifice some element of his existing situation, the price at which he was allowed to do so must have been in excess of the real value he attached to that sacrifice. The 'value' which a respondent attaches to improvements in his situation—relative to other variables— is the exchange rate which just brings about a marginal shift in his preference.

Of course, respondents could be asked to undertake their selection on several occasions using a different price structure each time. In this way, a picture of trade-offs associated with different rates of exchange could be used to determine the marginal utility values for each variable. An alternative would be to employ large matched samples using different price structures for each one. On the other hand, the number of alternative price structures that could be included in the test, by either method, would need to be very limited. It would obviously be more beneficial if some generalised conclusions about marginal utility value could be concluded from one or two attempts only.

One such generalised analytical method which has been partially explored is based on a probability approach. Suppose, for example, that the relative values of respondents corresponded exactly to the way in which all of the alternative positions had been priced. It would not matter to those respondents which of the many *combinations* they chose as their optimum, since each one would provide them with an identical level of satisfaction. In indifference curve terms, each of the combinations would appear on the same curve (or plane).

In practice, this means that, with large samples, each combination could be expected to occur by chance with equal frequency, simply because respondents are indifferent as to which they choose. By comparing *actual* choices for each combination with the expected choices (assuming complete indifference), we can determine whether each variable has been under-priced or over-priced. If a variable is chosen more frequently than would be expected by chance, then it can be concluded that, relative to respondents' values, it has been under-priced. Conversely, variables which are chosen less frequently than by chance have been over-priced, relative to respondents' values.

An actual/expected ratio can be calculated for each variable, as shown in Table 5 for our Brent sample. A ratio above unity indicates that the price allocated was below informants' values (that is they 'bought' the variable more than would have been expected if price structure had created indifference between choices).

TABLE 5. *Relations between actual and expected values given by the Brent sample*

	The average price attached to improvements from the base line	Actual/expected ratio
Journey time to work	£300	1·7
Noise from traffic	£200	1·6
Fumes from traffic	£100	0·8
Walking time to local park	£150	0·6
Travel time on weekend outing	£250	0·5
Parked vehicles on street	£400	1·0
Parking restrictions at shops	£250	1·0
Travel time on evening out	£200	0·4
Pedestrian safety	£250	1·2
Traffic in shopping centre	£300	1·0

These results, taken in conjunction with the earlier findings, generate some interesting hypotheses. For example, in the case of noise it appeared that respondents were not anxious to achieve major gains regarding this factor relative to other trade-offs in their existing situation. And yet, the actual/expected ratio of 1·6 suggests that, relative to values, improvements in this variable have been substantially underpriced.

The explanation for the different attitudes towards the underpricing of noise reduction appears to revolve around the concept of *marginal* exchange rates or trade-off values. The actual/expected ratio indicates the way in which the price substantially understated the exchange rate that respondents were prepared to accept *once they had achieved a reasonably balanced mix of the different factors*. At that point they would place a relatively high price on noise reduction. At their present position, however, they find themselves, relative to some other variables, with a slight consumer surplus regarding noise. They would be prepared to trade off some of this surplus at a price below the eventual 'balanced' exchange rate.

The converse appears to be true in the case of 'traffic in the shopping centre', where almost all respondents regarded their existing situation as very unfavourable relative to the other aspects. The price chosen represents a very acceptable exchange rate, which is used to achieve a substantial trade-off. But at the balancing point, at which an optimum mix was obtained, the price imposed was—if anything—regarded slightly unfavourably. Clearly, it was because their existing situation regarding the shopping centre was so much out of line, relative to the other factors, that the exchange price was regarded so favourably. In a substantially improved situation, the trade-off at the selected price would be much less dramatic and, at the margin, a price slightly below the present one would be acceptable. These results confirm those indicated earlier, that values must be assessed in the light of the current situation. As that situation changes, it would appear that sharp alterations in values will occur.

Another requirement of the analysis is to produce global monetary values suitable for inclusion in a balance sheet against other quantifiable items. This involves the transformation of relative priorities into absolute monetary values. Again, only limited steps have been made in this direction, but, in the 'modal choice' study, for example, one of the variables included was a monetary one. Trade-offs between journey fare and journey time made it possible to arrive at a relative value index which linked time savings to fare savings.

Amongst one such group of respondents who were offered time and fare savings at rates which assumed the value of time in relation to fare was 20p per hour, respondents were anxious to trade-off an element of their existing journey cost in order to gain in journey time, that is, this price understated the relative value.

In another matched group who were offered the same exchange but at a rate of 30p per hour, the choices made in relation to the existing situation were such that the 30p rate appeared to be an equitable one. Again, on the basis of the actual/expected ratios for the two groups, the conclusion reached was that an exchange rate around 30p per hour represented the marginal utility value in a reasonably balanced situation.

POSSIBLE APPLICATIONS FOR THE PRIORITY EVALUATION APPROACH

There are still many aspects of the basic approach which have to be advanced further. At the moment the method assumes no interdependence between variables, a weakness which needs to be overcome; the initial apparatus was fairly crude and a Mark II version is now being built which is easier for respondents to handle. There is a further limitation created by the discrete nature of choices, which will also be largely removed by the new version.

Similarly, there is still a great deal more to be learned about the methods of analysis and data interpretation. In general, however, it is clear that the method works and yields information about preferences which has not hitherto been available. One of the first tasks, now that the basic development work has been completed, is to establish the relationship between the preference data given by the 'Priority Evaluation' method and those concluded on the basis of behavioural observation. One such study, relating to commuter modal choices, is now being planned. A similar study could be undertaken based on recent house movers to identify the relationship between behaviour and underlying preferences.

To some extent, of course, these studies are part of the development and understanding of the basic approach, but they should also yield valuable information about preference patterns. A good deal of development work has taken place to turn the basic concepts into a workable research method from the point of view of data collection and data processing. An equal amount of development work is now necessary in terms of the *application* of the method as a problem-solving tool. As with all survey projects, the main strength or weakness of the Priority Evaluation approach rests not in the method itself but in its application. If the alternatives posed to respondents are too hypothetical or the situation too unreal, the method, however practical and simple, cannot be expected to yield satisfactory answers. Again, the way in which the data are interpreted is of crucial importance; for example, a set of modal choice preferences based on non-drivers cannot usefully form the basis for an explanation of the choice between public and private transport.

Thus, the Priority Evaluator in its present form cannot be used as a kind of simulator to replace or remove the need for experience. It is simply a means of communicating with the public in a way that permits some understanding of the ambivalent nature of their attitudes. If these attitudes are formed on the basis of inexperience or wildly inaccurate perceptions, the evaluator approach cannot provide a means of obtaining more realistic responses. At the same time, the approach, including the use of illustrations, offers a disciplined method of reminding people of similar experiences and enabling them to arrive at balanced judgments in the light of those experiences. This is not simulation in the sense that it is used when the object is to monitor reactions to test situations (for example, in the training of airline pilots); it only serves as a simulation technique insofar as it conveniently summarises the complex choice and trade-off situations which confront the public.

The first point, therefore, to make about the application is that it is not very meaningful to examine priority preferences, covering a wide range of variables, amongst respondents with only a very limited range of experience. But, on the other hand, it would be useful to interrelate preferences with the level of experience of the alternatives. Experience could be treated as an analysis variable to see how much preferences do vary between people with different backgrounds. In some situations, of course, the level and width of experience may be of no importance in influencing behaviour: in others it may be the really vital factor.

This relationship between experience and value is one of the avenues for very detailed exploration. The Priority Evaluator could well be used here as the basis for a range of comparative studies: minority samples of people who are badly off in certain variables, such as residents in an airport area or those forced to travel long distances, can be compared with samples of people who are particularly well-endowed with various environmental qualities. The relationship between the values of these extreme groups and their existing environment would be of immense value in providing an understanding of the value system and its dependence on experience.

There are really three different bits of information obtained from the Priority Evaluation approach:

1. It can be used to help people describe their existing situation and other situations which they perceive or have experienced. By attaching the correct 'weights' to the mix of variables a value for these situations can be obtained.

2. This involves the use of the apparatus to establish trade-off preferences. These preferences can be obtained for different price structures, from which both the direction and magnitude of change which is preferred by respondents can be derived.

3. From the preference information can be deduced the correct price which respondents would attach to the different variables to make them of equal value. Establishing a value of time of 30p per hour, for example, means that by juggling prices a 10-minute saving can be made to appear as attractive as a 3p reduction in fare. These 'corrected' prices form the weights, which can then be used to value both the existing situation and the trade-off preferences.

One of the possible applications of the third aspect is to see how these marginal utility values vary in different circumstances. For example, the value of time is likely to vary between short and long journeys; it is also unlikely that a ten-minute saving on a journey will be worth exactly twice as much as a five-minute saving. Differences will occur as well between different types of people; these too could be highlighted by the derivation of the marginal utility values. Of course, the same basic approach can be applied to other modal choice factors, such as reliability or comfort, as well as to variables outside the transport field.

One of the main applications of the Priority Evaluator in environmental issues would seem to be in arriving at a value of amenity loss (or gain) arising from an investment or planning decision. There are various ways of considering this but one, which is currently being planned, is to examine the trade-off preferences of a group of residents who have experienced a dramatic change in their environmental situation. These might be people who have benefited from a re-routing of through traffic onto a by-pass; or a community which is suffering the effects of temporary traffic re-routing whilst road construction is under way elsewhere. A whole series of examples can be given but the general purpose would be to identify samples of people with mixed experiences in the short term. From their trade-off preferences a correct set of prices can be deduced that correspond to marginal utility values. A detailed description from respondents of their pre- and post-situations can also be obtained; these descriptions can be 'valued' so as to arrive at the total worth of the amenity before and after the change occurred. The net difference between the two situations provides a monetary evaluation of the attitude towards the amenity loss or gain.

In the long term, it seems likely that there will be a large number of occasions on which the existing situation would be altered in quite a marked way: an airport may be closed; a traffic-free shopping precinct may be created; residential roads may be cleared of commuter 'rat-running'; access from side roads to main roads may be curtailed. Some of these alterations may be permanent; others may be temporary inter-ferences or experiments. In all cases this increased planning activity in existing communities would provide an opportunity for evaluation and measurement of the changing values which may arise from the newly created situations.

The principle of obtaining a difference in total valuation between two alternative 'mixes' can, of course, be applied to other types of problem. For example, commuters could be asked to evaluate all their alternative modal choices. As well as providing information about how these valuations are formed, it would also be possible to see where the regular modal choice scores over the rarely used alternatives. Here again the analysis must be limited to those with some experience of the alternatives.

Perhaps the main value and advantage, however, of the Priority Evaluation approach is its flexibility. It can examine the preference structure at a micro level in order to establish differences between different types of person, different types of situation, large and small changes in individual variables, and so on. It is a method which can be used to yield aggregate community values but, more important, it can be used to examine how these aggregates are formed. This makes it possible, for example, to see the variation in preferences between a slight reduction in traffic in the shopping centre and a full reduction; or again between a moderately quiet environment and a very quiet environment. It will be possible to see how the new generations have values different from their fathers; or establish the relationship between income and preferences; or find out how much people who possess a particular amenity value it in relation to those who do not have it.

The usefulness of this micro examination approach is self-evident. The success of cost/benefit analysis, for example, rests heavily on its ability to illustrate how the 'gains' and 'losses' are distributed between different sections of the community. The question of *who* place *what* values on *which* factors is as important as the compilation of an aggregate amenity value, and it is this aspect which is most appropriate for the Priority Evaluator approach.

Finally, it would be misleading to suggest that the method does not have problems and limitations of its own. Its very recent origins mean that a lot more development work needs to be done, and a great deal is also likely to emerge from its general application. However, sufficient has been done to suggest that the method can take its place alongside others as an evaluation tool to be employed.

REFERENCES

Metcalf, J. (1968) *Satisfaction and Housing Standards*, BRS-IN 159/67, Building Research Station, Garston, England.

McKennel, A. C. (1963) *Aircraft Noise Annoyance Around London Airport*, H.M.S.O., London.

Reynolds, I. and C. Nicholson (1970) *The Estate Outside the Dwelling*, H.M.S.O., London.

Skeffington, A. M. (1969) *People and Planning*, H.M.S.O., London.

Wilson, R. L. (1962) 'Livability of the city: attitudes and urban development', in *Urban Growth Dynamics in a Regional Cluster of Cases*, F. S. Chapin and S. F. Weiss, (eds.), John Wiley, New York.

The following references provide general background reading on the measurement and evaluation of community preferences relating to the residential environment:

Falk, E. L. (1968) 'Measurement of community values: the Spokane experiment', *Highway Research Record*, No. 229, Highway Research Board, Washington, D.C., pp. 53–64.

Highway Research Board (1969) *Transportation and Community Values*, Special Report of conference held at Virginia in March, Highway Research Board, Washington, D.C.

Howe, P. and P. D. Patterson, Jr., (1969) 'An environmental gaming simulation laboratory', *Journal of the American Institute of Planners*, 35 (6), pp. 383–8.

Kain, J. F. and J. M. Quigley (1970) 'Evaluating the quality of the residential environment', *Environment and Planning*, 2, pp. 23-32.

Landing, J. B. and R. W. Masons (1969) 'Evaluation of neighbourhood quality', *Journal of the American Institute of Planners*, 35 (3), pp. 195–9.

Langdon, F. J. (1966) *The Social and Physical Environment*, BRS Design Series No. 61, Building Research Station, Garston, England.

McKennel, A. C. and E. A. Hunt (1966) *Noise Annoyance in Central London*, H.M.S.O., London.

Shaffer, M. T. (1967) 'Attitudes, community values and highway planning', *Highway Research Record*, No. 187, Highway Research Board, Washington, D.C., pp. 55–64.

Voorhees, A. M. (1965) 'Techniques for determining community values', *Highway Research Record*, No. 102, Highway Research Board, Washington, D.C., pp. 11–18.

Wilson, A. G. and R. M. Kirwin (1969) *Measures of Benefit in the Evaluation of Urban Transport Improvements*, CES-WP43, Centre for Environmental Studies, London.

CHAPTER 7

The assessment of environmental standards

R. A. WALLER

The consideration of standards for the environment involves many alternatives. Many decisions involving human feelings have to be made. Most people regard this as an area requiring the exercise of judgment and of intuition. This is true, but there is a growing technology which facilitates the assessment of human feelings and enables better judgments and decisions to be made.

In terms of the physical environment the present state of technology means that almost any quality can be achieved. The limiting factor is the amount of resources which can be devoted to obtaining any particular quality. In the past the balance between improvements in environmental quality and their costs has not been studied in great detail. Much has been said but, in the main, it has represented personal opinions. This has been reflected in the way in which the control of noise, the provision of open spaces and so on have been tackled. Knowledge now exists of methods by which environmental quality can be quantified. It is possible to assess and to provide the environmental quality appropriate to the situation. There are, of course, many areas in which more work is required in order to develop suitable techniques and methods of extrapolating into the future, but the application of those which exist can have a profound effect.

This chapter is principally concerned with the physical environment and more particularly with the external physical environment as felt in people's homes and immediate surroundings. Many of the basic concepts, however, have a wider application.

STEPS IN SETTING ENVIRONMENTAL STANDARDS

Figure 1 shows the steps involved in the measurement and evaluation of a situation where one aspect of the environment is involved.

Such a situation would arise in looking at possible standards for the silencing of motor vehicles or aircraft.

1. *Describe the environment in physical terms*

Noise level is obviously such a term, but there are considerable restrictions on the physical measures that may be used. They must be capable of being correlated with the subjective effect, that is, with the opinion that people express about the physical effect. In the case of aircraft the important factors are the loudness of the individual aircraft and the frequency at which flights occur. These two factors are combined

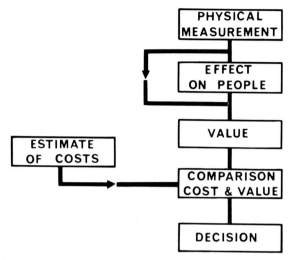

FIG. 1. *Steps involved in setting environmental standards*

together to produce what is called in the United Kingdom the Noise and Number Index (Wilson Committee, 1963).

The Noise and Number Index (N.N.I.) or its equivalent can be predicted from a knowledge of the operating conditions proposed for an airport. It is a relatively straightforward technical problem of prediction involving the knowledge of the laws of sound propagation and attenuation.

2. *Forecast effect on people*

With a knowledge of the physical measure which describes the environment and the correlation between this measure and the subjective opinion, the latter can be forecast. The difficulty arises in establishing this correlation in the first place.

3. *Evaluate*

Whilst it may be useful to know that certain noise levels will cause certain levels of complaint (Stevens *et. al.*, 1955; Kosten, 1961; British Standards Institution, 1967;) this does not entirely solve the problem. Instead of deciding how much it is worth paying to reduce aircraft noise, the question is merely changed to how much it is worth paying to reduce the complaints. It is necessary to go further and to try and evaluate the noise reduction in monetary terms (Waller and Thomas, 1967) and this goes some way to answering the problems of environmental design as they have been posed by several authors (for example, Studer, 1966).

4. *Compare*

Given that both sides of the balance sheet are now in monetary terms, comparison is straightforward. It is important to mention at this point that it is rarely a question of nuisance or no nuisance but rather a question of reducing it to some extent and, for example, balancing the benefits of a reduction in noise nuisance against the extra costs of silencing motor vehicles or aircraft.

5. *Decide*

To decide whether a particular standard should be adopted the criterion might be a minimum ratio of benefit to cost. Alternatively, if it has been decided to do something, then the standard chosen from among the alternatives may be that with the maximum ratio of benefit to cost keeping the cost within a given budget.

CORRELATION BETWEEN PHYSICAL MEASUREMENT AND EFFECT ON PEOPLE

There has been a vast amount of fundamental work done in the field of applied psychology in this particular subject. Fortunately, the relevant results can be summarised relatively briefly without significant loss of accuracy. Four general points emerge.

   1. A given ratio of a stimulus (for example, sound energy) will always produce a particular ratio in the response (loudness) (Stevens, 1962). In the case of sound, a ten-fold increase in sound energy will produce a two-fold increase in apparent loudness. This is true whatever the absolute level and a further ten-fold increase in energy will produce a further two-fold increase in loudness. This relationship holds for a large number of stimuli although the numerical relationships are different (see Fig. 2. and Table 1) (Stevens, 1966a). The same is probably true for the more social effects such as aesthetics (Stevens, 1966b).

   2. It would appear from the experimental work carried out that the most accurate way of assessing reaction to change in a stimulus is to compare it with another; for example, changes in the strength of a colour can be compared with changes in the loudness of a noise (Fig. 3) (Stevens, 1966a). It has been demonstrated several times that this can provide more consistent results than asking people to rate either of these parameters in terms of qualitative descriptions or in terms of the more sophisticated non-dimensional scales, such as 0 to 100 where 0 represents the least significant stimulus that could be imagined and 100 the most significant. (For a description of various scaling methods see Underwood, 1966 and Thomas, 1968).

   This means that it is sufficient to know, as it were, the rate of exchange between each of two currencies and a third in order to be able to determine the rate of exchange between the first two. This has the important result that, if this relationship cannot be obtained directly,

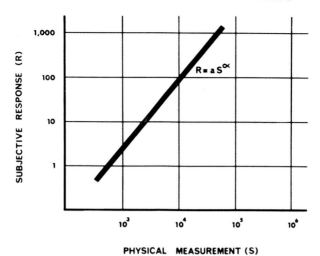

FIG. 2. *Relationship between subjective response and physical measurement.*

TABLE 1. *Typical values of the general relationship shown in Figure 2.*

	Physical measurement	x	Effect on R of × 10 increase in S
Smell of liquids	Vapour pressure	0·4–0·6	2·5–4
Loudness of sound	Sound energy	0·3	2
Brightness	Light energy	0·3–0·5	2–3
Area	Length²	0·7	5
Length	Length	1·0	10

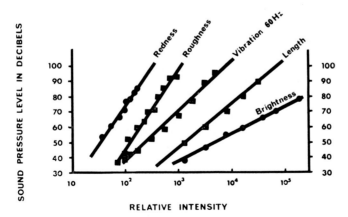

FIG. 3. *Matching of one stimulus against another.*

any intermediate variable (or currency) may be chosen which is the most convenient.

3. The prediction of physical parameters is easier than choosing the correct one to correlate with subjective response. Traffic noise from road complexes is a good example of this typical situation. The effect of individual vehicles has been assessed and correlated with loudness (Fig. 4) (Wilson Committee, 1963). The difficulty with traffic noise as

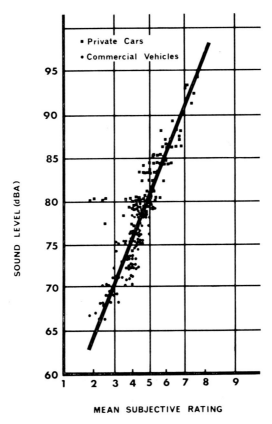

FIG. 4. *Correlation of vehicle noise with subjective rating.*

a whole probably arises because it fluctuates so widely and simple measures do not correlate well (McKennel, 1963). There is some suggestion that it correlates with a composite function of mean level and the amount of variation (Griffiths, 1968; Robinson, 1969). This is fairly fundamental. The response to most environmental effects is a function of the 'steady' level to which people are partially adapted and of the fluctuation to which people cannot adapt. For example, people in hot countries complain only slightly more of being too hot than people in the United Kingdom. On the other hand, they respond to a deviation from the normal temperature to an almost identical extent (Humphreys, 1970).

4. Almost all experimental results apply to groups of people and not to individuals. They also apply to particular situations or contexts. It is important to know whether or not experimental results can be applied to the groups under test. The above relationships are widely valid but there is less evidence about the absolute relationships between the various aspects of the environment, for example, what level of noise is equivalent to a given strength of colour. There is some evidence that such relationships may exist and be valid for relatively large groups of people and in some cases on a world-wide basis (Garth, 1931; Granger, 1952).

At this stage, the logic of such experimental studies becomes a little esoteric. The validity of evaluation techniques depends not on a philosophical justification in psychological terms but whether or not they work. There are eminent advocates of this approach (Hopkinson, 1966). Nonetheless, consensus of opinion between groups of people has to be watched and allowance made for the possibility that there are different groups (Lamanna, 1964).

PREDICTION OF PHYSICAL MEASUREMENTS

Although there is still some doubt as to the best measure for traffic noise, there is quite a considerable store of data about the physical properties of traffic noise. For example, data are available on the variation of noise level with time during the short term (Lamure, 1964). Traffic noise does, of course, vary throughout the day in addition to this short-term effect (Stephenson, 1967). One interesting effect about the short-term variation in noise level is that the difference between the mean noise level and the level exceeded for ten per cent of the time (L_{10}) decreases with distance from the road. This is because the noise is not so dominated by individual vehicles. Thus the Noise Pollution Level (L_{NP}), proposed by D. W. Robinson (1969) and based on the fluctuation as well as on the mean noise level, decreases more rapidly than L_{10} with distance (Fig. 5). There is also knowledge of how noise varies with the type and number of vehicles, gradient, speed and so forth.

EFFECT OF PEOPLE

In an experiment, a large group of people was asked to imagine themselves to be at home and a recording of traffic noise was played back to them (Robinson, 1966). The noise was at a high level and was probably the worst that could be experienced in this situation, and the people were asked to state their estimate of the compensation that would persuade them not to move under those conditions (Fig. 6). The range of the estimates was enormous. Six per cent of the people gave an estimate of zero, the average was £3,000 and the upper one per cent requested £30,000. This range of reaction is typical.

This wide variation in reaction to a given situation means that it is difficult to define what constitutes an acceptable level; clearly it is going to be impossible to satisfy everyone. It is somewhat salutary to look at the situation which exists with regard to party walls. In the United Kingdom there are two Grades, I and II; Figure 7 illustrates the situation. Although the figures are typical rather than precise, it is

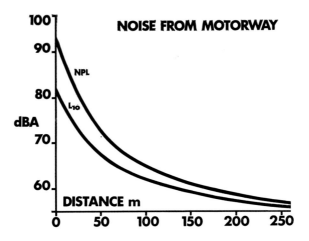

FIG. 5. *Noise versus distance from a motorway.*

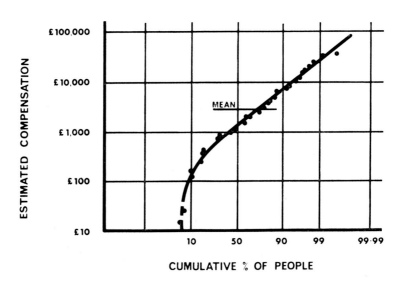

FIG. 6. *Variation of individual's estimates of loss of value owing to traffic noise (70 dBA median noise level indoors).*

clear that Grade II leaves nearly half the occupants dissatisfied and Grade I leaves as many as a quarter of them dissatisfied (Chapman, 1948; Bitter, 1955; Gray, 1958; Wilson Committee, 1963 and Northwood, 1964). In fact, it is technically difficult to improve more than marginally on Grade I as increasing the sound insulating properties of the party wall does not significantly reduce the amount of transmitted noise. This is because a large part of it will be coming via flanking paths through the floors and other walls. The improvement can only be obtained by building detached houses or flats isolated from the main structure.

How are the degrees of satisfaction or otherwise assessed? For some of the environmental aspects means of prediction are available. These were obtained by experiment or survey. Experiments (for instance, that producing Fig. 4) are useful to determine the way in which one particular aspect varies or correlates with effect or relates to others. A social survey is usually necessary to establish where effects studied in an experiment fit into the overall picture, and a more objective survey to relate what people do to what they say in order to fix their absolute values. The variation between people means that a large number of people must be involved in order that statistically reliable results can

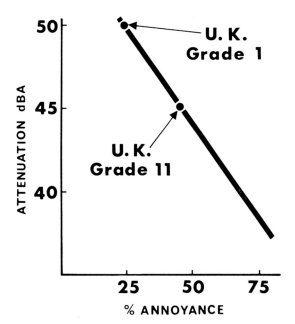

FIG. 7. *Illustration of noise insulation of party walls in houses.*

be obtained. In carrying out surveys it is usually necessary to ask a large number of questions in order to disguise the purpose of the survey as, otherwise, the answers obtained will be biased and meaningless.

It is encouraging, therefore, that work is being carried out to devise a system whereby observers can be trained to give answers which correlate with average reactions (Hopkinson, 1966). The trained observers do not necessarily form the same opinion as the general population. The idea is that there should be a fixed relationship between these opinions and that one can be predicted from the other. This method has, in addition, one important advantage, namely of taking into account the change of reaction with time. It is well known that not only do an individual's reactions vary in magnitude with time but the relative importance given to various aspects of the environment changes with time.

In the past the environment has been dealt with one aspect at a time and this has resulted in uneven environmental situations (Caldwell, 1963). The variation with time that has just been mentioned reinforces the need to consider the overall environment. When first presented with a situation, perhaps people moving into a new area, the initial reactions may well be centred on appearance either of the houses or of the countryside. A short while after moving in, reactions may shift away from this aspect and centre more on the quality of the house; for instance, on doors that do not shut. After a longer period still, judgment may be based on the reliability of the refuse removal service and the type of neighbour.

This view is borne out by several surveys carried out at Prestonpans (Byrom, 1966) where the number of adverse comments on a rather austere view declined with time compared with comments on other aspects. It was found, however, that even in the early stages when the volume of comments on the view was large, the adverse nature of these did not significantly affect the overall level of satisfaction with the environment (see also Willmott, 1964).

It may be that the need for aesthetic satisfaction is felt largely by those visiting the area and by people who have just moved into it. It might be said that to some extent view attracts, but it is the social experiences and such things as the ease of getting to and from work, that cause people to stay satisfied with their environment.

EVALUATION

This is the least studied of the steps involved in environmental design and it is in this area that the author of this chapter has concentrated much of his effort.

It is sufficient to know the relationship between each of a pair of environmental aspects and a third variable in order to define the relationship between them (see above and Fig. 3). It happens that it is difficult to measure the effects of the environment directly in monetary terms (see Bitter and van Weeren, 1955, for an interesting try). This is mainly because people, perhaps unconsciously, bias their judgments to their own advantage. It is generally better to get at the value through a third variable which has no emotive effect as far as the subjects of the experiment are concerned. Indeed, provided that the responses are consistent, the absolute values of this intermediate variable are not important. Any systematic error will be eliminated when the inter-mediate variable is calibrated. This calibration is probably best done by reference to actual market conditions so that real as opposed to hypothetical values are used.

Direct 'market' values can be obtained, but only with difficulty. In principle the loss of value due to annoyance with traffic noise could be assessed by establishing the correlation between traffic noise and the value of houses. Such a study was carried out in the United States but no statistically significant correlation was established (Kinney, 1966). This was probably because the measure of noise was not sophisticated enough and the variation in value due to noise was small compared to that from other causes. (Changes in value due to the introduction of noise, as when a new motorway is constructed, are likely to be more useful). Attempts have also been made to establish amenity values by direct correlation without success (Brigham, 1964).

It should be appreciated that the change in the value of a house does not necessarily reflect the value of the environmental effect to the owner. Moving house involves other expenses and the price is in any case also a function of market forces and of the extent to which an individual values his home over and above the market value (the householder's consumer surplus).

Such direct value relationships are hard to come by and the author and his colleagues decided to use an intermediate variable. This has the additional advantage that it can be related to many sources of annoyance. Its use also allows for the calibration between it and value to be drawn from a much wider range of situations. It also means that, if this intermediate variable could be established by experiment for a new effect such as the sonic boom, then the loss of value due to it can be predicted without any actual prior example.

An analysis on these lines has been carried out in relation to normal owner-occupied houses. The intermediate variable chosen was one of 'annoyance'. This scale can be broadly defined as representing the percentage of people 'annoyed' in a given situation and therefore, of course, represents the annoyance of a large group of people and not of individuals, as, for example, in the relationship between Noise and Number Index and annoyance. Not all these experiments were carried out with precisely the scale of annoyance used in this analysis and, where necessary, they have been modified numerically to correspond.

In Figure 8 the results of a number of market valuations have been related to the appropriate degree of annoyance. There are relatively few examples available at the moment but three additional factors should be borne in mind in judging the merit of the average line which has been drawn.

First, the mean line is expected to be approximately straight because the scale has been distorted to make this likely. (Abcissa, normal probability; ordinate, logarithmic).

Secondly, work has been done on the impairment of television pictures which suggests that the slope of the line should be taken so that the effect of the various sources of annoyance may be additive. In this

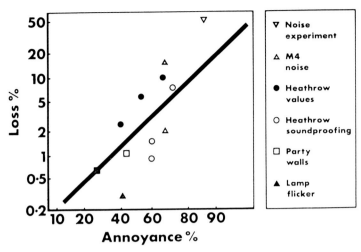

FIG. 8. *Loss of value of houses versus annoyance.*

case, the effect as measured in money allows the equivalent slope to be deduced to meet this condition. For example, the British Post Office's work (Prosser, 1964) and that of the British Broadcasting Corporation (see Lewis, 1965) suggests that two situations each producing an annoyance of 50 per cent will produce a combined annoyance of 67 per cent. In Figure 8, where 50 per cent annoyance produces a loss of value of £70, it would be expected that two such annoyances together give a loss of £140 which, in fact, roughly corresponds with an annoyance of 67 per cent.

Thirdly, most of the points represent inequalities. The numerical figures are in some cases above the actual loss of value and sometimes below. Judgment has been used to allow for this.

As an example (Fig. 9) the Heathrow points are based on a survey of estate agents' estimates of the effect of noise on house value (Commission on the Third London Airport, 1969). The annoyance due to aircraft noise had been established earlier (McKennel, 1963) (Fig. 10). It was judged that the estate agents probably over-estimated and so the mean line in Figure 8 is drawn below those points relating to Heathrow.

It is not proposed to discuss the details of cost-benefit and cost-effectiveness studies, but all expenditure has to be justified and, in deciding that a given scheme shall go ahead, it has surely been concluded that the benefits which will be derived will exceed the cost.

Unfortunately, many decisions are made without knowledge of the cost involved. A politician could be elected on a mandate to build more roads. His election would indicate the desire of the community for more roads but it does not necessarily indicate that the community is willing to pay. In general, it will not be sufficiently well informed on the costs of roads and of its own potential contribution to this cost.

Further, even if the community is informed of the costs of providing

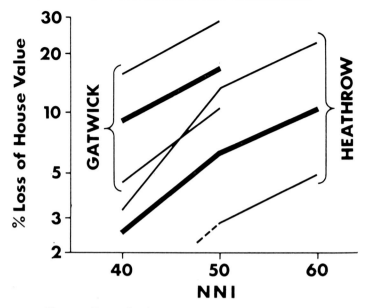

FIG. 9. *Loss of value of houses due to aircraft noise (thick lines—average price houses).*

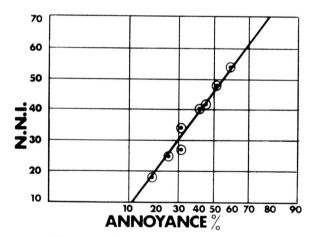

FIG. 10. *Aircraft noise versus annoyance.*

roads, and indeed of its own contribution to these costs, it does not mean that a referendum on the subject will necessarily produce the 'correct' overall answer. It is more than likely that the electorate would choose the alternative which resulted in them paying least at the present time, deferring as much as possible to the future. In short, they would choose the 'wrong' discount rates for the purpose of maximising benefit to the community as a whole.

It is suggested that the means exist to establish what it is worth to the community to have these new roads. An economic assessment can be carried out to produce a cost-benefit balance and to derive the optimum programme of road development. The cost-benefit balance could then form the basis of the justification as far as the electorate is concerned.

This is a gross simplification of the issues. Certainly the use of cost-benefit techniques does not eliminate the need for political decisions. Indeed, the present state of these techniques demands many such decisions. Typically such issues as the following need to be decided.

(a) Who should the planners wish to please with their schemes, the immediate client, the existing population or future generations?

(b) When do minority views cease to be overridden by those of the majority? Consider ten people, one of whom will gain £10 from a scheme and the other nine of whom will lose £1. If a vote were taken, presumably it would be thrown out by an overwhelming majority, but there is a net gain of £1 and the scheme is profitable.

(c) Is the value to the community of a scheme the same as the total value to the individuals making up the community?

(d) At what point in time or over what period should the benefit from a scheme be measured?

In general, a single factor will not be decisive and the overall cost-benefit balance will be a complex one made up of many contributory factors. The following example is, therefore, purposely simplified and relates to the noise problem arising from an urban motorway.

In Figure 11 can be seen the basic arrangement for a typical urban motorway where the optimum engineering design results in it being at ground level. The effect of various measures to reduce the noise has been considered and an estimate made of the improvement that they cause in environmental quality or amenity. The values quoted are based on the estimates of the loss of value of houses in Figure 8 and the relationship between Noise Pollution Level and Annoyance in Figure 12.

The conclusions that can be drawn are that it is probably worthwhile providing double windows on the motorway side of houses within 30m of it or noise screens 3m high. The other alternatives of putting the motorway in a cutting or enclosing it are not justified on the basis of noise considerations alone. There was a margin for error in the original valuations and it is important to note that the broad conclusions are not affected if the ratios value/loss are underestimated by a factor of more than ten.

The benefits of noise reduction and the cost of obtaining them are naturally paired together. If compensation is considered instead of noise reduction the situation would be different. Benefits might accrue from the construction of the motorways which would, to some extent, counteract the loss of value due to noise. Indeed, it might be that, as around major airports, the benefits of access to transport or lucrative employment sometimes outweigh the disbenefits due to noise.

Cost-benefit techniques are usually time-consuming to apply and are

appropriate for major schemes such as the construction of motorway net-
works and overall urban renewal requirements. For smaller issues it is
more appropriate to consider whether general answers can be derived

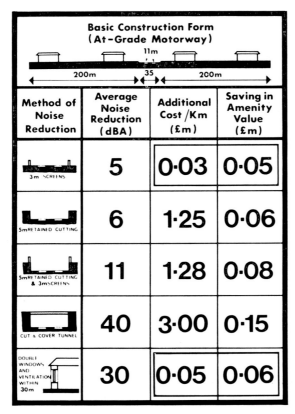

Basic Construction Form (At-Grade Motorway)			
Method of Noise Reduction	Average Noise Reduction (dBA)	Additional Cost /Km (£m)	Saving in Amenity Value (£m)
3m SCREENS	5	0·03	0·05
5m RETAINED CUTTING	6	1·25	0·06
5m RETAINED CUTTING & 3m SCREENS	11	1·28	0·08
CUT & COVER TUNNEL	40	3·00	0·15
DOUBLE WINDOWS AND VENTILATION WITHIN 30m	30	0·05	0·06

FIG. 11. *Cost versus benefit for schemes reducing traffic noise.*

(possibly by using cost-benefit techniques) and incorporated in some form
of standard or code of practice accepting a degree of sub-optimisation.

THE ROLE OF STANDARDS IN ENVIRONMENTAL CONTROL

In general, standards are a means of simplifying the design or planning
process; alternatively, they are capable of acting as a means of control
where economic sanctions do not apply. An example of the latter situation occurs in the control of vehicle noise. At the moment there is no
economic incentive for producing quieter motor vehicles in the United
Kingdom. In this situation the Government has to judge what reduction in noise level is worth the cost involved, a cost in this case to car
owners. The level of this balance between cost and benefit will have to
be varied as the years go by and as both the costs and the benefits vary.

In the past, many proposals for standards, particularly of noise levels,
have not been implemented. Perhaps the main reason for this has been

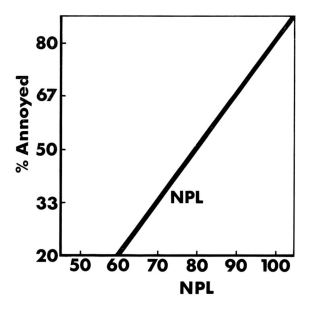

FIG. 12. *Noise pollution level versus annoyance.*

that the costs of implementation have been found to be too great in relation to potential benefit. The proposals for such standards certainly represented desirable levels but they have proved to be not desirable enough. For a standard to be both worthwhile and effective, it must be possible to assess the balance between cost and desirability quite accurately.

It may be that the use of the word 'standard' is a hindrance to some extent, because the balance between cost and desirability cannot be unique and will vary from situation to situation and as time goes by.

This can be illustrated by considering the case of choosing the the wall between two houses, from the noise point of view. Figure 13 is an attempt to represent the situation which arises. The abscissa represents the percentage of people who would be satisfied by the reduction of noise through the wall. The ordinate of £/house represents variously the cost of the party wall or the loss of value to the occupants due to noise which is transmitted between the houses. The chain dotted line in fact represents the latter as a function of the percentage of people satisfied. In other words, if there is a situation in which 90 per cent of the people are satisfied, the residual loss of value is only £10. Towards the other end of the scale, where only 10 per cent are satisfied, the loss is in the region of £400. (These figures are reasonable and are derived substantially from Figure 8). The datum is the situation where the cheapest wall from all other considerations is used. In the example such a wall produces a satisfaction of 40 per cent. The full line is then derived from this and represents the potential increase in value which will result from improving noise reduction. The reduction in loss of value or in the improvement in value to be obtained from increasing the satisfaction

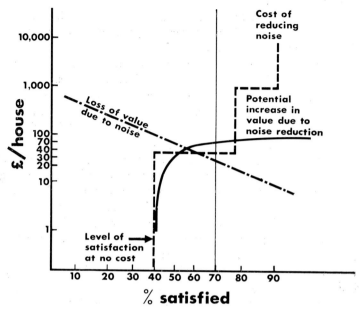

FIG. 13. *Methods of choosing standards.*

from 40 per cent to 100 per cent is about £100. Most of this is obtained at about 80 per cent satisfaction.

The dashed line represents the costs of the various alternative walls. The cheapest, of course, provides 40 per cent satisfaction. The next may well provide 75 per cent satisfaction and cost £40 per home more. The next alternative may cost £1,000 more. It is, in fact, difficult to achieve more than 75 per cent satisfaction with conventional forms of construction in terraced or semi-detached houses because of the amount of noise that is transmitted around the edges of the party wall and the only really significant improvement would probably be obtained by making the houses effectively detached. Only one of the alternative forms has a benefit which exceeds the cost and this is the second which achieves 75 per cent satisfaction at a cost of about £40 per home. This situation is somewhat analogous to that in the United Kingdom where the 11 inch cavity wall is preferred to the 4½ inch single leaf brick wall (British Standards Institution, 1960; see also Fig. 7).

A standard would divide Figure 13 into two areas; the area to the right of the line drawn through 75 per cent satisfaction represents an acceptable standard and the area to the left of the line represents unacceptable situations. Thus, any party wall in the left-hand region is unacceptable and presumably of infinite negative value and any party wall producing a situation to the right of it is no more value than one achieving 70 per cent. It is because of this that many standards and regulations miss the opportunity to provide an incentive for the improvement of environmental quality once the standard (often a minimum) has been satisfied.

Are there any alternatives to standards? One possibility, much discussed in relation to noise from motorways, is that of compensation for the affected householder (for example, Mohring, 1965). On purely practical grounds the compensation would probably have to be based on the average loss of value due to noise. This would result in half the householders receiving more compensation than the value of amenity lost to them and half less. It must, of course, be borne in mind that this does not eliminate the problem. Amenity may be lost in other directions, such as to people passing through the area whose enjoyment of it would be reduced. Nonetheless, the principle of compensation would seem to be a valuable one. It represents a means of underwriting the individuals' potential financial loss. Indeed, in the author's experience this potential financial loss is of more importance than the loss of environmental quality. If people were guaranteed no loss of value in their houses from the construction of a motorway, then most of the difficulties and complaints would disappear.

In most areas, however, it seems likely that standards will be politically desirable. Indeed, in many situations it would be uneconomical to assess afresh the balance between cost and benefit and this must be done on a countrywide basis.

There are few obviously totally undesirable environmental aspects and consequently few, if any, absolute standards of environmental quality. The variation between individuals makes it almost certain that in any situation it would be possible to find some people who are completely satisfied and others who are completely dissatisfied.

That there is no absolute upper limit for deficiencies in the environment is well illustrated by the problem of safety. In any form of rapid transportation there is a statistical risk of injury and of loss of life. These forms of transportation have large but finite values to the community and it follows therefore that loss of life has a finite value. There is no absolute standard that requires that no injury shall be caused but rather that things shall be so arranged that the rate of injury does not exceed a certain level. This level is set in a complex political way by pressure of public opinion and varies from place to place and from time to time. The same is true of all forms of travel. It is true of the construction industry where labour is recruited in the more risky areas by paying those working in them 'danger money'. The problem of safety is, therefore, recognised and the balance point between risk and cost is determined in a rather devious *ad hoc* fashion.

Standards are a convenient way of setting the point at which value to the community sufficiently exceeds cost to the community and determining indirectly the allocation of resources. It certainly does not mean that if the standard is met everything is perfect. If improvements over and above the standard can be obtained cheaply in a particular situation they may well be worth having. The converse is also true; there may be situations in which it is particularly expensive to meet the standard. In such situations, and particularly in the urban environment where costs are so high, it may be necessary to justify the expense by considering the adverse effects of allowing a standard to be eroded. This perhaps suggests that standards should not be produced unless there is an intention to keep them and to abide by the consequences. More importantly it means that the level set by standards must be decided only after the most careful consideration.

Standards, of course, need updating. To some extent people are 'educated' by improvements to their environment and come to expect more. Certainly as levels of real income rise the money available to improve the environment will increase. The values put on the various environmental aspects will rise and the balance points between cost and benefit will need continual revision.

REFERENCES

Bitter, C. and P. van Weeren (1955) *A Study of the Problem of Sound Nuisance and Sound Insulation in Blocks of Dwellings*, Research Institute for Public Health Engineering, T.N.O. Report No. 24, The Hague.

Brigham, E. F. (1964) *A Model of Residential Land Values*, Memorandum RM-4043-RC, Rand Corporation.

British Standards Institution (1960) *Sound Insulation and Noise Reduction*, British Standard Code of Practice CP3: Chap. III, London.

British Standards Institution (1967) *Method of Rating Industrial Noise Affecting Mixed Residential and Industrial areas*, British Standard 4142, London.

Byrom, J. B. (1966) *Courtyard Houses, Inchview, Prestonpans*, Architecture Research Unit, The University, Edinburgh.

Caldwell, L. K. (1963) 'Environment: A new focus for public housing?', *Public Administration Review*, 23, p. 134.

Chapman, D. (1948) *A Survey of Noise in British Homes*, National Building Studies Technical Paper No. 2, H.M.S.O., London.

Commission on the Third London Airport (1969) *Papers and Proceedings, Vol. VII*, H.M.S.O., London.

Garth, T. R., K. Ikeda and R. M. Langdon (1931) 'The colour preferences of Japanese children', *Journal of Social Psychology* 2(3), pp. 397–402.

Granger, G. W. (1952) 'Objectivity of colour preferences', *Nature*, 170, pp. 778–80, London.

Gray, P. G., A. Cartwright and P. H. Parkin (1958) *Noise in Three Groups of Flats with Different Floor Insulations*, National Building Studies Research Paper No. 27, Ref. No. 65, 128, H.M.S.O., London.

Griffiths, I. D. and F. J. Langdon (1968) 'Subjective response to road traffic noise' *Journal of Sound and Vibration*, 8 (1), pp. 16–32.

Hopkinson, R. G. (1966) 'The design of the built environment' in *Environmental engineering—its roles in society, Symposium Papers*, Society of Environmental Engineers, London.

Humphreys, M. A. and J. F. Nicol (1970) 'Thermal comfort of office workers', *Journal of the Institution of Heating and Ventilating Engineers*, 38, pp. 181–9.

Kinney, P. T. (1966) *The impact of traffic on residential property values and retail sales in Champaign, Urbana*, Engineering Experimental Station Bulletin 491, Illinois.

Kosten, C. W. and G. J. van Os (1961) 'Community reaction criteria for external noises', *The Control of Noise*, Symposium No. 12, National Physical Laboratory, H.M.S.O., London

Lamanna, R. A. (1964) 'Value consensus among urban residents', *Journal of the American Institute of Planners*, 30, pp. 317–23.

Lamure, C. and C. Aurou (1964) *Les Niveaux de Bruit au Voisinage des Autoroutes Dégagées*, Cahiers du Centre Scientifique et Technique du Bâtiment, No. 71, Cahier 599, Paris.

Langdon, F. J. and W. E. Scholes (1968) *The Traffic Noise Index—a Means for Controlling Noise Nuisance*, Current Paper 38/68, Building Research Station, Garston, England.

Lewis, N. W. and J. W. Allnatt (1965) 'Subjective quality of pictures with multiple impairments', *Electronics Letters*, 1, September.

McKennel, A. C. (1963) *Aircraft Noise Annoyance Around London (Heathrow) Airport; The Social Survey*, Report Ref. SS337, C.O.I., London.

Mohring, H. (1965) *Urban Highway Investments, Measuring Benefits of Government Investments*, The Brookings Institution, Washington D.C.

Northwood, T. D. (1964) 'Sound insulation and the apartment dweller', *Journal of the Acoustical Society of America*, 36, pp. 725–8.

Prosser, R. A., J. W. Allnatt and N. W. Lewis (1964) 'Quality grading of impaired television pictures', *Proceedings of the Institution of Electrical Engineers* 3, pp. 491–502.

Robinson, D. W. (1966) Private communication.

Robinson, D. W. (1969) *The Concept of Noise Pollution Level*, National Physical Laboratory, Aero Report Ae. 98.

Stephenson, R. J. and G. H. Vulkan (1967) 'Urban planning against noise', *Official Architecture and Planning*, May, pp. 643–7.

Stevens, K. N., W. A. Rosenblith and R. H. Bolt (1955) 'A community's reaction to noise. Can it be forecast?', *Noise Control*, 1(1), pp. 63–71.

Stevens, S. S. (1962) 'The surprising simplicity of sensory metrics', *American Psychologist*, 17, pp. 29–39.

Stevens, S. S. (1966a) 'Matching functions between loudness and ten other continua', *Perception and Psychophysics*, 1, pp. 5–8.

Stevens, S. S. (1966b) 'A metric for the social consensus', *Science*, 151, pp. 530–41.

Studer, R. G. (1966) 'On environmental programming', *Arena*, 81, pp. 290–6.

Thomas, R. J. (1968) 'Cash value of the environment', *Industrial Marketing Research Association Journal and Proceedings*, 4 (3), pp. 110–16.

The Times (1965) 'Life in the shadow of an overhead motorway', 30th June, p. 6.

Underwood, Benton J. (1966) *Experimental Psychology*, The Century Psychology Series, Appleton-Century-Crofts.

Waller, R. A. and R. J. Thomas (1967) 'The cash value of the environment', *Arena*, 82, pp. 164–6.

Wilmott, P. (1964) 'Housing in Cumbernauld—some residents' opinions', *Journal of the Town Planning Institute*, 50, pp. 195–200.

Wilson Committee (1963) *Noise*, Final Report of the Committee on the Problem of Noise, (Chairman, Sir Alan Wilson, F.R.S.), H.M.S.O. (Cmnd. 2056), London.

CHAPTER 8

The role of perceptions of professionals in environmental decision-making

W. R. DERRICK SEWELL

The publication of the First Annual Report of the Council on Environmental Quality in August 1970 (Council on Environmental Quality, 1970), was an important landmark in the quest for environmental revival in the United States. It pointed out that the rapidly deteriorating quality of the nation's streams, lakes, atmosphere, cities and rural landscapes posed a threat to survival. Even more important, it noted that if disaster was to be averted, fundamental changes in the approach to environmental management would be required. Past policies had clearly failed, and past mechanisms of decision-making had proved unsatisfactory. The public had not been provided with what it wanted or what it needed. Moreover, it had been increasingly alienated in the policy-making process. The time was ripe, the report suggested, for a serious re-appraisal of this process and the roles of the various participants in it. Similar conclusions appear to have been reached about past approaches in Canada (Canada, House of Commons, 1970), and in various European countries too (United Nations, 1971).

This chapter is intended as a contribution to the search for means to improve policy-making relating to environmental quality. It presents first a simple framework which may be used for the analysis of environmental quality policy-making. This framework identifies the various groups which participate in decisions and the roles which they play. Of the various groups involved, professionals appear to exert a considerable influence, either as technical advisers, administrators, or as advocates. This chapter then describes the results of some empirical investigations of two groups of professionals concerned with environmental problems, engineers and public health officials. It concludes with some suggestions as to the implications of the findings for environmental policy-making.

A FRAMEWORK FOR ANALYSIS

Policy-making in environmental quality management is a continuous process, involving several groups of participants (Fig. 1). The role of each group is conditioned in part by what the institutional framework

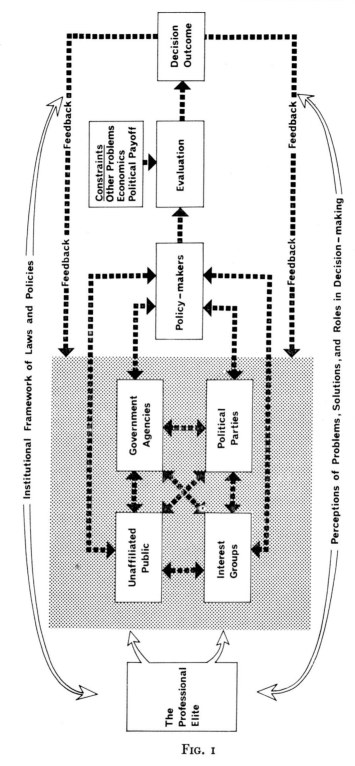

FIG. I

The Process of Environmental Quality Decision Making

of laws and public policies permits or encourages, and in part by individual perceptions, attitudes and motivations (Zisk, 1969). Thus, even though the law may permit direct participation of the individual, such as through membership of committees or presentations at hearings, he may not take advantage of the opportunity.

Five groups of participants may be identified: policy-makers (the ultimate decision-makers), government agencies (technical advisers and administrators), interest groups (such as manufacturers' associations, trade unions, or conservation societies), political parties, and unaffiliated individuals. The policy-makers are influenced in various ways by the other four groups, either because they require technical advice or because they are subjected to political pressure. The different groups are also affected by each other in their respective attempts to gain influence.

In decisions relating to environmental quality, considerable reliance is placed upon the advice of professionals, notably engineers, biologists, physicians, architects and planners. This is because the problems involved are often highly complex, partly because the individual feels that the exercise of his own judgment may result in disastrous consequences, and partly because of the salesmanship of the experts themselves. The consequence has been the development of a technical élite which has assumed responsibility for identifying problems and recommending solutions. Its advisory role has been institutionalised within the administrative structure, with various departments or branches of departments being staffed by particular kinds of professionals. Thus fisheries agencies are typically staffed by fishery biologists, forestry agencies by foresters, and water resources agencies by engineers. Their role, however, may not be confined solely to advice. They may also become policy advocates, either by drawing up agency proposals for acceptance by the elected official or by presentations through a professional society or other interest group.

One consequence of the increasing reliance of society upon professionals has been the alienation of the public in the policy-making process. This has led to adverse reaction in several parts of North America, in part because the public feels it has a *right* to be consulted, and in part because the professionals have often seriously misjudged what the public wants or how it would react to what is provided (Sewell and Burton, 1971).

It is pertinent to enquire, therefore, what are the problems perceived by the professionals and what are the solutions they recommend? How do they perceive their own role in policy-making and that of others? In what ways do such perceptions differ from perceptions of the public at large? The answers to these questions are not immediately clear, for as Kenneth Craik has pointed out, the environmental perceptions of environmental decision-makers have never been studied in detail, and those of professionals have hardly been investigated at all (Craik, 1970b). Studies undertaken at the University of Victoria in the past three years, however, have helped to identify perceptions and attitudes of two groups of professionals: engineers and public health officials. The research was not intended to be definitive in any way. Rather it was intended to be exploratory, aiming to develop a methodology and to identify factors that might be examined in greater depth in subsequent investigations. Nevertheless, the findings do appear to have some implications both for research and for public policy in the environmental quality field.

ENGINEERS AND PUBLIC HEALTH OFFICIALS

Engineers and public health officials both play critical roles in environmental quality management. Both have a long tradition of involvement in this area. Problems resulting from alterations in the physical environment are traditionally referred to engineers, especially when such problems affect Man's economic well-being. Thus engineers are usually called in to deal with alterations in the environment stemming from natural hazards such as floods, hurricanes, or earthquakes, or problems resulting from traffic congestion, industrial conglomeration or mining operations. In such instances economic costs can be clearly identified, and since the problems seem physical in origin, the expertise of the engineer is regarded as particularly appropriate (Gerstl and Hutton, 1966; Vallentine, 1967).

Public health officials have also been dealing with environmental quality problems for a long time (Brockington, 1961). The kinds of problems on which they work, however, differ from those involving engineers. Public health officials are mainly concerned with those aspects of environmental alteration that result in adverse effects on human health, such as the effects of disposal of industrial and municipal wastes into water bodies.

The two groups of professionals play similar roles in the policy-making process. They act as technical advisers and administrators, and sometimes as decision-makers as well. In these capacities they are instrumental in defining the problems to be solved, determining the solutions to be considered and, frequently, in selecting the strategy actually adopted. Inevitably in doing so they give expression to their views as to what society wants, and as to how it will react to what is provided.

ORGANISATION OF THE STUDIES

The study of engineers was undertaken in the summer of 1967. It was based upon a sample of thirty engineers, specialising in water resources problems, and drawn from government agencies, firms of private consultants, and from universities, all in Vancouver and Victoria, B.C. Care was taken to include engineers involved at various levels of responsibility and having differing degrees of experience. The sample was believed to be reasonably representative of the universe of the approximately 359 engineers specialising in water problems in the two cities from which it was drawn.

The study of public health officials was undertaken in the summer of 1969, based upon interviews with forty officials, who were located in the twenty health units which together cover the province of British Columbia. These were Medical Health Officers and Public Health Inspectors.

The Medical Health Officers (M.H.O.) and the Public Health Inspectors (P.H.I.) work together as a team, but they perform quite separate functions. The M.H.O. is ultimately responsible to the provincial Department of Health and to local Boards of Health. He is mainly an administrator, charged with the responsibility of interpreting government policy and ensuring it is carried out. The Inspector is the field representative of the Department of Health, and is generally regarded as 'its eyes and ears' in the region in which he operates. He carries out various tests to determine water quality, and acts as a sounding board to receive complaints and suggestions for policy change.

The two studies were based upon interviews, guided by a questionnaire. In both cases the interviews were conducted by a skilled interviewer and lasted about one hour. Open-ended and forced choice questions were used. The answers were recorded in shorthand. In the case of the public health officials, more detailed information was sought on certain matters and a questionnaire was left with the respondents to be mailed at their convenience to the researchers. Replies were received from all those who were interviewed.

The studies sought information on three main topics:

(i) the ways in which these professionals perceive problems facing society, and specifically those relating to environmental quality. Results of previous research have suggested that there are variations among individuals and among groups in the ways in which they perceive problems, and that such differences may account for variations in their responses to them (Craik, 1970b; White, 1966).

(ii) the ways in which engineers and public health professionals perceive solutions to problems with which they deal. Here, too, previous work has revealed that different individuals and groups perceive different kinds of strategy (Kates, 1962; Saarinen, 1966; Craik, 1970a), and that there are often major divergencies between solutions recommended by professionals and those perceived by the public (Appleyard, 1969; Lucas, 1966).

(iii) attitudes of the two groups as to their own role and the role of others in dealing with problems of environmental quality. Other studies have indicated that views differ among individuals and among groups as to the extent to which responsibility for initiating action lies with them, their agency, the government, or the public at large. Views also seem to vary as to the efficacy of individual versus collective action (White, 1966).

It is important not only to identify perceptions and attitudes, but also to account for variations in them. To this end information was sought on possible influences identified in other studies, such as socio-economic characteristics, training, experience, present responsibilities, and views about Man's relationship to Nature (Kluckhohn and Strodtbeck, 1961; White, 1966). The latter dimension has been found to be a significant factor in explaining variations in perceptions and attitudes relating to human adjustment to the environment in a variety of contexts (Lowenthal, 1967).

ANALYSIS OF THE RESULTS

Perceptions of problems

An attempt was made to determine the views of the two groups of professionals as to what are the major problems facing British Columbia, and how environmental quality problems ranked among these issues. As indicated in Table 1, most of the public health officials identified

TABLE 1. *Perceptions and problems*

| | Frequency of mention | |
	Public Health Officials	Engineers
Number One Problem facing the Province		
Environmental quality	32	5
Social problems (poverty, unemployment, education)	20	20
Urban growth and transportation	9	15
Lack of health facilities	8	—
Politics	6	—
Drugs, alcoholism, crime	4	10
Quality of the environment is deteriorating in B.C.		
Air	35	10
Water	34	20
Land	26	—
Other	3	—
Measures of water quality		
Coli count	39	NI
B.O.D.	36	NI
C.O.D.	13	NI
Visual characteristics	12	NI
Turbidity	12	NI
Taste	—	NI
Smell	—	NI
Major concern about water quality		
Hazard to health	31	5
Impairment of aesthetic values	9	5
Increased costs of production	—	15

NI = No information solicited.

environmental quality problems as the major issue facing the province, followed by various other social problems such as poverty, unemployment and education. Air pollution and water pollution were seen as the major causes of environmental deterioration, followed by land pollution in various forms. Little mention was made, however, of such things as noise, billboards or powerlines.

These results contrast somewhat with the findings of the engineers study. In this case problems of unemployment, labour unrest and juvenile delinquency were seen as the major issues facing British Columbia. Environmental deterioration ranked far down the list. Of the various forms of pollution, water pollution was regarded as the most important. These findings, however, should be interpreted with caution. The engineers study was undertaken in 1967, some two years before there was widespread public concern about environmental quality in British Columbia. If the study were undertaken today the results might be quite different. Nevertheless, it is interesting to note that the close relationship between problems on which the respondent worked and the perceived importance of the problem observed in the case of the public health officials was not found in the case of the engineers.

Other indications of the ways in which professionals perceive problems are found in the terms in which they describe them and the means they use to identify them. Both groups of professionals in this study described environmental quality problems in technical terms, principally in terms of 'standards' used by the public health profession. Thus coliform counts and B.O.D. levels were used to describe the degree of water pollution. Little mention was made, however, of parameters which are typically used by members of the general public to describe such pollution, such as colour, smell, or taste.

It was also clear that both groups of professionals generally rely on measurements of physical attributes to assess the 'seriousness' of a problem. The degree of public awareness or the extent of complaints is not normally regarded as an index of 'seriousness'. The public health officials noted that they do not usually go out to assess public awareness by surveys. The only measure they have is the number of complaints received by them or letters to newspapers.

A final indication of the ways in which the two groups of professionals perceived water quality was in the extent to which they saw it as a health problem rather than an impairment to aesthetic beauty or a cost of production. Interestingly, most of the public health officials saw it mainly as a health problem. Half the engineers viewed it as a factor increasing costs of production, and the remainder perceived it either as a hazard to health or an impairment of aesthetic values.

Perceptions of solutions

The solutions proposed by the two groups were clearly influenced by the conventional wisdom and practices of their respective professions.

The public health officials felt that the way to handle environmental quality problems was to discuss the matter first with the offender and suggest he find means of reducing the pollution, and if he does not do so, subject him to court proceedings (Table 2). This approach has long been the approach used by Departments of Public Health but it has often been unsuccessful. The more powerful the offender, the more likely it is he will be able to ignore the regulations. Those interviewed were well aware of the fact that this had been the case in British Columbia, but most of them were uncritical of the policies and pro-

TABLE 2. *Perceptions of solutions*

	Frequency of mention Public Health	
	Officials	Engineers
Strategy generally recommended		
Warning followed by litigation	40	2
Construction of facilities	—	28
Provision of subsidies	—	—
Imposition of charges	—	—
Public pressure	—	—
Present legislation		
Adequate	3	15
Weaknesses of present approach		
Lack of staff and facilities	10	—
Lack of time, money and research	16	—
Inadequate enforcement	20	20
Suggested improvements		
Enforcement and control	18	NI
Better testing facilities	11	NI
Improved criteria	9	NI

NI = No information solicited.

cedures used to combat pollution in the province (Table 2). Most of the officials were dissatisfied with present pollution legislation, but in the main their criticisms related to the lack of rigour in its application rather than to its relevance as a solution to the pollution problem.

There are various alternatives to legislation and regulation as strategies to deal with pollution, such as the imposition of charges for the use of water bodies, the provision of subsidies for effluent treatment, the development of non-polluting processes or products, or the imposition of public pressure on polluters (Bower and Sewell, 1970). None of these, however, was mentioned (Table 2). Suggestions were offered for a more forceful attack on pollution problems, but these all reflected the generally conservative bias of the officials. Tougher standards, more finances for laboratory facilities, and higher fines for offenders were among the suggestions most frequently offered. No radical departures from existing policies or procedures were suggested.

The engineers, too, perceived solutions in very conventional terms, reflecting standard practices of the profession on the one hand and an adherence to established government policy on the other. In their case this was expressed in the choice of 'Construction of facilities' as the most frequently recommended approach. Thus the solution to declining water quality was generally perceived as the provision of additional water to increase the assimilative capacity of the water body, or the installation of effluent processing facilities. Other alternatives, such as those noted above, were mentioned by a few of the engineers, but were dismissed as being 'unrealistic' or 'unacceptable by the public'. The engineers, too, seemed reasonably satisfied with present legislation and with the present approach to pollution problems in the province. Their main criticism was the lack of enforcement of regulations.

Attitudes toward roles and responsibilities

Attitudes to one's own role in dealing with problems and to the role of others appear to have an important bearing on one's perception of problems on the one hand, and on action proposed or taken on the other (White, 1966; Lowenthal, 1966).

The two groups of professionals saw themselves in a variety of roles in dealing with environmental quality problems. About twenty-five per cent of the public health officials regarded their role as being that of a technical adviser (Table 3). Sixty-five per cent of them, however, considered that they were decision-makers as well as advisers. The need to make quick decisions in the field (within the broad limits imposed by law and policy) no doubt accounts for this view. In contrast, ninety per cent of the engineers saw themselves principally as technical advisers, even though government engineers as well as consulting engineers were involved in the study. Only those concerned with issuing water licences thought they had any kind of a decision-making role. The decision-makers, suggested the engineers, are the politicians. As one of them put it: 'They make the policy and to a considerable extent they interpret it too. Our role is generally defined by Terms of Reference which set out in detail what the task is, and what actions we are expected to perform in undertaking it.'

A further indication of the way in which professionals perceive their role is the extent to which they feel that other groups have something useful to contribute to the solution of problems on which they work. To this end both groups were asked which other agencies or professions they consulted and how often, and in what ways they tried to assess public opinion. Contacts within an agency or a firm appear to be very frequent (Table 3). Consultation among peers is in fact an integral part of practice in both professions. Beyond the agency or firm, however, contacts become much less frequent and are generally very formal.

Public health officials seem reluctant to contact officials in other agencies or to establish formal links with groups in the general public. A partial explanation that might be offered for this reluctance is that

TABLE 3. *Perceptions of roles*

	Frequency of mention Public Health Officials	Engineers
Groups concerned with environmental quality		
Health officials	28	—
Recreation and service clubs	19	—
Educators	14	—
Anti-pollution committees	13	—
Civic officials and Chambers of Commerce	12	—
Lakeshore property owners and ratepayers associations	10	—
Provincial and federal agencies	4	—
Specific roles		
Adviser	10	27
Decision-maker	4	—
Adviser and decision-maker	26	3
Consultations		
Internal		
Within own office or other regional offices	39	30
With head office	32	30
External		
Other provincial or federal agencies	16	10
Municipal councils	29	5
Private agencies	11	5
Other (pressure groups etc.)	9	3
Perceived opposition		
'Abnormal' minority groups	13	NI
Politicians	26	NI
Industrialists and developers	6	NI
Individual members of the public	10	NI
Attitude of P.H.O. as to areas of responsibility		
Department of Health		
(1) All aspects of quality	20	NI
(2) Sewage disposal and treatment	15	NI
(3) Garbage disposal and treatment	11	NI
(4) Recreation	3	NI
(5) Indl. and comml. effluents	2	NI
(6) Drinking water	4	NI
Pollution Control Board		
(1) All aspects of quality	3	NI
(2) Sewage disposal and treatment	0	NI
(3) Garbage disposal and treatment	1	NI
(4) Recreation	2	NI
(5) Indl and comml effluents	15	NI
(6) Drinking water	0	NI

NI = No information solicited.

continuous contacts with other agencies might lead to a sharing of responsibility. This, as the views expressed on the perceived roles of the Department of Health and the Pollution Control Branch seem to suggest, is clearly not what the public health officials want. They wish to retain complete jurisdiction over control of pollution, at least as far as health considerations are concerned, and are willing to concede only that part involving major industries, which the officials feel require much greater power than the Department of Health can exercise, to control them.

Engineers are similarly jealous of the role which they perceive for themselves. They, too, have very few continuous external contacts. The rationale given is that they are sufficiently aware of the overall picture to be able to cast the problem into a broad framework, and they need to call in outside opinions only when they require specialised advice on a certain aspect. They felt that they were much more likely to be effective in the decision-making process than many other types of professional because they were 'precise and accurate, and have a reputation for offering workable solutions'. They contrasted the 'practical view' taken by the engineer with the 'idealism' that characterises proposals of many other professions, notably planners. 'Our projects usually get built,' said one of the engineers, 'whereas theirs usually end up on the shelf.'

The engineers were even less anxious to establish direct and continuous links with the public than were the public health officials. Most of them thought that 'the public is not well informed and therefore cannot make rational judgments' or that 'consulting the public makes planning much more difficult, and generally it delays or even precludes any action being taken.' Most of those interviewed thought that the conventional methods of consulting public opinion were satisfactory as guides, namely the public hearing, the referendum, and the ballot box. 'Here the public is presented with a clear choice of alternatives,' said one of them, 'Like any shopper you can decide whether to take it or leave it.'

The problem of consulting public opinion poses a somewhat different problem for the public health official than it does for the engineer. The effectiveness of the former in performing his tasks depends very much upon the extent to which his recommendations and regulations are understood and accepted by the public, and the extent to which he is able to overcome opposition (real or imaginary) from various groups. One way of dealing with this problem is to carry out programmes of public education through talks and lectures, and through encouraging the organisation of anti-pollution groups. Many public officials engage in such activities. However, most of them seem to feel that they are facing a dilemma in this regard: if they educate the public they may acquire increased support for their programmes, but at the same time they may be offered more advice than they desire as to what those programmes should be!

In summary, it seems that the perceptions and attitudes of the two groups of professionals studied have all the characteristics of a closed system. Their views seem to be highly conditioned by training, adherence to standards and practices of the respective professions, and allegiance to the agency's or firm's goals or mission. Both groups believe they are highly qualified to do their respective jobs and that they act in the public interest. Contact with representatives of other agencies or the general public, however, is considered either unnecessary or potentially harmful. There appears to be general satisfaction with past policies and practices, and few if any major alterations are suggested.

FACTORS CONDITIONING PERCEPTIONS AND ATTITUDES

The analyses of perceptions of problems and solutions, and of attitudes as to roles and responsibilities tended to confirm impressions gathered from other indicators of these views, such as statements of leading engineers or public health officials in professional journals, or in public hearings, and the courses of action they have recommended in the past to deal with certain problems. To an important extent these perceptions and attitudes differ from those which appear to be held by other professionals and by members of the general public, as statements in the technical and popular press and at public hearings clearly testify. What, then, are the factors that account for such divergencies in viewpoint? They may be rooted in the individual's training and experience, where he has lived, his interactions with others, or his views about the relationship of Man to Nature. Data were gathered on various factors which, it was believed, might have an influence upon perceptions and attitudes. These were examined by factor analysis to determine which were the most significant. Stepwise multiple regression was then used to discover the extent to which any of these factors could explain variations in the perceptions and attitudes.

The analysis also revealed five main variables relating to possible influences upon perceptions and attitudes, namely:

  (i) Years in the profession
  (ii) Rank and mobility
  (iii) Distinction between Medical Health Officers (M.H.O.) and Public Health Inspectors (P.H.I.)
  (iv) Nature over Man
  (v) Man over Nature

The analysis revealed some important relationships between the two sets of factors.

Years in the profession

The hypothesis that the amount of time one spends in an occupation conditions one's perceptions and attitudes about the problems with which it is concerned was clearly borne out by the analysis. As Table 4

TABLE 4. *Influence of years in the profession:*
results of multiple regression analysis

Dependent variable entering the equation	Sign	R	R²	Increase in R²	T-value To enter equation	In final equation	Level of significance
Environmental quality and sewage disposal	−	·423	·179	·179	2·874	3·511	·005
Dissatisfaction with role of public	−	·585	·342	·163	3·041	2·176	·025
Extra-agency consultation	−	·633	·401	·059	1·868	2·714	·005
Improved administration and standards	−	·674	·454	·054	1·840	2·735	·005
Organise groups	−	·706	·498	·044	1·737	1·660	·10
Adviser and decision-maker	+	·727	·529	·030	1·475	1·672	·05
Intra-agency consultation	−	·748	·560	·031	1·474	1·781	·05
Consultations with other provincial and federal agencies	+	·766	·587	·027	1·453	2·250	·025
Pesticides, noise and purification	−	·786	·618	·031	1·546	1·437	·10
M.H.O. role as a health administrator	−	·802	·643	·025	1·426	1·426	·10

indicates, the concern of the public health official about environmental quality problems tends to decline the longer he has been in the profession, as do his desire to involve the public more directly in decision-making, his propensity to consult with others outside his agency, his concern about the effectiveness of present administrative arrangements, and his scepticism about the validity of water quality standards. It seems also that the longer an official has been in an agency, the less anxious he is to promote change in either its structure, its policies, or the matters with which it concerns itself. In the present study it was mainly the younger, less experienced officials who tended to be most aware of deteriorating environmental conditions and most sceptical about the ability of present administrative arrangements and policies to improve these conditions. It was they, too, who were the most anxious to provide the public with a more direct link into the planning and policy-making processes.

One possible interpretation of the findings is that the longer a public health official has been in the profession, the more likely he is to become adjusted to his physical and institutional environments. He is less prone to want to move elsewhere, or to propose modifications to agency structure, standards of environmental quality, or public policies. So long as deterioration of environmental quality does not appear to be resulting in hazards to human health, the public health official does not feel any particular motivation to promote action or policy change. Modification of policies or expansion of responsibilities would obviously further complicate his task, a task which he believes is complicated enough already!

Years spent in public health appeared to be a good predictor of variations in perceptions and attitudes. It accounted for more than 64 per cent of the variance in ten significant dependent variables.

Rank and mobility

Several sociologists (Eiduson, 1962; Gerstl and Hutton; Gross, 1958) and others (Caldwell, 1967; Marshall, 1966) have suggested that an individual's view about the problems with which he deals and about his role in dealing with them are conditioned by his position in the employment hierarchy and by his identification with the organisation from which he works. It appears that those who occupy positions in the lower echelons generally feel divorced from responsibility for making decisions. They often develop an attitude of being a cog in a very large machine. As they ascend the ladder of responsibility, however, their feeling of commitment and of identification with the organisation's goals seems to grow (Zytowski, 1968).

The extent to which an individual has moved from one post to another also appears to have an influence upon his perceptions and attitudes. In some occupations, notably the academic profession and industrial management, transfers from one location to another are a generally accepted means of moving up the hierarchy (Gerstl and Hutton, 1966; Caplow and McGee, 1958). In many government agencies, experience in the field is often a prerequisite in obtaining a post at the head office (Corson and Paul, 1966; Caplow and McGee, 1958). Having ascended to the top rung of the ladder, however, the individual then tends to become more sedentary. Generally there is nowhere else to go, except to another organisation, and there is also the knowledge that others are also anxious to reach the top positions. The individual, therefore, can be expected to defend both his own position and the aims and policies of the organisation for which he works.

Seniority and mobility (i.e., the number of previous moves) were found in the analysis to be closely related and were combined into a single factor for the regression studies. This factor seems to have an important influence on perceptions of public health officials, accounting for more than fifty per cent of the variance in six variables (Table 5). The more senior the official, the more likely it is that he has a fairly narrow view of problems facing society and that he identifies solutions in terms of the conventional practice of his agency. It seems also that seniority affects perceptions of the role of the public. The more senior officials are much more sceptical about involving the public in planning and policy-making than are the junior officials. Finally, it appears that seniority brings with it an increasing degree of dedication and commitment to the agency. The more senior officials spend a good deal of time outside their office hours informing themselves about environmental problems (such as through reading journals or attending meetings) and trying to inform the public.

These findings provide some interesting comparisons and contrast with the results of the engineers study. As in the case of public health

TABLE 5. *Influence of rank and mobility:*
results of multiple regression analysis

Dependent variable entering the equation	Sign	R	R²	Increase in R²	T-value To enter equation	T-value In final equation	Level of significance
Broad perspective	−	·514	·264	·264	3·695	5·041	·005
Environmental quality and sewage disposal	+	·580	·336	·072	2·008	2·089	·025
Organise groups	+	·631	·398	·062	1·913	2·520	·02
Adviser and decision-maker	−	·667	·445	·047	1·713	1·609	·10
Adequate legislation	+	·695	·483	·038	1·607	1·731	·05
Dissatisfaction with role of public	−	·717	·514	·031	1·452	1·510	·10
Pesticides, noise and purification	+	·728	·530	·016	1·037	1·037	*

* Statistically insignificant.

officials, seniority is attained partly through experience acquired through working in a variety of places on a variety of problems. No characteristic patterns could be detected in transfers. It seems, however, that engineers may transfer at least three times before they settle into a post for more than five years. Like the senior public health officials, the senior engineers indicated a close allegiance to the agency for which they worked and support for past recommendations made by it. In contrast to the public health officials, however, they tended to perceive a wider range of problems facing society, and their off-duty activities were much less related to their work. In particular, they were seldom involved in public lecturing or in organising groups.

Distinction between the Medical Health Officer and the Public Health Inspector

As noted earlier, responsibilities relating to public health in British Columbia are shared between Medical Health Officers and Public Health Inspectors. The essential difference between them is that the former are principally administrators while the latter are the field representatives. This distinction appears to have an important bearing on their perceptions, attitudes, and behavioural responses. M.H.O.s participate much more actively in intra-agency consultation than do P.H.I.s, and especially with their head office. P.H.I.s, in contrast, are much more frequently in contact with representatives of private industry and the general public. While M.H.O.s are generally fairly sceptical about involving the public in policy-making, the P.H.I.s tend to support such involvement.

The two main groups also differed in their views as to their roles as advisers and decision-makers. The former saw themselves as both advisers and decision-makers, whereas the latter tended to consider

themselves as advisers only. This, of course, reflects the kinds of functions which they perform in the agency, particularly in connection with
environmental policy.

Differences in perceptions resulting from differences in functions
performed by subgroups of a profession were also observed in the case
of the engineers. The government engineers saw themselves as public
servants, using their talents and training to promote the general welfare.
All were strongly attached to the agency for which they worked and
referred constantly to its goals, activities and achievements. They spent
much less time describing projects on which they had worked themselves. They contrasted their role with that of the consulting engineer.
The latter, they thought, was brought in only to answer specific questions on a specialised topic and was not answerable to the public.
'Consulting engineers', said one of the government engineers, 'do not
have to be as aware of government policy or of potential public reaction
as we do. They are able to operate in a detached manner whereas we
have to be ready to field comments and criticisms long after the report
is completed or the project is built.'

The consulting engineers tended to concur with the government
engineers' image of them. They, too, saw themselves as specialists on
specific topics, participating as advisers in the planning and policy-
making process when called upon to do so. They contrasted their role
with that of the government engineer. The latter, they thought, carried
out important functions as watchdogs, planners and administrators, but
their job was neither as challenging or precarious as that of the consulting engineer. As one of them suggested, 'The consulting engineer
can afford much less to be wrong than the government engineer.'

Man's relationship to Nature

As noted earlier, several studies have shown that views about Man's
relationship to Nature have an important bearing upon perceptions of,
and attitudes towards the environment. The views of the public health
officials on this relationship were sought in several ways. First, the
respondents were asked whether they thought technology had the
answer to most problems faced by Man. Next they were asked for their
views on three technological innovations that are now on the horizon
and which are likely to alter the environment in important ways:
namely, the large-scale diversion of water from Alaska to Mexico, the
NAWAPA scheme (Sewell, 1967); the purposeful modification of the
weather (Fleagle, 1968); and the Supersonic Transport Plane, S.S.T.
(Shurcliff, 1969). Finally, they were asked who should be put in charge
of decisions about the control of Nature. Their views in these connec-
tions were then correlated with their perceptions of problems, solutions
and responsibilities.

Opinion was sharply divided on the extent to which Man is in control
of Nature and vice versa. Over one-half of the public health officials felt
that technology cannot solve many of the major problems now faced

by Man (Table 6). The rationale given for this view was that there are some problems that are not amenable to 'the technological fix', such

TABLE 6. *The efficacy of technology*

	Frequency of mention Public Health	
	Officials	Engineers
Does technology have the answer to all problems?		
Yes	16	24
No	24	6
What are its deficiencies?		
Cannot deal with problems of human relations	15	6
Is limited by time or money	15	4
Creates problems	7	5

as the Watts Riots, poverty, or drug addiction, and that in many cases technological solutions create more problems than they solve. In contrast, those who felt that technology does have the answer pointed to the fantastic material progress made in the past three decades as a result of technological advances. To the technological optimists, the only limitations were money and the need to develop institutional means of ensuring innovations were adopted.

Opinions were also divided on the desirability of the three techno-logical innovations, with roughly half in favour of them and half against. Those who favoured them spoke of improvements in income, additions to food supply and more rapid communications. Those who were against them pointed out uncertainties as to impacts on the environ-ment and the lack of a clearly demonstrated need for the innovation.

Man now has the technological capacity to make vast alterations to the environment and perhaps even destroy it. To provide another indication as to attitudes towards the Man-Nature relationship, the respondents were asked to suggest a group of persons to whom they would entrust the control of technology and decisions as to its use. Opinion was divided on this matter too (Table 7). Varying proportions

TABLE 7. *Allocation of responsibility for control of technology*

	No. of respondents Public Health	
	Officials	Engineers
Scientists	7	7
Politicians	8	1
Scientists and politicians	10	2
Scientists and the general public	15	20

of scientists and laymen were proposed. The only point of agreement was that no one would trust either a group of politicians, a group of laymen, or a group of scientists to make such decisions!

The views of the public health officials on the role of technology showed both interesting similarities and interesting differences with the views of the engineers. Knowing that the fundamental goal of the engineering profession is the control of Nature, one would naturally assume that engineers would feel highly confident that technology has the answer to most problems and that major technological innovations would be looked on with favour (Hertz, 1970). Analysis of the answers to the questions on technology reveals that, in contrast to the public

TABLE 8. *Views on three technological innovations*

	No. of respondents	
	Public Health Officials	Engineers
Weather modification		
Aware of the innovation	39	30
Is it feasible?	32	26
How far should we go?		
Do not attempt it	19	—
Small scale	10	26
Large scale	11	4
S.S.T.		
Advantageous innovation	9	18
Disadvantageous innovation	31	12
Advantages		
Increased speed of communication	9	16
Increased trade	4	7
Increased understanding	2	2
Challenge to the imagination	2	16
Disadvantages		
Noise	20	10
Space requirements	10	8
Jet contrails	2	2
Ecological disturbances	2	—
NAWAPA scheme		
Advantageous innovation	18	8
Disadvantageous innovation	22	22
Advantages		
Solution to growing water needs	16	8
Source of revenue	8	6
Challenge to technology	6	8
Disadvantages		
Involves water export	22	22
Cheaper alternatives available	18	14
No demonstrated need	8	12
Potential ecological disaster	3	4

health officials, most engineers are confident about the ability of technology to solve human problems, yet they, too, have reservations about the desirability of certain kinds of innovations (Table 8). There was greater support for the S.S.T., based on the view that reductions in travel time were still a desirable social goal. Some mentioned problems of noise but these were believed to be surmountable. Attempts to alter the weather drew much less support and most of the engineers thought such attempts should be strictly controlled, pending much better understanding of the processes involved. There was almost unanimous opposition to the proposed NAWAPA scheme, based partly on technical and economic considerations, but mainly on the fact that it involved export of Canadian water. Mention of the scheme seemed to trigger considerable emotion in many of the respondents, revealing a variety of attitudes about resource ownership, economic dependence and so on.

Views about Man's relationship to Nature appear to have an important influence on perceptions and attitudes. In the study of public health officials, those who regarded water quality mainly as a health problem, those who were sceptical about public involvement in environmental health decisions, and those who were particularly concerned about pesticides, noise pollution and water purification tended to hold the view that Nature is in control of Man (Table 9).

TABLE 9. *Influence of views on Nature's control over Man: results of multiple regression analysis*

Dependent variable entering the equation	Sign	R	R²	Increase in R²	T-value To enter equation	In final equation	Level of significance
Dissatisfaction with role of public	−	·315	·099	·099	2·045	1·424	·10
Water quality as a health problem	+	·412	·170	·071	1·771	1·852	·05
Adequate legislation	−	·492	·242	·072	1·358	1·179	*
Pesticides, noise and purification	−	·522	·273	·030	1·209	1·412	·10
Extra-agency consultation	+	·547	·299	·027	1·142	1·050	*
Improved administration and standards	−	·565	·319	·020	0·964	1·053	*
Intra-agency consultation	+	·580	·336	·017	0·933	0·898	*
Opposition from vested interests	−	·591	·349	·013	0·785	0·785	*

* Statistically insignificant.

The view that Man is in control of Nature, however, appeared to be an even better predictor of perceptions and attitudes. It accounted for forty-seven per cent of the explained variance in nine significant variables (Table 10). Those who held this view also tended to feel that consultation beyond the public health unit is generally not essential, that public involvement often leads to unsatisfactory results, that present water quality criteria are valid, and that pesticides, noise and

TABLE 10. *Influence of views on Man's control over Nature: results of multiple regression analysis*

Dependent variable entering the equation	Sign	R	R^2	Increase in R^2	To enter equation	In final equation	Level of significance
Extra-agency consultation	−	·352	·124	·124	2·316	3·386	·005
Focus on physical criteria	−	·462	·213	·090	2·050	1·627	·10
Environmental quality and sewage disposal	+	·536	·287	·074	1·930	2·196	·025
Opposition with vested interests	−	·586	·343	·056	1·727	2·139	·025
Adviser and decision-maker	−	·624	·389	·046	1·600	1·672	·05
Satisfaction with role of public	−	·642	·412	·023	1·153	1·416	·10
Pesticides, noise and purification	−	·658	·433	·021	1·089	1·457	·10
Broad perspective	+	·674	·454	·021	1·088	1·157	*
Water quality as a health problem	+	·683	·467	·012	0·843	1·647	·10

* Statistically insignificant.

water purification problems are not a matter for great concern. One possible interpretation of these results might be that the public health official not only sees Man in control of Nature, but also he sees his official role as occupying an especially vital position in helping Man to deal with problems involving the physical environment. Believing that his background and experience furnish him with the necessary expertise, and that others are either less capable or uninterested in dealing with the problems with which he concerns himself, he feels a strong personal commitment to his job. At the same time he knows that other professionals, other agencies and the general public are developing a concern about the environment. This poses a dilemma. On the one hand it could mean that there will be vastly increased public recognition and support for his work. On the other it could result in criticism, opposition and perhaps an erosion of his position.

IMPLICATIONS OF THE RESULTS FOR ENVIRONMENTAL QUALITY MANAGEMENT

The solution to the emerging environmental crisis will require at least three major changes in the present approach to environmental quality management. First, it will necessitate the adoption of a holistic rather than a fragmented view of the problem. Instead of water pollution being considered in isolation from air pollution or land pollution, and instead of the physical dimensions being considered apart from the human dimensions, a conscious attempt will need to be made to consider them together. Likewise, the overall effects of the adoption of any solution on the environment and on Man will need to be taken into account in policy decisions.

Second, it will be necessary to involve the public much more directly in the planning process. It is already clear that the public feels alienated in this process and that conventional means of consulting public opinion do not accurately reveal their preferences. Presenting the public with a few discrete alternatives has the advantage of simplifying the process of choice, but unless the alternatives reflect the values held by the public rather than the planners, they may all be rejected.

Third, and as a corollary of the first two requirements, there will need to be changes in administrative structures, laws and policies to ensure that a broader view is taken, enabling the various aspects of environmental quality problems to be considered in an integrated fashion and ensuring that the public enjoys a satisfactory sense of participation.

The results of these studies seem to suggest that such changes will not be easily accomplished. In fact, the likelihood is that they will be vigorously opposed. Holism, for example, is the antithesis of the approach upon which different professions depend for their recognition, and is likely to be rejected by them. It is possible that some attempt will be made to broaden the viewpoint of certain professions by establishing training programmes which expose members to ideas and methods of other disciplines, and by setting up formal and informal links among professions. This process is in fact already under way, generally under the banner of environmental science or environmental studies. Almost always, however, one discipline or profession dominates the scene, and only in rare instances does it appear that several professions can work together in a truly integrated fashion on a problem of mutual concern.

It also seems that professionals, particularly in the physical sciences and the natural sciences, are sceptical about involving the public in policy-making. For the most part they appear to take the view either that the public is not well informed, or that so many different opinions will appear that policy-making will become impossible. The alternative is to present the public with solutions conceived by the planners. The only choice then is to accept or reject them. If they are rejected, the problem remains unsolved. As the rows of unimplemented plans on planners' shelves testify, this is frequently the case.

Finally, it is clear that experts are not in favour of institutional change, especially if it means that their own role will be altered. Accordingly, they resist suggestions that new agencies should be established, new laws should be passed, new solutions should be tried, or that other professions should become involved. Such resistance appears to increase with seniority. There is in fact an inverse relationship between the perception of the need for change and the power to accomplish it.

It is obvious that society will always need experts and expertise. The question now is, what kinds of experts and expertise are needed to solve environmental problems. Unless our present experts broaden their views and integrate their activities, they may well contribute more to the promotion of the environmental crisis than to its solution.

REFERENCES

Appleyard, D. (1969) 'City designers and the pluralistic city' in L. Rodwin *et al.* (eds.), *Regional Planning Development*, M.I.T. Press, Cambridge, Mass.

Brockington, C. F. (1961) 'Organisation and administration of health services' in W. Hobson (ed.), *The Theory and Practice of Public Health*, Oxford University Press, London, pp. 305–20.

Bower, Blair T. and W. R. Derrick Sewell (1970) *Selecting Strategies for Management of Air Quality*, Queen's Printer, Ottawa.

Caldwell, L. (1967) *Politics, Professionalism and Environment*, University of Indiana Institute of Public Administration, Bloomington.

Canada, House of Commons, Special Committee on Environmental Pollution (1971), *Minutes of Proceedings and Evidence, Ottawa.*

Caplow, T. and R. J. McGee (1958) *The Academic Marketplace*, Basic Books, New York.

Cooley, R. L. and G. Wandesforde-Smith (1970) *Congress and the Environment*, University of Washington Press, Seattle.

Corson, J. and R. S. Paul (1966) *Men Near the Top*, Johns Hopkins Press, Baltimore.

Craik, K. H. (1970a) 'The environmental dispositions of environmental decision-makers', *Annals of the American Academy of Political and Social Science* (May), pp. 87–94.

Craik, K. H. (1970b) 'Environmental psychology', in T. M. Newcomb (ed.), *New Directions in Psychology*, Holt, Rinehart and Winston, New York, pp. 1–122.

De Bell, G. (ed.) (1970) *The Environmental Handbook*, Ballentine Books, New York.

Eiduson, B. T. (1962) *Scientists: Their Psychological World*, Basic Books, New York.

Fleagle, R. G. (1968) *Weather Modification: Science and Public Policy*, University of Washington Press, Seattle.

Gerstl, J. E. and S. D. Hutton (1966) *Engineers: The Anatomy of a Profession*, Tavistock Press, London.

Gross, E. (1958) *Work and Society*, Crowell, New York.

Hertz, D. B. (1970) 'The technological imperative—social implications of professional technology', *Annals of the American Academy of Political and Social Science*, pp. 95–106.

Hewings, J. (1968) *Water Quality and the Hazard to Health*, Natural Hazard Research Working Paper No. 3, University of Toronto, Department of Geography, Toronto.

Kates, R. W. (1962) *Hazard and Choice Perception in Flood Plain Management*, University of Chicago, Department of Geography, Research Paper No. 70, Chicago.

Kluckhohn, F. R. and F. L. Strodtbeck (1961) *Variations in Value Orientations*, Row Peterson, Evanston, Illinois.

Lowenthal, D. (1966) 'Assumptions behind public attitudes', in H. Jarrett (ed.) *Environmental Quality in a Growing Economy*, Johns Hopkins Press, Baltimore. Md.: pp. 128–37.

Lowenthal, D. (1967) *Environmental Perceptions and Behavior*, University of Chicago, Department of Geography Research Series No. 109, Chicago.

Lucas, R. C. (1966) 'The contribution of environmental research in wilderness policy decisions', *Journal of Social Issues*, 22 (October), pp. 116–26.

Marshall, R. (1966) 'Politics and efficiency in water development', in A. V. Kneese and S. C. Smith (eds.), *Water Research*, Johns Hopkins Press, Baltimore, Md., pp. 291–310.

Nicholson, Max (1970) *The Environmental Revolution*, Hodder and Stoughton, London.

Saarinen, T. E. (1966) *Perceptions of the Drought Hazard in the Great Plains*, University of Chicago, Department of Geography Research Paper No. 105, Chicago.

Sewell, W. R. D. (1967) 'NAWAPA: pipedream or practical possibility?', *Bulletin of the Atomic Scientists* (September), pp. 8–13.

Sewell, W. R. D. and I. Burton (eds.) (1971) *Perceptions and Attitudes in Resources Management*, Queen's Printer, Ottawa.

Shepard, P. and D. McKinley (eds.) (1969) *The Subversive Science: Essays Towards an Ecology of Man*, Houghton Mifflin, New York.

Shurcliff, W. A. (1969) *SST and the Sonic Boom Handbook*, Ballentine Books, New York.

Sommer, R. (1963) *Expertland*, Doubleday, New York.

U.N. General Assembly, Preparatory Committee for United Nations Conference on the Human Environment (1971) *Second Report*, Geneva.

U.S. Council on Environmental Quality, (1970) *First Annual Report*, U.S. Government Printing Office, Washington D.C.

Vallentine, H. R. (1967) *Water in the Service of Man*, Penguin Books, Harmondsworth, Middlesex.

Watt, K. E. (1968) *Ecology and Resource Management*, McGraw Hill, New York.

White, G. F. (1966) 'Formation and role of public attitudes' in H. Jarrett (ed.) *Environmental Quality in a Growing Economy*, Johns Hopkins Press, Baltimore. pp. 105–27.

Zisk, Betty H. (1969) *American Political Interest Groups: Readings in Theory and Research*, Wadsworth Publishing Co. Inc., Belmont, California.

Zytowski, D. G. (1968) *Vocational Behavior*, Holt, Rinehart and Winston, New York.

CHAPTER 9

Costs of environmental quality — the role of cost-benefit analysis

P. M. S. JONES

This chapter presents a personal view of the role of cost-benefit analysis (C.B.A.) in studies of environmental quality. These are usually aimed at providing an input to decision processes concerning potential changes in the environment. The reasons why such appraisals are necessary, the difficulties and limitations in practical studies of environmental economics, the uses of the output and the methodological framework are discussed and related to pollution, noise, visual intrusion and other areas of environmental interest.

THE NEED FOR COST-BENEFIT ANALYSIS

If all markets functioned perfectly there would be no need for C.B.A. since classical economic theory leads to the conclusion that prices will act as reliable indicators of the value set by society on the goods or services available. Under such idealised conditions market forces would ensure that resources were utilised in an optimal fashion for the prevailing pattern of wealth distribution.

Markets in modern society are rarely, if ever, perfect. Government or local authorities provide services in fields such as health, defence, highways, sewage disposal and water supply for which the user does not pay directly and where charges to the individual are not related to consumption. In the environmental field the polluter and the polluted usually lack knowledge of the true nature and extent of the pollution effects and can therefore set no meaningful value to them. The structure of the market may also be such that there is no direct link between the polluter and polluted. The expenditure by an individual on pollution control does not bring him any direct benefit and by increasing his costs may put him at a positive disadvantage in relation to his competitors if he is a manufacturer or supplier of services. The beneficiaries from his control are under no obligation to reward him and there is therefore no direct economic incentive to incur expenditure. Social pressure or regulation are the only forces that can operate.

This theme has been discussed by many authors in relation to air pollution (Wolozin, 1966, p. 162; Crocker, 1966, p. 61; Gafney, 1964; Kneese, 1968) and several economists have debated the possible use of taxation or other means of restoring 'proper' functioning to the market.

Alfred Marshall (1920, p. 804) well over a half a century ago was suggesting a 'fresh air levy' on property owners to be spent by local authorities on air quality control. He voiced the opinion that the owner would recoup much of this by increased valuation of his property. J. E. Meade (1952) has suggested that when the social returns to scale are constant a proper tax on the negative externality (pollution) will yield the proper revenue to subsidise the damaged party. The nature of a 'proper' tax is further explored by E. S. Mills (1966, p. 40). R. H. Coase (1960) discusses transferable rights (e.g., a right to clean air) and says that when these are well defined and easily traded, their initial ownership by either the polluter or the damaged party will lead to the same ultimate resource allocation, provided the wealth effects of changing the endowment pattern leave prices unchanged. Such a system would remove the need for collective action by regulation or tax. On a practical plane the U.S. government is currently reported to be contemplating a tax on fuels related to their sulphur content, primarily to encourage reductions in sulphur oxide pollution rather than to compensate for market deficiencies.

These methods of restoring the functioning of the market demand that the taxes or levies are related to the damage done by pollution, i.e., that some measure of the real costs to society is available. The proposal for transferable rights is more flexible but presupposes that owners of rights are aware of their real value in terms of the effects they will suffer after their sale. Ignorance on the part of the vendor could lead to perpetuation of inefficient resource utilisation.

If a government or local authority decides that a policy of laissez-faire in the environmental field will produce socially, politically, or economically unacceptable consequences then decisions have to be made concerning such matters as levels of investment and degree of control. These decisions could be left to the market if some suitable schemes such as taxation or transferable rights could be devised. Alternatively, controls could be introduced by statute or regulation or public money invested to produce change. These regulations or investments could be based either on subjective appraisal and personal judgment or on in-depth objective analysis of the causes and effects and the costs and benefits of change.

The role of the cost-benefit analyst is to provide the analysis and data base necessary for underpinning objective decisions on change whether they be related to taxation systems, control regulations, or public investment in highways and the like, and even decisions that no changes are necessary. The measurement of the effects and value of change, albeit imperfect, must assist the decision-taker and should help to improve the quality of decision.

THE NEED FOR A SYSTEMS APPROACH

Before any meaningful discussion can be held on the costs of pollution or environmental effects, it is necessary to establish the framework within which the problem is to be considered. This framework will include both geographical and economic constraints. It may be appropriate to limit a study of the costs of visual intrusion, noise or odour to the proximity of the offending source. On the other hand, the effects of some pollutants may be global, e.g., the long-term build-up of carbon dioxide in the atmosphere. The decision on the appropriate boundaries for particular studies will depend on the sponsor's area of decision and the nature of the decisions to be influenced.

A study of one aspect of environment such as air pollution, in isolation from others, e.g., water pollution and solid waste problems, can only yield a sub-optimal basis for decision since it is possible to exchange one form of pollution for another. For example, refuse can be dumped inland, discharged to sea or burnt; some noxious gases and dusts can be discharged into the air or scrubbed out into an aqueous effluent or filtered and collected as solid waste. In practice, bounds have to be drawn and allowances for this type of exchange effect introduced as necessary. The constraints appropriate to different types of study can now be considered.

Air pollution

Pollution of the atmosphere can arise from emissions from combustion processes: from domestic or industrial chimneys, from motor exhausts or even from burning operations such as the burning of stubble after the harvest or burning of leaves or unwanted solid refuse. It can also take the form of emissions of other unwanted gases which are side products or waste from processes, such as acid gas emissions from smelting operations, odours from sewage works, abattoirs and chemical plant of various types, and particulate materials from processing and handling operations, as in coal yards and cement works.

These pollutants enter the atmosphere at different heights, different temperatures, and different locations from which they gradually disperse either by becoming diluted into a larger volume of air or by returning to the ground as dusts or dissolved in rain water. The seriousness of the effects of pollution will depend on the emission factors, on local topography, and on the climate and weather conditions at the time of the release. The initial effects may be felt locally but subsequently the pollution can spread over very much wider areas and in the extreme could be regarded as producing a world-wide effect.

The most obvious effects of air pollution are the soiling it causes and the physical damage to structures. The smoke and dusts emitted from combustion processes lead to deposition of soot and dirt over the exterior of buildings which is particularly noticeable in the case of stone or brick buildings in the major conurbations. Exterior paintwork and windows also become soiled more rapidly in a polluted atmosphere and it seems likely that internal decorations will be affected. People, their garments, and the fabrics used in furnishings are also soiled. The acid content of combustion emissions can cause physical damage by increasing the rates of corrosion of metallic material, by causing physical degradation in protective films such as paints, and by causing degradation of the cellulosic materials in textiles, paper, etc. To counteract these degradation processes, protective coatings such as zinc or paint may be put on exposed surfaces, the rate of attack can be decreased by improved design and improved maintenance and cleaning procedures can slow down the rate of damage and preserve the integrity of protective films. An alternative choice would be to allow the physical damage to occur and to renew the whole damaged article at more frequent intervals than would be necessary if protection had been adopted.

In addition to the effects on inanimate materials, pollution can affect living systems and may affect the yields of agricultural crops and the health of livestock. In extreme cases of severe exposure both crops and livestock have been known to die, but a more general effect is likely to be small decreases in yield. In the case of crops this can result from direct damage to leaves, thus reducing the ability of the plant to synthesise materials for its further growth, the adherence of dirt, which reduces the ability of the plant to breathe and photo-synthesise, and reductions in sunlight intensity by general obscuration in the atmosphere. There are also some benefits from air pollution since ammonia and sulphur oxides from industrial and combustion processes produce the fertiliser ammonium-sulphate, sulphur oxides are known to inhibit certain fungal diseases, and additional atmospheric haze can help to reduce the incidence of frost.

If air pollution affects health there will be economic consequences resulting from lost production caused by absence from work due to sickness or premature death, and there will also be social costs in the form of increased suffering to the affected individuals and their families.

The quality of the environment may suffer as a result of the effects of pollution. It will be dirtier, possibly smellier, and the variety of vegetation is likely to be reduced. Those living in the environment will be suffering a disutility which they would be prepared to spend money to alleviate, and those travelling through the environment will also be suffering a loss of enjoyment.

In the very long term pollution may affect the world's climate. It is generally thought that the build-up of carbon dioxide owing to combustion of fossil fuels will gradually increase the average world temperature, whilst dust and the contrails from high-flying aircraft will produce an opposite effect. The precise magnitude and time scale over which these effects will become apparent is far from certain because the natural processes by which carbon dioxide returns to the biosphere and the sea are not fully understood. Clearly, the effects of world temperature on rainfall and the extent of the polar ice caps could have very major effects on all aspects of our existence.

If it is desired to control the emission of pollutants to the environment then the costs of this control have to be borne. The same processes may be continued and an attempt made to trap the emissions using precipitators, filters or scrubbers; alternatively, discharge may be attempted at such height and temperature that the emissions are so diluted that they produce no significant damage; or finally, the processes can be completely modified in such a way that the emissions themselves are avoided at source. In the case of combustion processes this latter aim can be achieved by using different fuels where practicable.

The effects in terms of changes in patterns of expenditure, consumption, and general levels of amenity resulting from a decision to change the level of air pollution can be best appreciated by building a simple model (Fig. 1).

What is beneficial to one section of the community may not be beneficial to others and the net effect of a decrease in the level of pollution will be the release of resources of labour, materials and land, with an equivalent release of cash which should enable the resources to be diverted to more beneficial activities within the community. In order to make use of such a model as a decision aid, it is clearly necessary to have factual information on the different costs and benefits, with particular attention to the transfers between different sectors of the economy, showing what benefits and disbenefits will accrue and to whom, and what the net overall effect will be.

Because air pollution is no respecter of regional or international boundaries, the model of transfers has to be applied across fairly large areas, except in situations where a single readily identifiable source of pollution is concerned from which the effects are known to be confined to a small area, e.g., odour or cement dust. The constraint would normally be related to the resources (such as people, materials and land) within the area for which a decision maker is responsible, e.g., a British government study might cover the United Kingdom only, whereas the Organisation for European Cooperation and Development might sponsor a pan-European study.

Water

Environmental quality is related to the supply, location and pollution of water. Both pollution and the construction of reservoirs interact with the supply and use of water, which is an increasingly scarce resource, and both involve social and economic costs. Provided the supply of water greatly exceeds demand and alternative means of storage are available, the costs of pollution and its control or the provision of additional storage can be treated in isolation. If these conditions are not satisfied, the two are inextricably mixed with the supply problem and a systems overview would be necessary.

The water available in a region arises from its rainfall, from underground supplies that may have their source external to the region and from artificially purified waters such as those produced by desalination.

The needs of the users are met by abstracting water from rivers or by tapping underground aquifers by means of wells. Some aquifers were

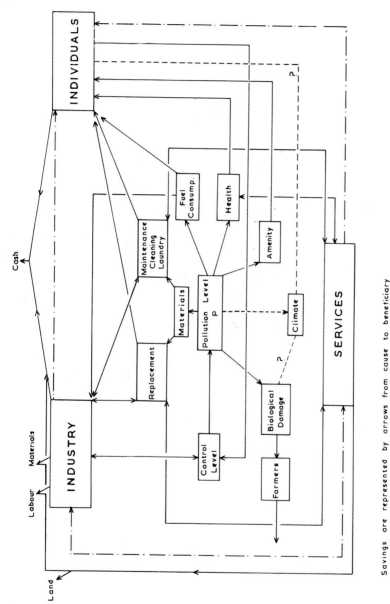

FIG. I. *Transfer model (pollution decreasing)*

formed in the distant past and have no current contact with the hydrological cycle. If such aquifers are tapped or if aquifers are drained at a
rate which exceeds the maximum rate of replenishment from rainfall
and surface water sources, the level of reserves in the aquifers will
gradually decrease. In order to minimise the risks of water shortages
during dry spells or to assist in the transfer of water from regions of high
rainfall and low demand to regions where the demand exceeds the
supply, storage methods are adopted. These may also assist in flood
control. Such storage can take place in natural lakes, artificial reservoirs, in artificially charged underground aquifers, or in estuaries confined by barrages. In addition to the external supplies of water, individual users, particularly industry, may choose to have internal recycling
of water, thereby providing additional storage in the system.

The transfer of water from place to place occurs naturally *via* rivers
but may be assisted by canals made specially for that purpose or for
transport, or it may be transferred through special pipelines where
necessary. Waste water from domestic and industrial users is normally
returned to the water courses either directly or through treatment
works or by percolation through the soil and possibly into aquifers.

Water leaving the users will contain a wide variety of organic and
inorganic wastes and residues which, if not removed, can lead to pollution of waterways and interference with other people's sources of supply.

The domestic user makes use of water in disposing of domestic
sewage, and detergents, dirt, disinfectants and bacteria are all added as
a result of human action. Industrial users may leave residues of chemical
process as waste products and products of corrosion in their effluent.
Fertilisers and animal wastes added to the land deliberately or naturally in the course of farming practice can be eluted through the soil and
enter the water courses in quite large quantities. Water supplies may
also become polluted by infiltration of brackish or saline waters owing
to excessive demands on underground reserves.

If polluted water is returned to water courses, any downstream users
will have to process the water to a standard which is satisfactory for
their own requirements. This is clearly of great importance where the
water is required for drinking. The presence of phosphate residues from
detergents and nitrates from fertilisers can cause eutrophication of the
water, leading to excess growth of algae and the de-oxygenation of the
river. This, or the introduction of toxic industrial wastes, can result in
the death of water organisms and fish. Pollution can also lead to foul
odours and to the growth of sewage fungi.

It will be seen from this listing of effects that the consequences of
returning polluted water to water courses include the costs associated
with the necessity for additional water treatment and incurred to deal
with specific pollution problems in an *ad hoc* fashion when the volume
of protest becomes too great. The foaming of rivers prior to introduction of bio-degradeable detergents and the removal of algae from lakes
might be quoted as examples. The loss of marine life and the conversion

of rivers to malodorous and visually unattractive sewers cause a loss of amenity and are reflected in a reduced desire of people to live adjacent to the river, and the absence of leisure activities such as fishing, boating and swimming.

There are many processes of water treatment which offer a number of alternative ways of achieving purity and which can be used in parallel or sequentially. Decisions have to be made upon the most appropriate according to individual circumstances so that these alternatives must form an integral part of any systems approach to water conservation and utilisation. The methods have been summarised conveniently by W. W. Eckenfelder and D. L. Ford (1969, p. 110).

Any co-ordinated plan for the exploitation of water resources must involve an integration of the water supply and treatment models and compare the costs of treatment with the costs of new sources of supply by desalination, tapping underground sources or building reservoirs, including the costs of pumping and piping of water where this is necessary (Fig. 2).

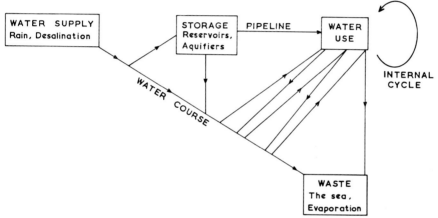

FIG. 2. *Water supply model*

The systems would be optimised by minimising the cost of water where:

Cost of water = Supply Cost + Storage Cost + Transfer Cost + Pre-Use Processing Cost + Post-Use Processing Cost + Amenity Cost

Subject to given constraints such as:

Rate of Supply ⩾ Rate of Consumption (Net)
Overall at all times

Rate of Supply ⩾ Rate of Demand (Gross)
at all points and times

The social and economic costs of processing water after use and of pollution could only be isolated from the regional supply model if there were a surplus of water which was not wanted for re-use. The

appropriate geographical constraints for optimal overall resource use
may not correspond with political (regional or national) boundaries.

Solid wastes

Solid wastes arise in a number of ways. Domestic solid wastes arise from
natural biological processes, the residues of food preparation and processing, from unwanted paper, glass and metal containers, from worn-
out and broken household articles and clothing, and from combustion
of solid fuels. Industrial solid wastes arise in the form of unusable scrap,
by-products of processes, waste products from packaging, fuel burning,
and worn-out or redundant equipment and plant. Agriculture also
produces solid wastes as by-products.

In many instances, the disposal of solid waste is an uncontrolled process. Leaves are burnt on the garden fire, old tyres, timber and other
combustible products may be burnt in an industrial yard or back
garden. More durable residues, such as vehicles and mattresses may be
sold as scrap or may be taken to some convenient deserted spot and
abandoned. In less affluent times and with smaller populations, such
uncontrolled disposal did not get out of hand, except perhaps in the
form of industrial slag and spoil heaps in mining and metal-working
areas. The durability of modern materials and the development and
packaging and short-life commodities has increased the problem enormously in this century.

Controlled disposal for the most part involves the collection of solid
wastes, either privately in scrap yards or publicly by local authorities.
The scrap business, in metals, cloth, paper and other materials, depends
upon recycling of the scrap for use in new articles, and economic factors
help to minimise the level of unusable residues. Local authorities col-
lecting solid refuse may attempt to salvage the reusable portions, they
may burn the waste or as much of it as is convenient, or they may dump
the waste in carefully chosen localities as infill which can subsequently
be grassed over and eventually built upon or put to other use. Some
portion of solid waste is disposed of by households with the liquid
wastes and these are separated off and reduced in bulk by bio-degradation. Residual organic wastes of this form or from farming processes may
be spread upon land to act as soil conditioners and nutrients. The
increasing use of artificial fertilisers has diminished the demand for
natural soil treatment and this, together with factory farming, is
likely to pose significant problems of waste disposal in areas of intensive
farming in the future.

Dumped waste is failing to make use of economically attractive
materials, may be occupying land that will have value in other uses, is
interfering with visual amenity and may be causing offensive odours.
Some industrial wastes may be toxic and poison the soil or percolate
into water courses and cause further pollution problems elsewhere.

There are several alternative means by which the disposal of solid
wastes can be controlled and these can be illustrated with reference to

the domestic situation. The wastes can be separated by the producer and the different categories treated in a different fashion, thereby simplifying the centrally co-ordinated disposal functions. Alternatively, all wastes could be collected as a mixture and transferred either by vehicle or by pipeline in a dry or suspended form to a central processing unit. On the domestic side, segregation is already practised to a different degree in different areas. Solid biological products and some food residues are passed with waste water into the sewage systems. In the United States and to a lesser extent in other western countries, particularly where people are housed in apartment blocks, paper and other domestic refuse is shredded for deliberately mixing with the fluid residues. Garden refuse may be burnt or composted. Papers may be separated for salvage and bulky articles disposed of at scrap yards or by other special means. Surplus containers and other miscellaneous domestic refuse are then collected by local authority vehicles. There is no reason to suppose that, with a deliberate process of education, the public could not be persuaded to alter the manner in which they handle refuse, thereby simplifying the problems of the local authorities.

The cost of pollution by solid wastes is clearly inextricably mixed in with the manner of disposal and interacts considerably with water pollution. The framework within which it could be treated is indicated in Figure 3.

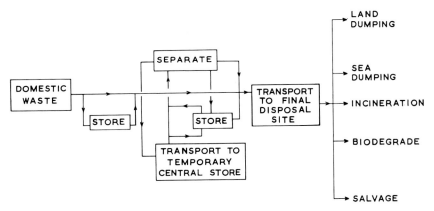

FIG. 3. *Solid wastes*

As in the case of water pollution described above, an attempt can be made to minimise the costs of solid waste disposal. These costs are equal to the cost of collection of refuse or waste, or alternatively of its transport by pipeline or other means to the final disposal site, plus any storage costs necessitated by the means of collection or transfer (domestic dustbins, scrap yards, or temporary rubbish tips), plus the costs incurred in separation and segregation of rubbish to make its subsequent disposal easier, minus any savings achieved from salvage or use of waste (re-use of metals or paper, use of sewage sludge as a fertiliser, or use of combustible wastes such as tyres or paper as a means of generation of heat or other energy), plus the costs of treatment of the waste (such as compaction, bio-degradation), plus the cost of waste disposal (e.g., costs of infill sites, transportation to these sites, pipework out to sea, and cost of incinerators), plus any social costs incurred as a result of the selected means of storage, transportation and disposal (e.g., odour, litter and vermin).

As with water supply there are constraints. The capacity of the system for dealing with solid wastes must have an average rate of solid waste disposal that is greater than, or equal to, the rate of production of solid waste, and the system designed for waste removal must give a rate of removal at all points greater than, or equal to, the rate of production at all points within the system.

Solid waste disposal is a far more local problem than either air pollution or water pollution since the solid wastes are for the most part confined within the locality in which they are generated. Land infill may be carried on at some distance from the site of generation but again this must be by agreement with the relatively local area affected by the site. The only case where this is not true is where waste is deposited into a river or into the sea when offence can be caused over a wide area and other towns may have to take steps to clear up their beaches. If incineration is adopted then again the effluent from the incinerator itself may be a form of pollution which will affect the surrounding environment. This transfer of pollution from one phase to another is discussed again later.

Noise

Unlike water and solid waste pollution, noise cannot be collected or dealt with in a centralised fashion. Like air pollution it is all-pervading and has to be stopped at source or ameliorated at the reception site. It is still debatable whether noise should be treated as an overall problem or solely related to the decisions relevant to specific noise sources. If it were only factories or aircraft or vehicles that created the problems then each specific noise source could be treated in isolation on its own merits. The only grounds for looking at noise from the systems standpoint are if society as a whole, in its normal process of living, creates noise that demands a centralised action or specific steps in planning. Alternatively, if the combination of noises from large numbers of unexceptionable sources is itself sufficiently large to be undesirable, then again some centralised policy of co-ordination might be required.

For any given decision it might appear reasonable to attempt to minimise the costs of noise, which will be equal to the sum of the economic penalties (such as lost output, waste of resource) plus the economic and social costs consequent on effects on health, plus the value attached to any loss of amenity by society, plus any costs of noise control at source, plus any expenditure on amelioration of noise.

Unlike water pollution and solid waste, noise does not have to be supplied or removed and it disperses of its own accord in conformity with well-defined physical laws. There are therefore no constraints in this simple cost model.

Visual intrusion

Visual intrusion, like noise, is confined to the immediate vicinity of the cause. Its effects are limited, however, and are likely to be largely reflected in the market since individuals can see and fully appreciate them: there are no subtle or delayed health effects. The construction of new buildings, pylons, scrap heaps and so forth, will be reflected in property values and the cost-benefit analyst may be concerned with valuing the social and economic penalties of the construction in relation to the benefits that will flow from it, such as new jobs and power for industrial growth. The 'system' to be considered will be entirely dependent on the nature and purpose of the construction.

INTEGRATED APPROACHES

The simple frameworks described above confine themselves to single aspects of environmental quality. Can these be integrated into a more comprehensive systems approach?

One possibility has been developed by A. V. Kneese and R. U. Ayres (1968, p. 636) in which they look at the residuals, the unwanted final end products, arising from processes or from filling specific needs of society. For example, the manufacture and use of the motor car produces solid, liquid and gaseous residuals in the mining and processing of ores, the manufacture of metals, rubber and plastics, the fabrication of the vehicle, the use of the vehicle and the manufacture of its fuel and lubricants and finally in the disposal of the worn out vehicle and its parts. The costs and benefits associated with the provision of personal transport can therefore be treated within a self-contained framework.

This approach can be broadened to cover a region of population with defined needs for energy, food, water and manufactured products. The residuals can be transferred from one phase to another and some recycling introduced to minimise the net level of residuals (Fig. 4). One could aim to minimise the residual unwanted pollutants, measured in terms of their damaging effects rather than quantity, by maximising the cycle process. Clearly minimising residuals may itself be a sub-optimal solution in the eyes of the population, since more may be spent on salvage operations than the benefits as they perceive them. Cost-benefit studies can treat residuals as costs to the citizen for comparison with the benefits associated with chosen ways of life. The problems of obtaining the data base on which to operate this model make perfection unachievable at the present time. However, a better understanding of the full system and the implications of transfer of resources from one

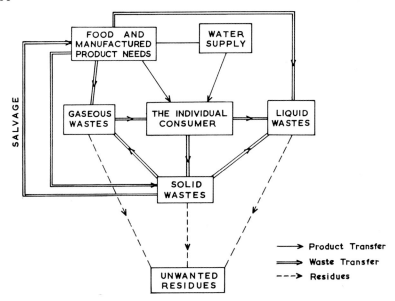

FIG. 4. *Composite system*

activity to another or pollutants from one sphere to another are clearly beneficial to the decision-taker and planner.

An alternative approach to an integrated analysis would be to treat a region in input-output terms, listing all those items that contribute to the quality of life and examining the cross impacts of one sector on another. These impacts could be listed in terms of net gains in social welfare, and a composite social welfare function equivalent to Gross Domestic Product (G.D.P.) in conventional input-output determined. The effect of changing the different inputs on the net social welfare function could then be explored. A list of possible items for inclusion is given in Figure 5.

1. Food	9. Health
2. Water	10. General welfare
3. Housing	11. Manufactured goods
4. Energy	12. Air pollution
5. Transport	13. Water pollution
6. Education	14. Solid waste
7. Roads	15. Noise
8. General construction	16. Visual amenity

FIG. 5. *Items for inclusion in social welfare matrix.*

DETERMINING THE COSTS AND BENEFITS

There are four general categories of cost that are relevant in cost-benefit studies of environmental quality:

(a) Costs of control or avoidance of environmental damage.

(b) The directly measurable economic costs of damage, such as corrosion or soiling or loss of output due to illness resulting from air pollution.

(c) The indirectly measurable costs where monetary values are not usually applied but where market values can be inferred from suitable proxies. Examples can be seen in losses of leisure time, loss of amenity due to noise or pollution and loss of housewives' services due to illness.

(d) Unmeasurable costs where no market values are readily ascribable, such as the costs of suffering or premature death.

These categories are not distinct and frequently they overlap. Benefits from improvement in environmental quality arise either from reductions in the costs itemised in (b) to (d) or from the creation of additional utility as by time saving or increased amenity.

It is not often practicable or sensible to talk in terms of absolute costs and benefits since the complete abolition of all pollution or nuisance is prohibitively costly. The relevant parameters relate to the changes in costs and benefits associated with proposed changes in environmental quality.

There is little to be said regarding costs of control or avoidance of damage. These have to be determined by looking at the specific processes or activities leading to the effects and how these could be improved: for example, the costs of filters or scrubbers or low sulphur fuels to reduce air pollution; costs of sewage treatment plants to reduce water pollution; the costs of incinerators or landscaping to reduce solid wastes or conceal them; the costs of undergrounding power cables or buildings to avoid visual intrusion, or of new roads or means of transport to decrease journey times. Each cost has to be determined as a function of the degree of environmental improvement obtained: a single figure is rarely likely to be of use. Care has to be exercised to ensure that the control route adopted is the cheapest and to watch for step changes in best-options; thus the costs of undergrounding power cables may be so high that it becomes cheaper to move or subdivide the source of electricity generation. Similarly, the costs of scrubbing flue gases may be so high that a radical change of production processes may be preferable.

The directly measurable economic costs of damage also appear simple but this is often far from true in practice, particularly with the more diffuse effects (Jones, 1971a). Corrosion caused by a pollutant can be measured in laboratory or ambient air environments, but the costs of corrosion arise in many ways. Extra expenditures may be incurred to use corrosion resistant or specially treated materials, maintenance by cleaning and painting may be increased, the materials may be allowed to corrode and replacement becomes more frequent, or the item susceptible to damage may be specially housed to protect it from the environment. The cost of each of these alternatives as actually adopted must be determined as a function of environmental quality.

The actual costs incurred then need to be determined from knowledge of the ambient environmental conditions and the distribution of susceptible materials, neither of which may be known with any great degree of reliability. Some of these difficulties are reduced when localised effects are involved, but it is still very difficult to determine how much corrosion or paint damage is due to pollution and how much to poor surface treatment and normal weathering by sun and moisture.

The loss of output due to bronchitis can be approximated by multiplying number of days off work due to this illness and average wage, taken as a measure of marginal product, but care is needed. Short period illness is not notified to the Department of Social Security so the information underestimates the number of days off. The average wage may not be appropriate if the bronchitic, through his illness, is necessarily employed on tasks with below-average remuneration, particularly since chronic bronchitis is predominantly a disease of the older members of the community. The big question of what proportion of bronchitis is attributable to, say, air pollution has also to be resolved. The use of multiple regression techniques is fraught with problems. Smoke pollution is at its highest in regions of dense housing with open coal fires, predominantly in the North of England. A reasonable correlation between pollution and numbers of bronchitics is inevitable and the relevant parameter is bronchitics per unit at risk. A remaining correlation may reflect such factors as social differences and climate, which may be difficult to isolate on the basis of available statistics.

The cost of soiling by air pollution or killing of river life by water pollution may be equated to the extra costs incurred in restoring the situation, but this is properly determinable only in situations where major deviations from the norm result in once for all effects. In chronically polluted environments the standards of cleanliness may be allowed to deteriorate and the fish may not be replaced. If the conditions are improved the gain may be one of amenity (category c) rather than economic, or some combination of the two.

The economic costs of introducing a new source of noise (highway, airport) or visual intrusion into a region might be properly argued to include the costs of removal of those who cannot stand the change, but information on the past behaviour of people in such circumstances does not exist.

The third category of costs is the one under most active investigation by economists at the present time, and is an area where opinions still differ widely. The value of time saving, for example, is usually equated to average wage or salary when the time saved is business time and can be assumed to be put to productive use; but is a few minutes saved of real value? It clearly depends on the use to which the time is to be put. If the saving makes the difference between catching or missing a train with a possible long wait, it may be far more valuable than if the time is dissipated over a number of activities with no observable change of output.

Leisure time, on the other hand, can be viewed from a number of perspectives. It could be argued that leisure time was at least equal in value to working time or the individual would find some remunerative work to do in its place. Alternatively, leisure could be valued in relation to the activity undertaken. If one did not dig one's own garden one would need to employ a gardener. In practice, transport economists have looked at the price people appear to be prepared to pay for time savings where alternative transport modes at different cost cover the same journey (Quarmby, 1967). There are many difficulties in applying these figures to decisions involving new forms of transport, new highways and the like; means of transport differ in comfort and are seldom exactly equivalent in convenience or frequency; returns to scale are assumed linear, i.e., 60 savings of 1 minute = 1 saving of 1 hour; results from test areas may differ from those applicable to the decision area for social or other reasons; generated traffic may erode or destroy the expected benefits and this changes the nature of the benefit in kind and value. Other approaches to valuing time savings have involved looking at the choice of routes where journey length or toll introduce differences in cost (Lee and Dalvi, 1969, p. 213) or correlating property prices with journey times into London from the commuter belt (Wabe, 1970). Many other factors have to be taken into account (see below), but the method was claimed to yield satisfactory agreement with the pure transport approach, viz. 27 new pence compared with 15 new pence from Quarmby (1967).

The use of property values as a general means of measuring disutility associated with living in a particular environment is attractive because the economist postulates that the value of a good (the house) is equal to the discounted present value of the future stream of benefits deriving from its ownership. If identical properties exist in identical markets with identical access to all amenities but different levels of a specific single disutility, such as noise from a highway, an ugly refuse tip causing visual or odorous offence, or air pollution, then the property with the disutility will have a value lower by an amount that equals the individual's valuation of this disutility. Equally a property with a good view will command a premium. This approach is satisfactory provided a proper market exists where individuals are able to trade off disutility for cash and provided the purchaser knows of the disutility and its effects.

This latter point has been contested by R. J. Anderson and T. D. Crocker (1970) who claim that 'buyers need only know that they prefer one property to another, and other things being equal, are willing to pay more for preferred properties. It is hypothesised that one of the factors which causes some properties to be preferred is the relative absence of the effects of air pollution, irrespective of whether the cause of these effects is known to buyers. The notion of cause and effect rest wholly in the mind of the theorist and not necessarily in the mind of the property buyer'. This may suit academic economists but is clearly a

nonsense as soon as it is appreciated that the effects of pollution themselves are not always evident. Houses in neighbourhoods that tend to
be odorous in winter conditions will be sold in summer and the
purchaser can scarcely know that purchasing one house will make him
more liable to bronchitis in 30 years' time than purchase of another.
The market can only properly reflect obvious disutilities, such as visual
intrusion and dirt, and this is reflected in Ridker's studies of public
awareness of effects (Ridker, 1966).

The price of a property will in fact depend on a large number of
factors: the local market in terms of supply and demand, its size, age,
state of repair, the local housing density, proximity to work, schools,
shops and entertainment, the quality of the neighbourhood and its
amenities, local taxes, availability of public services, and finally
environmental quality. To isolate the relative dependence of price on
a single aspect of environmental quality is no mean task. R. G. Ridker
(1966) has attempted to do this for air pollution in St. Louis by multiple
correlation methods using sulphation rates as an indicator for pollution.
J. A. Jaksch (1969) has eliminated many of the market and neighbourhood problems by looking at a compact area with uniform amenities
and principal variables of size, housing density and pollution (measured
by dustfall only). A further study by Ridker followed the time dependence of property value in 'identical' areas after a new source of pollution was introduced which affected one but not the other. Each of these
studies gave a measure of the relative change in property value per unit
of pollution. Ridker's regression data have been criticised by Anderson
and Crocker (1970) who re-evaluated them on the basis of the theory of
consumer behaviour put forward by K. J. Lancaster (1966, p. 132).
Their answer gave a significantly higher dependence of price on
pollution.

Absence of readily available data on house prices in the United
Kingdom makes surveys of property value difficult, but the author has
reported one study in which estate agents were used to estimate subjectively the difference in property values for identical properties with
identical amenities situated in smoke controlled and uncontrolled
zones of their own cities (Jones, forthcoming). The average differentials
were small, corresponding to 1·05% on a £5,000 house in heavily polluted areas and 0·4% in low pollution areas, with an overall mean of
0·8%. The differential increased with property value. There was a lag
between introduction of smoke control and changes in property value,
with a mean value of 1·7 to 2 years. These results were in surprisingly
close agreement with those of Jaksch and Ridker when normalised for
pollution level and property value. This value of about £40 per property relates to predominantly domestic smoke pollution (and sulphur
dioxide) in urban areas. Severe local pollution from industrial or other
sources (such as sewage works and abattoirs) can have a far larger
impact as judged by the work of both Ridker and the author with
changes measured in £100s rather than £10s. The Warwick study

(Wabe, 1970) interestingly gave a capital value appreciation of £276 associated with ready access to the London Green Belt.

The use of property values as a measure of the disutility of pollution, noise and the like suffers from many disadvantages in reality. Decisions on house purchase are actually composed of a series of complex intuitive trade-offs by the purchaser, which is one good reason for using market models like those of Lancaster (1966). Secondly, property type may correlate with the disutility, e.g., high density nineteenth century dwellings are generally sited close to industrial areas and tend to have high domestic smoke pollution, whilst modern and/or larger dwellings are usually situated in the less polluted areas. Lastly, without proper attitude surveys it is difficult to tell what aspects of disutility are being taken into account. This latter point has been discussed (Jones, 1970a, p. 103) and possible solutions offered using a novel experimental technique developed by Hoinville in which individuals are asked to allocate limited notional resources between various alternative changes in environmental quality (Hoinville, 1970; see Chap. 6). In the author's study the capitalised disutility of pollution is roughly equated to the present value of disutility from soiling and extra maintenance costs determined by independent means. Those clearly are the obvious outward manifestations of pollution which one would expect to be appreciated by a purchaser.

In situations where the environmental quality is improving, it is appropriate to use the property value change (or its expected value by analogy with other situations) as a measure of gain of utility. Where deterioration occurs, individuals may feel obliged to move and the disutility then exceeds the price differential in a normal equilibrium market by an amount equal to the costs of removal and the loss of consumer surplus vested in the property by the vendor, i.e., the amount over and above the normal market value he would have had to be offered to induce him to leave his friends, garden and other attractions of his present house in the absence of the new disutility. This problem has arisen particularly with regard to noise intrusion (Commission on the Third London Airport, 1970). The questions of the effect of environmental change on land values offers a similarly wide range of problems (Brigham, 1965, p. 325; Jones, 1969a; Holmans, 1970).

Numerous other examples can be cited involving the inference of value from market proxies. Minimum notional values for housewives' services (which may be lost through illness) can be assessed by arguing that their families must value their services at least as highly as those of the average working woman, otherwise she would work. Alternatively the costs of replacing all her services by paid labour might be taken (Mansfield, 1970).

The value of a leisure activity (Burton and Fulcher, 1968; Smith and Kavanagh, 1969) or of holiday areas (Mansfield 1970) has been assessed by finding out what people are prepared to pay to reach it from different distances. The assumption that the proportion of the population prepared to pay these sums is constant at all distances then allows one to construct a price-demand curve and evaluate the consumer surplus derived by those who pay less (because of their location) than they would be prepared to do. There are limitations to this approach since the journey itself may be regarded as an attraction rather than a cost and the attractiveness of one region can only be measured relative to competing attractions. Results from existing amenities are therefore difficult to relate to proposals for changes in environmental quality caused by such features as new reservoirs or parks.

The final class of costs incurred from poor environment relates to the incommensurables such as suffering, premature death and poor education. These typify things that no individual can value rationally even if he can appreciate the degree of disutility. This topic has been reviewed briefly by the author (Jones, 1973). Some attempts have been made in the United States to determine what people would be prepared to pay for a change in the probability of death over a defined time period and to extrapolate this data to gain a current valuation of life (Schelling, 1968). General experience indicates, however, that what people say they would do and what they will do differ widely so that the results of such enquiries need to be treated with considerable scepticism.

Alternatively one can attempt to examine what society currently spends or wants to spend on reducing death and injury on the roads, in factories and elsewhere or on alleviating suffering by medical treatment. This approach gives widely variable results and demands some stepwise change in expenditure which can be tied with a measurable effect, either real or readily predictable. Thirdly, one can examine court awards to see what value the courts have attached to disutility (Jones, 1973, Dawson, 1967). This only applies to non-lethal effects in British courts. Where death is concerned, awards are related to economic loss alone. Finally, one can allocate arbitrary sums based on subjective consideration of the data from the previous sources and explore the implications of using these or alternative values so that the decision-taker can make a choice.

It is in this area of cost that emotion clouds objectivity and many people feel morally averse to the use of cash values. However, every decision concerning expenditure on safety or health carries an implied valuation of life or injury, as do many others, and there is much to be said for having some uniform basis for decision, at least in the public sector.

USING THE DATA

Once a framework has been agreed and the costs and benefits of changes in environmental quality appraised against that framework, the question of using the data to full effect arises. The maximum benefit or minimum cost is clearly achieved when the sum of control or avoidance costs and damage or loss costs is minimised over the whole population covered by the framework (Fig. 6). In an unrestricted free market society the damage (or loss) curve would merely be the cost penalty incurred by the polluter for wasting fuel (smoke), product (cement), or by-product (sulphur, hydrogen chloride), to take an example from air pollution, or energy losses and excess wear in the

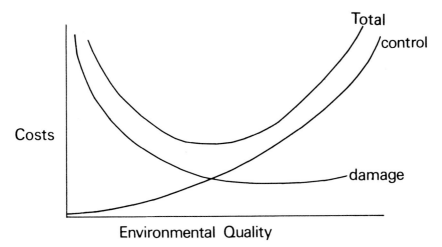

FIG. 6. *Optimum strategy.*

case of noisy plant. If the economic costs to society as a whole are included the damage cost curve rises and the minimum moves to higher levels of environmental quality. If the social penalties to society are added (the non-G.N.P. costs) the minimum will move to still higher quality. This argument is spelt out more fully for air pollution elsewhere (Jones, 1971a).

The cost-benefit data can therefore be used as an aid to formulating policy goals for environmental quality, but is no more than an aid (Jones, 1971c) since the economists' ideal is unattainable in practice. First, for a true optimum, each individual source would need to be controlled independently, a generally impossible aim. Secondly, in the case of pollution, the basis of control should be damage cost not emission. The relationship between the two is a complex function of location, including topography and nearness to sites where damage can be inflicted and, for air pollution, weather and wind conditions, emission height and temperature and nature of the emissions. Identical sources of environmental damage located at different places produce quite different damage costs so that each would need to be reviewed separately. A visual intrusion or noise emission may cause far more disutility in a residential area than at an industrial or isolated rural site. For some pollution the emission may remain constant but the damage may vary by the hour depending on such features as water flow in rivers and wind speed for noise. Thus truly optimum control would need to vary not only from source to source but from day to day.

An economically sub-optimal compromise method of control may therefore be adopted aimed at average conditions and possibly average locations. Alternatively, political decisions may favour a threshold policy similar to that in the atomic energy field where emissions have to be controlled to below the level at which they can do any damage. This is a very costly method and only practicable in situations with isolated point sources of disutility since, for multiple sources, the degree of control will vary every time an additional source is created or one removed.

Clearly single isolated changes to the environment can be considered individually but for these and more general cases, knowledge of the costs and benefits can be of considerable value in formulating policy. Questions such as 'is one large power station at one site more damaging to the environment than several smaller ones?', or 'will a given plant be more acceptable at one site or another?' are always likely to occur.

A further use of the cost-benefit study is to examine the 'transfers' of money or social welfare that may follow postulated changes in environmental quality. The differential impact on particular sectors may lead to decisions to modify control features or introduce them more gradually. It may be obvious that if one bans all noise sources above certain levels in residential areas, then particular activities will cease, but it may be less apparent that a change in pollution emission regulations will introduce economic penalties to particular firms which will force them out of business and create local unemployment problems, or that a change of process to avoid a control regulation may increase environmental damage in some uncontrolled way.

The data on damage costs, control or avoidance costs, and benefits are invariably sparse, imprecise, and difficult to come by. In consequence high levels of uncertainty attach to the output of most cost-benefit studies, although this is rarely explicitly recognised. The recognition of the uncertainty in the base data, allied with knowledge of the policy being followed with regard to environmental quality, can give a guide to the upper levels of investment that ought to be made to improve the data base and reduce the uncertainty (Jones, 1969b, 1971b). The effects of potential improvements in waste recovery, reduced control or avoidance costs, and improved methods of minimising damage, such as corrosion protection or noise screening, can be explored using the cost-benefit data and the value of such improvements used as a guide to the deployment of resources for research and development (Jones, 1971a, 1971b).

Overall it will be seen that cost-benefit data can provide a useful input into a number of aspects of planning, control and resources allocation, especially at governmental level.

FORECASTS

Whilst data on current costs of environmental damage may be of value for short term policy formulation, there is a need to look to the future to determine how environmental quality will alter if things continue as they are doing. How much reduction in air pollution will result from continued introduction of smoke control and the switch to closed boiler central heating systems? How much refuse and sewage will be produced by the region of interest at future times? How much noise will the individual be exposed to, how many power stations will there be and what will they be like? Such forecasts of technology and demand will initially be surprise free and assume that no specific alteration is made in policy. Armed with the prospects, the policy-maker can decide what changes, if any, are needed to maintain the *status quo* or to improve environmental quality.

Two particular aspects are of interest to the cost-benefit analyst. First, research into control, avoidance and the like is likely to take many years before it can be implemented (Jones, 1969c) and the benefits of the research need to be determined in relation to the situation as it will be at implementation, not as it is now. Secondly, the change in level or nature of pollution may be accompanied by changed attitudes in society so that the current values attached to disutility will alter and, for example, a good environment may become of greater importance relative to the possession of material wealth. It is evident that such changes have taken place in the United States and in Western and Eastern Europe during the past five years (Jones, 1970b). Public pressure has prevented the building of power stations, roads, reservoirs and other structures solely on amenity arguments. One role of cost-benefit analyses may be to bring perspective and objectivity into such debates, but nevertheless if the analysis is to be an objective aid to decision making, it must take account of changing social values.

Few attempts have been made to look at this problem and the author's experience has highlighted the difficulties (Jones, 1970b, 1973). There is great difficulty in finding any reliable quantitative indicator of socia lvalue or expectation. Much research is needed in this area if only to identify or establish indicators for future use. In some instances simple behavioural or causal models may be used as a forecasting aid and one for looking at vehicle pollution has been described elsewhere (Jones, 1970c).

A further role for forecasting is to be found in attempts to identify future threats to environmental quality before they arise (National Academy of Sciences, 1969; Starr, 1970, p. 409) and hence to establish the costs and benefits involved as a guide to whether or not the changes should be allowed.

THE PROBLEMS

There is a tacit assumption in the preceding discussion that, whilst there are difficulties in finding the right values to attach to costs, these 'right' values exist. Unfortunately this is not the case and there can be considerable doubt as to whether a particular cost should or should not be included. For example, if one buys a house facing on to a rubbish tip and thereby gets it for a lower price than an equivalent house elsewhere, should the disutility one suffers, which is quite real, be included in the overall sum of disutilities or should one be regarded as having recouped this cost and cancelled the disutility. The answer may appear self-evident, but as a result of one's loss the rest or some part of society —perhaps the ratepayers—have benefited from lower costs for waste disposal than they would otherwise have had. Should they continue to benefit to the detriment of other people? To take another example, one may choose in a polluted area to accept a lower standard of cleanliness and maintain other modes of consumption. Again there is 'measurable' disutility, but if one is taxed to ameliorate this disutility one is forced into an expenditure pattern one had rejected.

It is common experience that people resist change and this has been observed with smoke control. When control is first mooted strong opposition often builds up, whereas after introduction equally strong approval is voiced. The apparent value attached to the gain in utility changes with experience, but which is right? The implication from the cleanliness case might be that the pre-existing situation gives proper values whilst the smoke control situation suggests that the administration know best.

The market values attached to environment have no unique correctness. Each different distribution of wealth in society will give a different market equilibrium and a different set of values (McKean, 1968). The distribution of wealth is regulated to some extent by taxes in the light of political philosophy; only if the distribution is accepted as right, can cost-benefit values be right and then only if the changes envisaged in the environment are marginal. If the values lead to decisions to make non-marginal changes, the distribution changes and can no longer be 'right' so that further compensating action will be needed.

A further problem has also to be appreciated. Democratic decision is based on the principle of one man, one vote. In a referendum everyone has an equal say. Parliamentary rule is majoritarian where, in the absence of proportional representation, the system is likely to be biased away from the national average. Cost-benefit analysis, or better, the principle of economic pareto-optimality, biases decision towards the wealthier members of society compared with the referendum (Self, 1970a).

P. Self (1970b) and A. Coddington (1970, p. 579) have questioned the validity of the all embracing cost-benefit study such as that on the Third London Airport, on the grounds that many factors defy evaluation (the long term infrastructure effects, in particular) and that adding soft numbers (social and inferred costs and benefits) to hard facts (such as real capital expenditures) confuses rather than helps.

All these criticisms have some validity; nevertheless, it is hard to see how decisions made in the absence of factual information, albeit uncertain, can be better than those made with the data. The fact that some items remain unquantifiable is only of overwhelming import if one has subjective reasons to believe that these greatly exceed all other items. In such a case it may not be worthwhile pursuing a cost-benefit study since the decision is necessarily subjective; nevertheless, the study of the redistributional effects ensuing from decisions could still merit examination. The objections to addition of 'dissimilar' things expressed in monetary units can only be sustained if the decision-taker or objector believes the monetary values to be wrong and to yield incorrect weightings. He always has the option of saying so and of opening a dialogue on an objective basis. Refusal to contemplate such a process reduces decision to the level of black magic. Other arguments in the same vein are given by M. Peston (1969, p. 563).

SUMMARY AND CONCLUSIONS

It has been argued that decisions have to be made concerning environmental quality and that a necessary basis for such decisions, if they are to be objective, is an analysis of the costs of environmental damage and its avoidance and the benefits of environmental improvement. Such costs and benefits need to be analysed in relation to changes in quality and great importance has to be attached to selecting the proper framework and constraints. One of the main criticisms levelled at the Third London Airport enquiry was that the constraints (terms of reference) had been too limiting. Whether such criticism is valid can be judged only by examining the effect of changes in the constraints, always provided that this does not magnify the task much.

The determination of the costs of environmental damage is far from simple even in apparently straightforward cases such as damage by corrosion or soiling, and when social disutility is involved the costs are not absolute and have no permanence. They are determined partly by political decision, partly by observed social preference and partly by the existing patterns of wealth distribution. Attention must always be given to the changing values of society and the temporal relevance of pollution costs to the decisions in hand.

Despite all these complexities there can be little doubt that cost-benefit analysis can provide a valuable input into policy formulation and into decisions on control or avoidance of damage or creation of fresh amenities, it can be used to test proposed changes in the environment and to aid decisions about investment in research and development. The problems of quantification can be overcome with a little ingenuity, but the uncertainty in the final values and the assumptions must be clearly spelled out so that the sensitivity of the decision to the data can be fully appreciated.

So long as the cost-benefit analyst does not attempt to usurp the role of the decision-taker and recognises that there are other value systems besides that of economic efficiency, there can be no real dispute between the decision-takers, the planners and the analysts. It is the task of society, through government, to decide what criteria it wants applied to decisions on environmental quality. The analyst should accept these criteria and content himself with exploring and explaining their implications.

REFERENCES

Anderson, R. J. and T. D. Crocker (1970) *Air Pollution and Residential Property Values*, University of Wisconsin, Milwaukee, Report to U.S. National Air Pollution Control Administration.

Anon. (1970) 'What will you pay for amenity?', *Economist*, May 23rd, p. 76.

Brigham, E. S. (1965) 'The determinants of residential land values', *Land Economics*, 41, pp. 325–34.

Burton, T. L. and M. N. Fulcher (1968) 'Measurement of recreation benefits—a survey', *Journal of Economic Studies*, 3, pp. 35–48.

Coase, R. H. (1960) 'The problem of social cost', *Journal of Law and Economics*, 3, pp. 1–44.

Coddington, A. (1970) 'Soft numbers and hard facts', *New Society*, October 1st, pp. 579–81.

Commision on the Third London Airport (1970) *Report*, H.M.S.O.

Crocker, T. D. (1966) 'The structuring of atmospheric pollution control systems', in *The Economics of Air Pollution*, H. Wolozin (ed.), Norton & Co., New York, pp. 61–86.

Dawson, R. F. (1967) *Cost of Road Accidents in Great Britain*, Road Research Laboratory Report LR 79, Garston.

Eckenfelder, W. W. and D. L. Ford (1969) 'Economics of waste paper treatment', *Chemical Engineering*, p. 110.

Gafney, M. M. (1964) *Economic Analysis and Air Conservation*, Ph.D. Thesis, University of Wisconsin, Milwaukee.

Hoinville, G. (1971) 'Evaluating community preferences', in *Cost Benefit Analysis in the Public Sector*, Institute of Municipal Treasurers and Accountants, London, p. 23.

Holmans, A. E. (1970) 'Changes in land prices as a measure of benefits and dis-benefits in cost benefit analysis', in *Cost Benefit in the Public Sector*, Institute of Municipal Treasurers and Accountants, London, pp. 15–21.

Kneese, A. V. (1968) *Economics and the Quality of Environment*, Social Sciences and the Environment, reprinted Resources for the Future Inc., Washington.

Kneese, A. V. and R. U. Ayres (1968) *Environmental Pollution*, Federal Programs for the Development of Human Resources, Vol. 2, p. 626, U.S. Govt. Printing Office, Washington.

Jaksch, J. A. (1969) *Residential Property Values in Toledo, Oregon*, M.Sc. Thesis, Washington State University, Seattle.

Jones, P. M. S. (1969a) 'Land, amenity and infrastructure in cost-benefit studies of air pollution', Treasury Management Accounting Unit Seminar, Sunningdale, September.

Jones, P. M. S. (1969b) *Decisions on Levels of Investment in Research, Feasibility Studies and Market Research*, PAU Report M8, H.M.S.O., London.

Jones, P. M. S. (1969c) *Technological Forecasting as a Management Tool*, PAU Report M.10, H.M.S.O., London.

Jones, P. M. S. (1970a) *Preliminary Thoughts on Social Forecasting*, PAU Report M.16, H.M.S.O., London.

Jones, P. M. S. (1970b) 'Determining priorities and investment levels in scientific research and development', *Policy Sciences*, 1, p. 299.

Jones, P. M. S. (1971a) 'Some aspects of the economics of pollution', Paper to Society of Environmental Engineers Conference on Pollution, Olympia, London, June.

Jones, P. M. S. (1971b) comment, in *Cost Benefit Analysis in the Public Sector*, Institute of Municipal Treasurers and Accountants, London, p. 103.

Jones, P. M. S. (1971c) 'Lessons from the objective appraisal of programmes at the national level—implications of criteria and policy', *Research Policy*, 1, p. 81.

Jones, P. M. S. (1973) 'The use of cost benefit analysis as an aid to allocating Government resources for research and development' in *Cost Benefit and Cost Effectiveness Studies and Analysis*, J. N. Wolfe (ed.) George Allen & Unwin Ltd., London, pp. 155–81.

Lancaster, K. J. (1966) 'A new approach to consumer theory', *Journal of Political Economy*, 74, pp. 132–57.

Lee, N. and M. Q. Dalvi (1969) 'Variations in the value of travel time', *Manchester School*, 37, p. 213.

McKean, R. N. (1968) 'The use of shadow prices', in *Problems in Public Expenditure Analysis*, S. B. Chase (ed.), Brookings Institute, New York, pp. 33–65.

Mansfield, N. (1971) 'The estimation of benefits accruing from the construction of a major recreational facility, in *Cost Benefit in the Public Sector*, Institute of Municipal Treasurers and Accountants, London, pp. 41–71.

Marshall, A. (1920) *Principles of Economics*, 8th edn., Macmillan & Co., London.

Meade, J. E. (1952) 'External economies and dis-economies in a competitive situation,' *Economic Journal*, 62, pp. 54–67.

Mills, E. S. (1966) 'Economic incentives in air pollution control', in *The Economics of Air Pollution*, H. Wolozin (ed.), Norton & Co., New York, pp. 40–50.

National Academy of Sciences (1969) *Technology—Processes of Assessment and Choice*, Report to the Committee on Science and Astronautics, U.S. House of Representatives, July.

Peston, M. (1969) 'Cost benefit analysis', *Town and Country Planning*, 37, p. 563.

Quarmby, D. A. (1967) 'Choice of travel mode for the journey to work', *Journal of Transport Economics and Policy*, 1, pp. 273–314.

Ridker, R. G. (1966) *The Economic Costs of Air Pollution*, Praeger and Sons, London.

Schelling, T. C. (1968) 'The life you may save may be your own', in *Problems in Public Expenditure Analysis*, S. B. Chase, (ed.), Brookings Institute, New York, pp. 127–62.

Self, P. (1970a) 'Nonsense on stilts: cost-benefit analysis and the Roskill Commission', *The Political Quarterly*, 41, pp. 249–60.

Self, P. (1970b) 'Nonsense on stilts: the futility of Roskill', *New Society*, July 2nd, pp. 8–11.

Smith, R. J. and N. J. Kavanagh (1969) *Recreation at Grafham Water*, Faculty of Commerce, Birmingham University, Discussion Paper Series B, No. 15.

Starr, C. (1970) 'Technology assessment. Pt. 1, Weighing the benefits and risks of new technologies', *Research Management*, 13, p. 409.

Wabe, J. S. (1970) *A Study of House Prices as a Means of Establishing Journey Time*, Warwick Economic Research Papers No. 11, University of Warwick, Coventry.

Wolozin, H. (1966) 'Setting criteria for public expenditures on air pollution abatement', in *The Economics of Air Pollution*, H. Wolozin, (ed.), Norton & Co., New York, pp. 162–91.

CHAPTER 10

Urban environments and mental health

A. E. PHILIP

'Mental health' is a useful blanket term which covers not only the treatment and prevention of pathological mental process but is also, in its social meaning, concerned with the dynamic equilibrium between man and his environment. It is a concept which has much wider scope than its apparent opposite 'mental illness'. There are many environmental pressures and interpersonal stresses which cause distress in individuals without producing mental illness; indeed, the treatment of such distress is perhaps better seen as the province of the social work department rather than the mental hospital. In the context of this book it is the social aspects of mental health that are most relevant.

MENTAL HEALTH AND LIFE IN SELECTED URBAN ENVIRONMENTS

This chapter examines some recent examples of studies which have attempted to relate mental health to some environmental features, life in high flats, in a new housing estate and near a large airport. It will also present some findings based on a series of ecological studies in Edinburgh. These findings can be used to estimate the degree of importance of the environment in producing socially disruptive, personally distressing behaviour. The paper by D. M. Fanning (1967), in which he compared the frequency with which families living in flats and families living in houses consulted general practitioners, provided evidence that flat dwellers had a greater overall medical morbidity than those who lived in houses. The greatest differences were seen in the incidence of respiratory infections and in psychoneurotic disorders. He thought that these last, which are of interest in the present context, were due to monotony, boredom, isolation and experiencing difficulty in looking after children. The most illness-prone groups were those mothers with young children and older women who, Fanning thought, were less able to adapt to a changed mode of life.

Articles in the popular press on high flats have stressed the feelings of isolation and loneliness which some people experience as well as the difficulties which occur when, for instance, lifts break down. Fanning's article carries weight because it was written by a medical man and published in a medical journal. However, it seems to have been forgotten that the flats about which he wrote were not fifteen-storey monsters but 'three- and four-storey blocks', tenements 1960 style, in fact. Now most Scots have some experience of life in three- or four-storey blocks of a much older style, and the author personally recalls that a great deal of interaction between tenants took place. Much of the interaction was unfriendly, and the petty quarrels which spring up when people are in close proximity can be very stressful; but Fanning makes no reference to these things and one can only assume that there was no 'tenement life' as we know it in Scotland.

This lack of community life has also been blamed by some for their findings regarding the poor health of people in new housing estates. For instance, F. M. Martin, J. H. F. Brotherston and S. P. W. Chave (1957), in a study of a new housing estate in North London, found that there was a high rate of mental ill-health and that this rate could be attributed partly to the shock of re-housing and partly to the poor social facilities on the estate which led to 'a degree of loneliness and social isolation incompatible with positive mental health'. E. G. Hare and G. K. Shaw (1965) compared a new housing estate with an old-established area to ascertain whether factors peculiar to new estates, as opposed to urban areas in general, were in operation. For most of their indices of mental health the two populations did not differ. Such differences as existed were explicable in terms of factors such as family size and distance from hospitals. Expressions of general dissatisfaction with the environs were equally common in the new estate and the older area, some fifteen per cent of people in each location being dissatisfied. From this study Hare and Shaw concluded that the lack of social amenities on the new estate had no appreciable effect on mental health, or if it had an adverse effect, this was offset by other factors. People who were in poor health mentally also tended to be of poor physical health; these people were more often those who were dissatisfied with their neighbourhood.

Noise has been recognised as an important hazard to health and a group of doctors practising near Heathrow Airport found that there was a higher rate of admissions to a psychiatric hospital among people living in the area of maximum noise (Abbey-Wickrama et al., 1969). Although being cautious about attributing 'cause and effect' the authors clearly implied that aircraft noise had something to do with the higher rate of admission. Their findings were later challenged on a number of points relating to areas of maximum noise and characteristics of the area (Chowns, 1970). It is not credible that aircraft noise per se would lead to admission to mental hospital.

These three areas of research, flats, new estates and living on the line of a busy aircraft flight path, are ones where people have to adapt to some environmental change. Now people will adapt in their own characteristic ways; some will miss the close proximity of relatives, while others will develop new relationships. People even adapt to incessant noise although physically they do become impaired. This seems to indicate a rough and ready rule: where an environmental

factor has some adverse effect on almost all people, what might be
called a universal effect, then there is a clear indication that action
should be taken to deal with that factor; where an environmental
factor has an adverse effect only on some people, where there is a
differential effect, then action is required to deal not with the factor
but with the people who react badly to it. As regards mental health it
must be considered doubtful whether any non-human environmental
factor falls within the universal-effect category. The author's own
interest and contribution to the study of relationships between urban
environment and mental health has come about through his research
on suicidal behaviour (McCulloch and Philip, 1972). In its medical,
psychological and social aspects this behaviour is a mental health
problem of considerable magnitude. Completed suicide, with a national
rate of some thirteen per hundred thousand, accounts for the same
number of deaths per year as road fatalities. Both are far behind the
death rates for cancer and coronary heart disease, which account for
about 210 and 250 deaths per hundred thousand, but while road
fatalities are at least occasionally the subject of public concern and
attention, suicide is ignored as a public health problem. Suicidal
behaviour which does not result in death is a much more common
phenomenon, the current annual rate in Edinburgh is just over two
per thousand; in other words, close on one thousand people each year
make some attempt on their lives. Financial hardship, material circumstances, interpersonal difficulties, physical or mental illness are all
factors which can precipitate an episode of self-poisoning. In situations
which might be called crises of despair, some people injure themselves
in order to appeal for help, to spite others or to submit themselves to
trial by ordeal.

SUICIDAL BEHAVIOUR IN EDINBURGH

Very early in the research programme of the Medical Research
Council Unit for Epidemiological Studies in Psychiatry into suicidal
behaviour in Edinburgh it became apparent that some areas of the
city contributed more than their share of admissions to the Poisoning
Treatment Centre. It was soon apparent that high rates for attempted
suicide were related to high rates for overcrowding, family dislocation
and areas where known criminals resided; in other words, where there
was a lot of social disorganisation. These and other findings led to
further examination of the ecology of suicidal behaviour in Edinburgh.
Like every large community, the city is a patchwork of many diverse
areas each of which has its own kind of people, activities, physical
characteristics, life styles and traditions; in brief, its own sub-culture.
The investigation and analysis of these variations has in the past shed
useful light on deviant behaviour, mental disorder and physical illness.
The most commonly used areal units have been census tracts or
electoral wards; in either case, provided there is a fair amount of varia-

tion *between* wards (or census tracts), and a degree of uniformity or lack of variation *within* these wards (or census tracts), it is usually profitable to analyse data in this ecological fashion. Such analyses provide information on some of the structural and cultural properties of cities and their constituent wards. By good fortune the city of Edinburgh has developed in such a way as to make ecological research particularly worthwhile. Of Edinburgh's 23 electoral wards the first three, in numerical order, encompass the centuries old, multi-storied buildings of the Royal Mile (Fig. 1). In these wards are to be found Edinburgh Castle and Her Majesty's Palace of Holyroodhouse in close proximity to numerous less desirable premises, such as lodging houses and cheap hostels. Wards

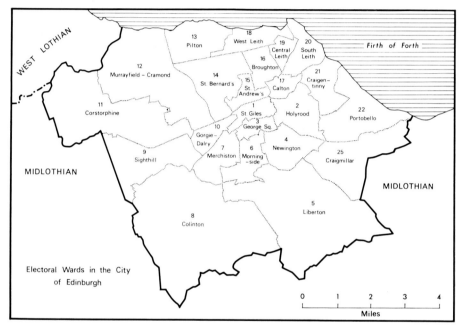

FIG. 1 *Based on a figure from the census report*

15 to 20 extend north-eastward from the city centre to the Firth of Forth and the port of Leith; for the most part this area comprises ageing nineteenth-century industrial tenement buildings. Immediately to the south and west of the town centre lies an inner ring of spacious, old-established dwellings, traditional homes of Edinburgh's well-to-do professional workers interspersed with high density flats and tenements. An outer ring of more recent buildings of modest amenity and undistinguished architecture completes the city. Three of these outer wards are marked by being predominantly local-authority housing schemes, the others are areas where owner-occupied houses predominate. Slum clearances over the past three decades has left the central wards with steadily declining populations, very little new domestic building having taken the place of the old. Two wards, number 1 (St. Giles) and

number 23 (Craigmillar), have a special relationship. The latter ward, on the south-eastern perimeter of the city, has as its core a housing scheme of the 1930s initially populated by families from the slums of the central ward (see Chap. 12). Although removed from their old physical environment, many of these families took with them their old behaviour and characteristic ways of life.

Such has been Edinburgh's pattern of development that most of these electoral wards show differences between one another while having a fair degree of uniformity within themselves. Advantage was taken of this favourable state of affairs to compare the distribution of suicidal behaviour in various parts of the city with a variety of social information, most of which was readily available from Census tables and the annual reports of various departments of the local authority.

When the correlations between these social variables were analysed, it was found that they grouped themselves into a number of clusters, one of which was particularly interesting and is shown in Fig. 2.

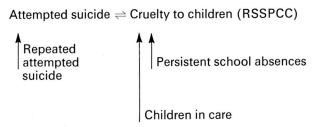

Fig. 2. *Close correlates of high attempted suicide rates*

Contact with those who had behaved suicidally had made the investigators aware of the appalling difficulties such people experienced in their personal relationships. The cluster of variables in Figure 2 reflects these relationships as they appear, using an ecological technique, and highlights a particular facet, namely a peculiar parent-child relationship. High rates for attempted suicide are related to high rates of cruelty to children, high rates for children being taken into the care of the local authority and high rates of school absence for reasons other than sickness (persistent truancy and being kept off school by parents). Among variables which were significantly related to rates for attempted suicide but which did not appear in the core cluster shown in Figure 2 were high rates for juvenile delinquency, much overcrowding, high rate of suicide, and high incidence of divorced persons.

Three measures of suicidal behaviour were included in the study, viz., attempted suicide, repeated attempted suicide and completed suicide. Five social variables had significant relationships with all three forms of suicidal behaviour; these were juvenile delinquency, children taken into care, overcrowding, referrals to the Royal Scottish Society for the Prevention of Cruelty to Children, and divorce. Where the rates for suicidal behaviour were high then the rates for these other variables were high also. Ecological data, although they can point to possible relationships between variables, cannot determine whether these variables occur together in the same individual. In order to determine whether these social variables held together for individuals, a number of persons who had attempted suicide was interviewed and asked if they had ever been taken into care, been persistent school absentees and the like. It was found that the associations established at an ecological level hold good at the individual level. Other members of this M.R.C. Unit later sought to determine whether the inter-ward differences in rates for suicidal behaviour could be explained away as simply reflecting differences in certain social and demographic characteristics (Buglass *et al.*, 1970). The characteristics they considered, viz., sex, age, marital status, social class, overcrowding and unemployment, when combined reduced the variation between wards to a considerable extent but did not account for all the variations between wards. Wards 1 (St. Giles), 3 (George Square) and 23 (Craigmillar) still produced much more than their quota of attempted suicides.

The historical link between St. Giles and Craigmillar has been pointed out. Physically the two are quite different but some of their inhabitants share the same cultural background. Many of them have suffered from early deprivation of one form or another and in adult life show difficulties in dealing with the world. Here it is necessary to return to the rule of thumb involving universal and differential effects. Not all inhabitants of St. Giles or Craigmillar behave in a suicidal manner, not even all of those who live in the most desperate of material and personal conditions. So while indices of the quality of the physical environment are useful, in so far as they reflect trends and patterns of poor mental health, they cannot really be blamed for *causing* it. The suicide population is clearly one which is characterised by poor early personality development and a subsequent inability to cope with life in an effective, satisfying way. The interpersonal environment is much more important than the physical, the quality of a man's friendships more vital than the quality of the house in which he lives.

In brief, the argument presented here is that where there are factors in urban life which can be demonstrated to be harmful to the well-being of almost all people, then these factors must be dealt with; where there are factors which appear to be harmful to a minority of people then the fault may lie in the people, not in the factor. Regarding mental health it seems that most factors appear to be of the latter variety.

REFERENCES

Abbey-Wickrama, I., M. F. a'Brook, F. E. G. Gattoni and C. F. Herridge (1969) 'Mental-hospital admissions and aircraft noise', *Lancet*, 2, pp. 1275–6.

Buglass, D., P. Dugard and N. Kreitman (1970) 'Multiple standardisation of para-suicide ('attempted suicide') rates in Edinburgh', *British Journal of Preventive and Social Medicine*, 24, pp. 182–6.

Chowns, R. H. (1970) Correspondence, *Lancet*, 1, p. 467.

Fanning, D. M. (1967) 'Families in flats', *British Medical Journal*, 4, 382–6.

Hare, E. G. and G. K. Shaw (1965) *Mental Health in a New Housing Estate*, Oxford University Press, London.

McCulloch, J. W. and A. E. Philip (1972) *Suicidal Behaviour*, Pergamon Press, Oxford.

Martin, F. M., J. H. F. Brotherston and S. P. W. Chave (1957) 'Incidence of neurosis in a new housing estate', *British Journal of Preventive and Social Medicine*, 11, pp. 196–202.

CHAPTER 11

Perceptions of environmental quality on housing estates

CONNIE BYROM

Perhaps there are other people who suffer from a kind of amnesia whenever words such as environment and quality are used; what do these expressions mean and are they at best anything more than a cover for the loosely thought out and incomplete? Like most covers they convey a sense of simplicity to something which is in fact infinitely subtle and elusive. Perusal of the professional journals reveals no shortage of expressions relating to the 'quality of the environment', but rarely does anyone try to list what is or is not included under these terms: meaning has largely to be sought through inference alone.

ENVIRONMENTAL QUALITY IN RELATION TO HOUSING ESTATES

Many features commonly mentioned under environmental quality overlap to a large extent, and it is usually the outside of dwellings which are considered in this context. One often quoted constituent of environmental quality concerns the development of open space as an integral part in the overall design and the provision of unity between the open spaces and the buildings. According to planners, architects and landscape designers, the provision and treatment of spaces between dwellings has a considerable effect not only upon general appearance but also on the way the housing group works in practice. Environmental quality certainly involves appearance, a difficult item to define in aesthetic terms but something which runs counter to 'the monotony, dreary repetition of individual units, a bleak and boring kind of orderliness' which is characteristic of so many housing estates (Bauer, 1951). A satisfactory and convenient solution for car parking both for residents and visitors (the present standard of provision of one car space per dwelling is likely to become inadequate by 1975), and the means of access for car and pedestrian somehow resolved without conflict arising between the two are other measures of environmental quality; so, too, is the provision of play facilities appropriate to the different age groups (more than two families out of five in Britain contain children under sixteen years old), carefully sited and designed to take into account the noise likely to be generated, accessibility, safety, attractiveness and so forth. Ideally, children should be free to roam the length and breadth

165

of an estate without causing nuisance to anyone. Environmental quality also concerns such intangible items as privacy, territory and individuality; somehow a balance has to be achieved between privacy for the individual on the one hand (freedom from disturbance by noise, overlooking into the house and garden, and perhaps most important of all, freedom to live one's own life without unwanted interference and intrusion from those living round about) and complete isolation on the other. A sense of belonging and involvement, and an extension of identity beyond the immediate front doorstep area are essential parts of the quality of the environment, however elusive each aspect might be. Availability of shops, transport services, schools, nursery schools and play groups, places of entertainment and worship, public houses and so on are again important features. Good environmental quality assumes a high standard of management and maintenance of the buildings and the outside spaces and a high standard of design and equipment; these are important requirements.

After a brief review of some of the general and historical aspects of environmental quality in housing, this chapter describes the results of a number of studies which have collected information on the subject from the user's point of view; the implications of the material are then discussed and a number of practical points raised. Throughout, the term 'housing estate' is used to include not only those provided by local authorities but also those built by private developers for owner occupation (about half the houses in England and Wales are owner-occupied although only twenty-nine per cent in Scotland) and by housing associations and societies for cost rent or co-ownership.

PRESENT-DAY INTEREST IN ENVIRONMENTAL QUALITY

In recent years, several people from a variety of backgrounds have drawn particular attention to the pitiful conditions of many local authority housing estates, both old and new, which seem completely devoid of anything remotely approaching good environmental quality. Their comments are curiously similar; estates are described as: 'Places of unutterable boredom, so gross, so unlovable and so unliveable' (Richardson, 1970), '. . . monstrosities of contempt for the common people: concrete deserts without amenities, thousands of people with no cinemas, no dance halls, few public houses and shops . . .' (Dewhurst, 1971), and 'Bleak windswept deserts of sterilised spaces that meet all the rules but miss the point' (Brown, 1968). It is true that many of these estates date from the time of acute housing shortage when the main aim was to complete houses as quickly as possible: the external environment was very much of secondary importance. These conditions no longer apply to anything like the same extent; as a result, we now have time for critical assessment. In particular, many people feel that the standards required within the home should be matched by ones which can be applied to the outside (Ministry of Housing and Local Government,

1961). This consideration is becoming more crucial as housing densities increase and pressure on external space becomes more acute.

A report published in 1970 by the Scottish Housing Advisory Committee entitled *Council House Communities: a Policy for Progress* has come as a timely reminder of the serious consequences of disregarding environmental quality. Evidence for this report was partly based on a number of social surveys which were carried out on various estates in Scotland. The report emphasised the need for urgent action to avoid 'the grave social and economic consequences' of the alarming and sometimes barely tolerable conditions in many local authority housing schemes in Scotland; several schemes were in fact felt to be degenerating into the slum conditions they had been designed to replace. A list of common deficiences mentioned included defects in the house plan, misuse of external space, traffic congestion, parking difficulties, lack of shops and places of entertainment, and the absence of social facilities.

The private housing sector, too, with one or two notable exceptions, has also been criticised for its poor standards of environmental design; more hopeful is the work of housing associations and societies which appear to be achieving a good reputation for well designed housing in attractive and convenient surroundings.

AN HISTORICAL PERSPECTIVE

It is too readily assumed that concern for environmental quality in housing is some new concept; certainly its relevance is now much greater as there are many more houses and estates than in the past, but interest in the environment beyond the individual dwelling goes back much further. What is so sad is that, for one reason or another, there has been a failure to take sufficient notice of what has happened before: to learn from the numerous examples of good housing coupled with good environment. It is also sad that many sound and far-sighted recommendations contained in government reports published over the years have largely gone unheeded.

The eighteenth- and nineteenth-century residential squares of London, Bath and Edinburgh, for example, are remarkable for the balance achieved between the man-made and the natural; somehow a distinctly urban and civilised quality was achieved. Lewis Mumford (1961, p. 398) considers that the order and unity of these developments were chiefly due to a unified attitude to life, the unified ownership of land and the unified control of the architect and builder.

Such developments provided gracious living for the aristocracy and the well-to-do, but the early and middle years of the nineteenth century also saw considerable effort on the part of many philanthropists who were disturbed by the cramped standards and environment of the working people, men such as Edward Akroyd, who acquired land in 1855 at Harley Hill near Halifax, and set out to develop a small town where working people could become owners of their houses, through

the assistance of the Halifax Benefit Building Society. Akroyd's desire
was to 'awaken the innate taste of the people for the beautiful in outline'
(*Builder*, 1883). John Crossley (the carpet manufacturer) was another
example with his model dwelling at West Hill Park near Halifax, as
was Sir Titus Salt, with his model village of Saltaire (his architects
were instructed to spare no expense to render the dwellings of the
operatives a pattern to the country). All these men were inspired to
create adequate space and amenity standards not only within the
dwellings but also the external environment; hence parks, open spaces,
community halls, schools and hospitals were provided. The latter part
of the century saw a further significant contribution in the attempts
by a number of individuals to work out standards for healthy, convenient and attractive houses and surroundings for houses. George
Cadbury's work at Bourneville (1879) is a notable example; here one
of the aims of the management has always been to make clear in
practice that it really does care for the good appearance of the estate.
This example was followed by a housing project developed by Joseph
Rowntree (architects: Raymond Unwin and Barry Parker) at New
Earswick, York (1901). One point of interest about New Earswick is
that ever since the first houses were completed the residents have been
consulted about the development of the village and their views sought
about the design of the houses. Lord Leverhulme's work at Port Sunlight (1888) provides another example.

The concept of an all-embracing social community, integrating
design of dwellings with their surroundings, was to follow in the
Garden Cities of Letchworth (1903), Welwyn (1920) and Hampstead
Garden Suburb (1925); great emphasis was placed on the need to provide social and cultural facilities and on residents' participation. In the
opinion of one well-known landscape designer, Ian McHarg (1956), the
garden city movement represented the peak of British influence in
the field of housing and its distinction lay not in the architecture but in
the quality of the environment created.

When the Housing and Town Planning Act of 1919 first introduced
a state subsidy for housing and thus launched local authority housing
as it is known today, awareness and concern for environmental quality
did not suddenly cease. Indeed, the Tudor Walters Report (Local
Government Board, 1918) of the preceding year stressed the need for
full advantage to be taken of all the opportunities offered by a site and
that 'It is not enough merely to cover the ground with streets and
houses'. Thus it was felt that, in the planning of housing schemes,
suitable land should be reserved for larger houses, shops, schools,
business premises, places of worship, clubs, institutions and for open
space and playgrounds.

Several council house estates later, a not dissimilar set of comments
was being repeated in the Dudley Report published in 1944 (Ministry
of Health, 1944). This report states that 'good design implies good
layout, good internal arrangement, good equipment and good appear-

ance. It is the lack of design that has produced so much dreary and monotonous development in the past. Our evidence shows a widespread if rather inarticulate dissatisfaction with this state of affairs and an innate desire for well ordered and pleasant surroundings.' The mistakes made in the planning and layout of estates in the interwar years are listed: these include the development of large estates where private and municipal housing are conspicuously separated; insufficient attention to the provision of schools, clubs, shops, churches, open spaces and other amenities; the location of estates too far from the tenants' places of work; too rigid interpretation of density zoning, resulting in insufficient variety of types of dwelling; lack of smaller open spaces and playgrounds; and 'the failure to appreciate the value to a neighbourhood of good design applied not only to the houses themselves but to their setting'. The report stressed that more attention should be paid to the satisfactory grouping of buildings in relation to each other.

In 1948 the Central Housing Advisory Committee produced a report entitled: *The Appearance of Housing Estates* (Faringdon Report). At the R.I.B.A. conference in the same year, which took as its theme housing layouts, J. H. Forshaw (Chief Architect, Ministry of Health) in reply to a question why such a report was necessary, said that 'the answer is written across the face of all the dreary localities in which so many of the English people have their homes. This is the first time that the state has made a comprehensive effort to improve the visual quality and amenity of housing'. Aneurin Bevan (then Minister of Health) also addressed the conference and stated his own belief that 'If people live in squalid and ugly surroundings, or even in unimaginative and unbeautiful surroundings, it profoundly affects their spiritual and mental character'. The Faringdon Report contained twenty-six small but important recommendations for improving the appearance of estates; these included such items as the colour washing of walls, the use of climbing plants, the planting of forest trees, and advice being available to tenants on simple garden layout.

Much time has elapsed since these reports were published, yet the message has changed little over the years. The familiar expressions continue to be repeated at intervals . . . the need for a suitable variety of dwellings, the need for open space near dwellings, the need for dwellings to be conveniently sited in relation to shops, schools and open spaces, the need for housing areas as a whole to be conveniently sited in position and scale to the rest of the town (Ministry of Housing and Local Government, 1952, p. 2); the need for the designer to meet requirements of access, off-street parking, garages, children's play space, community buildings, and to provide at the same time 'an attractive landscape environment as a setting for the buildings and for outdoor activity' (Ministry of Housing and Local Government, 1958); the need for space about buildings to be well designed ('Areas of asphalt separated by stretches of worn and neglected grass are not the right setting for a modern home' (Ministry of Housing and Local Government,

1967)) and so on and so forth. Since the 1950s (when new types of layout and multi-storey developments began to make their impact) more attention has been focused on environmental design in relation to high density housing and there is now more talk of 'landscaping', but apart from these features, little change in the overall tone can be detected; the basic ingredients of environmental quality have not, it seems, greatly altered.

THE USER'S POINT OF VIEW

So far little comment has been made on the extent to which residents of housing estates are themselves aware of the environment outside their own home, or what in fact environmental quality means to them—if anything. How far is the quest for environmental quality which has been haphazardly pursued over the years really desired by the public, what kind of value is placed upon it and is it, in fact, something which is worth making a fuss about anyway?

As far as is known, there have been no studies specifically concerned with the perception of environmental quality on housing estates; but there is information, based on a number of investigations designed with other aims in mind, which bears on the subject. In assessing the material, it must be remembered that people vary a great deal in their sensitivity to the environment and that many factors can condition and influence response, for example, age, stage in the life cycle, social class, and a person's own experience and knowledge of housing. Account must also be taken of the fact that, until fairly recently, user studies in housing research have concentrated mainly on design requirements within the home rather than within the estate as a whole, and that more work has been done with local authority tenants than with other groups of occupiers. At best, the present state of knowledge is still very incomplete.

Rather than become entangled by all the different elements which contribute to environmental quality this discussion concentrates mainly on one feature, the appearance of housing estates; this in itself seems to encompass many of the other aspects and some interesting material is available on it. One of the earlier studies in which information about tenant response to appearance is recorded and discussed was carried out in the 1950s by the Building Research Station in one of the larger Scottish burghs (Hole, 1959). The new estate, a fairly low density one, consisted of three-storey blocks of flats and two-storey houses built in groups of two and four. At the time of the interviews, one section of the estate was still being used as a municpial rubbish dump and litter blown from it lay strewn about the streets; in the middle of the estate was a large disused colliery bing. Tenants had moved from nineteenth-century tenement property. During a series of interviews which were conducted with a sample of residents in their first year on the scheme, almost no spontaneous comments were recorded about these unsightly features, and the monotonous effect of houses in block layout prompted little criticism. Similar attitudes to the external appearance of an estate had apparently been found in another survey (also in a Scottish town) undertaken by the Building Research Station at about the same time. Here one section of the estate consisted of three and four storey blocks of flats of similar design and arranged in rows on either side of the street; in a separate section, a small site had been designed by the architect in a coherent plan. Existing trees and shrubs were retained wherever possible and the blocks of maisonettes and old people's dwellings were grouped around an open courtyard with the object of affording a sunny aspect combined with privacy in all the living rooms. In discussing these two different forms of layout the tenants failed to distinguish between the part which followed the older style of local authority design and that which was more in keeping with the layout standards then recommended (Department of Health for Scotland, 1958). The retention of trees and shrubs in the second example was, in fact, criticised because of the resulting untidiness from leaves, twigs and insects. Although the external appearance of the dwellings and the estates studied prompted so little critical response, the research worker felt that this was largely because tenants were not only unfamiliar with better standards of housing layout and design but also tended to dissociate themselves from the layout and general appearance as it was something beyond their control; a common remark made was in fact: 'the outside doesn't really matter, it's the inside that counts'. Indeed, it was found that most tenants had taken a lively interest in the interiors of their dwellings and this at least was thought to be an encouraging sign.

Up to a point, satisfaction with the new home itself appears to divert or at least offset some of the finer feelings residents may have for the outside appearance and environment which, in any case, is outwith their control. F. Zweig, in his study of Cumbernauld, (1970), found that, when householders were asked what they liked about the New Town, they tended to give three typical replies, viz., the clean fresh air, ideal for kids, and a comfortable house, with often an added remark to the effect that the house was 'drab outside but nice inside'. Thus, in a study carried out by the Architecture Research Unit (Byrom, 1966) of a local authority scheme of single storey courtyard houses at Prestonpans, it was found that most tenants had at least some misgivings about the uncompromising external appearance of the scheme; however, these did not appear to count for much in the assessment of general satisfaction, largely because the houses themselves were well liked. After a year on the scheme most housewives had, in fact, begun to take the appearance for granted, or as one resident remarked: 'If you're indoors it doesn't bother you.'

Nevertheless, evidence from a number of recent studies carried out by the Sociological Research Section of the Department of the Environment indicates that the awareness of tenants of the outside appearance of their estates is now becoming much more critical and it seems to form a major component of the satisfaction of residents with the environment. One of these studies, based on three high-density estates at Liverpool, London and Leeds, which included low-, medium- and high-rise dwellings, found that attitudes to the estate centred to a great extent on the appearance and upkeep of the estates, on their surroundings, on play facilities, on relations with neighbours and on access to shops, schools and work (Ministry of Housing and Local Government, 1970). In a later investigation, 'the layout study' (which looked at various features within housing layouts, such as arrangements for car parking, refuse, children's play and open space), information was collected from a sample of housewives living on six high-density estates (Reynolds and Nicholson, 1969); the results of this survey showed that satisfaction with the estates was closely related to whether the housewives thought the estates were attractive and well-maintained, and whether they liked the views from the living room and kitchen (Telford, 1970). This was so whether respondents lived on or off the ground. An attractive estate to these housewives was one with light, bright colours, not too enclosed, with trees, grass and flowers, where there was a variety of buildings and spaces, and where the standards of detailing, finish and maintenance were high. In general, residents were less satisfied with their estates than with their dwellings. One further study carried out by the Sociological Research Section on four high-density low-rise estates, appears to confirm these previous findings (Burbridge, 1971). Again, it was found that tenants satisfied with the estate outside the dwelling tended to find their estates attractive. In particular, they liked the approach to their front door, the appearance of the blocks of flats, the appearance and size of the open space between the blocks and the colour of the bricks, and in that order of importance.

A case study undertaken by the Architecture Research Unit in 1968 has also revealed some interesting information on the subject of appearance and response to the estate outside the dwelling (Byrom, 1969). This study, which was commissioned by the Scottish Special Housing Association, looked particularly at the condition and usage of open space on a 9·5 acre local authority housing scheme at Niddrie Mill in Edinburgh, in order to make recommendations for carrying out improvements. The scheme was completed and occupied in 1957 and consists of 35 identical blocks of 3-storey flats at a density of about 97 bed spaces per acre; 18 of the blocks are grouped to form two large courtyards. The site lies some three miles east of the city centre and adjoins a similar but much larger scheme of local authority flatted houses built between 1930 and 1936 to rehouse families displaced by slum clearance and generally regarded as a tough and undesirable area. The study was largely prompted by the anxiety among officials responsible for housing management that a prevalence of rent arrears among the tenants of Niddrie Mill and a low standard of upkeep of gardens and drying greens might be indications that this newer scheme was being blighted by the reputation of its older neighbour (see also Chap. 12). Information about the estate was collected from several sources, including a tenant survey based on a one in four random sample of all the dwellings. On the subject of the scheme's appearance, the findings showed that only twenty per cent of the informants expressed dislike of it and most of the points which would have caught an architect's eye were largely passed over. No one, for instance, seemed very aware of the lack of an adequate balance of established planting, only a small number sensed monotony in the layout and only two felt any awkwardness in the relationship of blocks at street corners. Of those informants who liked the scheme's appearance, most singled out the balconies as its best feature (balconies being one of the features which distinguishes this scheme from the older Corporation estate referred to) in spite of the clutter of items stored in them. On the other hand, most informants had decided views on what should be done to improve the scheme's appearance; suggestions centred on the need for open spaces to be tidied up, for the size of gardens to be reduced and for doors to be fitted to the stairways. Perhaps the most worthwhile aspect of this study was the overall attitude shown by those interviewed; the majority appeared to be good tenants who had spent considerable time, money and energy in improving their homes. But their concern did not stop here; most were undoubtedly very much aware of the external environment even although their level of perception was fairly limited in aesthetic terms. They were certainly quite clear about the estate's inadequacies—the lack of children's play facilities, storage and off-street parking, the untidy open spaces and the complete failure of the drying greens. Many expressed considerable dismay at their inability to bring about any improvement.

All the data quoted so far have been confined to local authority housing. Evidence from studies of owner occupiers suggests, not surprisingly, that those buying in the lower price ranges are mainly concerned with the house itself and its price while those in more expensive houses consider environmental reasons as well when they come to choose a house (Todd, 1969; Urban Land Institute, 1966). Some firms, notably Wates and Span, have pioneered a new concept of environment in speculative housing estates by providing landscaped open space maintained communally by the house purchasers; both firms refer in their publicity to the quality of the environment provided in their estates. Follow-up studies of a number of these estates have shown that, although residents were initially attracted to the estates because of the houses themselves (modern, easy to run, the right price, the right area), they do come to appreciate and value the high standards of the layout and landscaping and this contributes substantially to their overall satisfaction (Research Services Ltd., 1965; Shankland Cox and Associates, 1969). Opinions about the general appearance of these schemes seem to be almost identical to the opinions expressed about the landscaping and planting, and the better landscaped areas were always more popular. Rather interestingly, the studies found that whenever architecture was mentioned it was criticised; the authors concluded that, on the whole, people were more satisfied when landscaping and plants masked the buildings.

Concern for environmental quality in housing is no new cause; it has been pursued over the years with little real success. There are a few scattered examples of good housing coupled with a good environment and a legacy of government reports all testifying to the need for higher standards in the external environment; yet in all forms of housing the achievements are far from impressive. Failure to learn from past experience is indeed one of the most worrying aspects.

At present we are experiencing another wave of 'something must be done', but are the signs any more hopeful now than they were twenty years or so ago, when the Faringdon Report was published? To some extent they are. In the first place, it does seem, from the evidence of the various studies quoted, that there is an increasing awareness of the environment outside the home and that it does matter to people; a higher standard of living, a higher standard of education and better press and television coverage should help to foster this awareness and at least make for a much more demanding and critical public. There are very real signs that this is already happening; some councils are now embarrassed by a number of 'choosey' applicants on their lists who refuse the offer of houses on certain estates with the reputation for inferior housing in all senses of the word. Secondly, there is perhaps a greater sense of urgency and pressure now than previously: rehabilitation work on housing schemes with environmental deficiencies is recognised as a costly business and at best no more than an expensive facelift; to continue creating similarly deficient estates just does not make sense.

When all the material is assessed it is difficult to escape the conclusion that, while the precise nature of environmental quality may be difficult to define, people as individuals think they have a fairly shrewd idea of what it is all about, of when an estate has it or does not and of the extent to which it is important or otherwise. Undoubtedly there is room for much more research into the different orders of priority people attach to obtaining various features in their environment, yet there is sufficient evidence that, for the most part, present-day standards of environmental quality are not good enough. What can be done?

First, it is necessary to aim at better standards of design outside the immediate dwelling and be prepared to pay more generously for it. The value of professional advice in the design of open spaces in housing is now fully recognised, but all too often only lip service is paid to it. Secondly, the management and maintenance of outside areas is of critical importance; no matter how good the original design, damage of all kinds will immediately increase if standards deteriorate. Where there is any ambiguity about responsibility for maintenance, conditions are likely to deteriorate all the faster. The higher the densities, the higher must be the standards of maintenance and management; intensity of use is bound to lead to more wear and tear and more money will be needed to keep the open spaces and communal facilities up to standard. As a third suggestion it seems that greater participation by local authority tenants in management decisions, particularly where these relate to improvements, can only be of benefit; they need to be much more involved than they are at present and to have a greater control over the external environment. A private member's bill introduced into Parliament by Mr. Dick Leonard in 1971 (Council Housing Tenants Representation Bill), which provides for housing advisory committees to be set up with council tenant members, indicates one possibility: these committees could deal with matters such as repairs, colour schemes for external painting, layout of open spaces and children's playgrounds. Another proposal first put forward by Della Nevitt is that a National Tenants Association should be set up which would perform the same service for its members as the Automobile Association does for the motorist (Morton, 1971). Fourthly, it would certainly help if there was more co-operation and exchange of criticisms and ideas between planners, architects, landscape designers, engineers, housing administrators and sociologists at different stages in housing projects. This does happen occasionally, but not very often. A crucial problem today is the failure of architects to recognise the design implications of management policy and of management to appreciate the significance of new forms of housing layout. How many architects, or even housing committees, ever return to have a good look at their own work. There is so much to be learnt from just walking round on estates that it is a pity this is not done much more often. Finally, the private developer is not likely to change his habits without a great deal more pressure, either through the general public (a slow process) or through planning authorities being more alert and demanding in their standards. Some authorities are doing a lot to encourage environmental quality in housing developments; alas, they are all too few.

Colin Buchanan and Partners, who have recently completed a report for the Nationwide Building Society (1971), have come to the conclusion that four out of every ten inhabitants of Great Britain live in areas that do not meet present-day environmental needs; however, they have sufficient faith 'in the resilience and energy of our society' to believe that the country will achieve the kind of housing it needs for a 'fuller and richer life'. How justified is such optimism?

REFERENCES

Bauer, C. (1951) 'Social questions in housing and community planning', *Journal of Social Issues*, 7 (1 & 2), p. 20.

Bevan, A. (1948) 'Housing layout in theory and practice', *Royal Institute of British Architects Journal*, 55 (9), p. 383.

Brown, M. (1968) 'Landscape and housing', *Housing Review*, 17 (3), p. 96.

Buchanan, Colin & Partners (1971) *The Prospect for Housing*, Nationwide Building Society, London.

Builder, The (1883), 21, p. 110.

Burbridge, M. (1971) 'Low rise high density housing', *Official Architecture and Planning*, 34 (4), April, p. 278.

Byrom, J. B. (1966) *Courtyard Houses, Inchview, Prestonpans*, Architecture Research Unit, The University, Edinburgh.

Byrom, J. B. (1969) 'Rehabilitation case study: Niddrie Mill, Edinburgh', *Housing Review*, 18 (3), pp. 89–96.

Central Housing Advisory Committee (1948) *The Appearance of Housing Estates*, (Faringdon Report), H.M.S.O., London.

Department of Health for Scotland (1958) Scottish Housing Handbook, No. 1, *Housing Layout*, H.M.S.O., Edinburgh.

Dewhurst, K. (1971) 'Bath without getting wet', *Guardian*, January 27th, p. 8.

Dewhurst, R. (1960) 'Saltaire', *Town Planning Review*, 31 (2), p. 138.

Forshaw, J. H. (1948) 'Application of principles in layout', *Royal Institute of British Architects Journal*, 55 (9), p. 387.

Hole, V. (1959) 'Social effects of planned rehousing', *Town Planning Review*, 30 (2), July, pp. 161–73.

Local Government Board for England and Wales and Scotland (1918) *Report of the Committee Appointed to Consider the Question of Building Construction in Connection with the Provision of Dwellings for the Working Class*, (Tudor Walters Report), Cmd. 9191, H.M.S.O., London.

McHarg, I. (1956) 'Can we afford open space?', *Architects' Journal*, 123, p. 261.

Ministry of Health (1944) *The Design of Dwellings*, (Dudley report), p. 10, H.M.S.O., London.

Ministry of Housing and Local Government (1952) *The Density of Residential Areas*, H.M.S.O., London.

Ministry of Housing and Local Government (1958) *Flats and Houses: Design and Economy*, H.M.S.O., London.

Ministry of Housing and Local Government (1961) *Homes for Today and Tomorrow*, Report of a Sub-Committee of the Central Housing Advisory Committee, (Parker Morris report), H.M.S.O., London.

Ministry of Housing and Local Government (1967) *Landscaping for Flats*, Design Bulletin 5, p. 2, H.M.S.O., London.

Ministry of Housing and Local Government (1970) *Families Living at High Densities: a Study of Estates in Leeds, Liverpool and London*, Design Bulletin 21, H.M.S.O., London.

Morton, J. (1971) 'Society at work: in defence of amalgamated tenants associations co-ordinating committee', *New Society*, 441, pp. 396–7.

Mumford, L. (1961) *The City in History*, Martin Secker and Warburg Limited, London.

Research Services Limited (1965) *Living on a Wates Estate*, Research Services Limited, London.

Reynolds I. and C. Nicholson (1969) 'Living off the ground', *Architects' Journal*, 150 (34), p. 460.

Richardson, M. (1970) Letter in *Royal Institute of British Architects Journal*, 77 (10), p. 441.

Scottish Housing Advisory Committee (1970) *Council House Communities: a Policy for Progress*, H.M.S.O., Edinburgh.

Shankland Cox and Associates (1969) *Private Housing in London: People and Environment in 3 Wates Housing Schemes*, Shankland & Cox, London.

Telford, A. (1970) *Criteria for Sunshine, Daylight, Visual Privacy and View in Housing*, Social Science Research Council project, Internal progress report, June, Department of Building Science, Strathclyde University.

Todd, A. (1969) *New Home Owners in Kent Villages*. First report for Span (Kent) Limited, University of Kent, Canterbury.

Urban Land Institute (1966) *Open Space Communities in the Market Place*, Technical Bulletin 57, Washington.

Zweig, F. (1970) *The Cumbernauld Study*, Urban Research Bureau, Wates Limited, London.

CHAPTER 12

Environmental perceptions in a deprived area

UNA MACLEAN

Raymond Pahl has recently stressed the importance of investigating the life styles of distinctive groups in the population. But it is not only urban sociologists who are concerned with such studies, for, from the point of social medicine, research can cast light upon the operation of the health and welfare service in parts of cities which are known to possess a large number of special medical and social problems. In such places the way in which potential clients or patients view the various available services will affect the differential use they make of them, influencing their decisions as to where or whether to seek help for difficulties in their private lives.

The very designation of certain districts as 'problem areas', 'urban ghettoes' or 'socially deprived neighbourhoods' constitutes a derogatory labelling process which serves to perpetuate the stigma attaching to residence there. The prevailing odium cannot fail to be felt by the people concerned, so that those who live or work in a part of town which is habitually deplored by the larger community are obliged to add the consciousness of a bad public image to their own total perception of the environment. So an investigation into the manner in which certain dwellers in a municipal housing estate conceptualise their social and physical situation may be rewarding from other angles, too, illustrating what the 'quality of life' implies for those who dwell far from the homes of most middle-class environmentalists and indicating how they manage to come to terms with both the practical and psychological frustrations of their enforced station. Any effort to alter or ameliorate the circumstances in which many members of the local community presently exist should ideally take cognisance of their personal response to their surroundings and ought to enlist their active co-operation.

However, one of the paradoxes of this recurring theme (which is so familiar to the modern practice of preventive medicine) lies in the fact that the very people who most need help may be the least able to communicate their needs or effectively to criticise existing agencies or institutions, whose official aims they may not fully comprehend and whose activities frequently appear to be arbitrary and confusing. The profession of medicine is an ancient one and, although the public's view of medicine may well be out of date, incomplete or unrealistic, people have had centuries in which to formulate their conception of the doctor's role in society, so that there is a fair degree of consensus over the physician's supposed ability to help and heal a wide variety of human misfortunes. The public image of social work, on the other hand, is probably considerably more vague and ambivalent, relating to a very new profession whose own spokesmen have been known to disagree about primary aims. There is, for instance, still some debate between the exponents of a purely welfare role for social workers, who are to concentrate upon directing clients towards the appropriate sources of practical aid, and those who stress the psychotherapeutic function of long-term case work.

THE RESEARCH AREA

The research reported in this chapter relates to a large ward on the outskirts of the City of Edinburgh. Now housing over 24,000 inhabitants, it has grown rapidly since its original establishment as a municipal housing estate during slum clearing operations in the 1930s. The original long terraces of three-storeyed buildings, sub-divided into flats, have now been supplemented, as fashions have changed, by a succession of architectural styles, including some blocks of high-rise flats and groups of attractive single dwellings.

The older parts of the estate convey a desolate impression of neglect and dilapidation. The windows of unoccupied flats are boarded up against the depredations of 'vandals', few gardens survive and the open spaces are strewn with rubbish and broken glass. The area is generally short of amenities, shopping facilities are limited and a journey to town is necessary to secure anything but the barest essentials. Added to these physical limitations, which the area shares with many similar council housing estates in industrial Scotland, is the unfortunate reputation which it holds in the eyes of the rest of Edinburgh. It is a discredited and discreditable place, regarded by horrified middle-class citizens as a hot-bed of crime and, moreover, the resort to which the city housing department is reputed to send all 'problem families'. The old stereotype of 'slum clearance' has not faded with time and most current accounts of the area act as a self-fulfilling prophesy, confirming its long-standing notoriety.

At the time when municipal housing schemes were first begun in Scotland the relationship between poor living conditions and social problems of one kind or another had been realised. It was appreciated that infectious diseases generally and tuberculosis in particular spread more easily in overcrowded and insanitary surroundings. A naively optimistic spirit expected the relief of many social ills from the simple expedient of transplanting large sections of the population from the old city tenements to suburban green fields. Today it is no longer possible to believe in such simple solutions to the inequalities of urban existence and, although both health and living standards generally have improved enormously over the past forty years, society still experiences and maintains marked gradients and disparities in regard to both physical morbidity and social pathology.

Initially it was the health problem of this urban community which attracted the most attention. Shortly after the inauguration of the National Health Service in 1948, S. A. Sklaroff and L. Stein (1952) conducted an investigation among a sample of households. The picture of health and sickness which they uncovered led them to conclude that there were differences in group perceptions of what constituted 'conspicuous sickness', the kind of disturbances likely to prompt medical consultation. The authors considered that measurements of sickness in different communities might differ because of their relationship to group characteristics and attitudes, and that they could only be interpreted in the light of detailed knowledge of local norms.

Since then considerable numbers of research projects have focussed upon the area, probably the most influential being that undertaken by the Medical Research Council Unit for Research in the Epidemiology of Mental Illness (Philip and McCulloch, 1966; Hope, 1969 and Chap. 10). Each ward of the city was ranked according to its position on a scale built up from a number of social indices. These were calculated from many existing sources of data including, for example, rent arrears and eviction notices, children taken into care, adolescent psychiatric referrals, incidents of self-poisoning or attempted suicide, juvenile delinquency, truancy and perinatal mortality.

On the basis of multiple statistical correlations it was clearly demonstrated that this particular ward constituted an area of high social morbidity. Although this had always been suspected, its confirmation in strictly measurable terms was sufficient to convince the local health committee of the need for positive action and a 'Health, Welfare and Advice Centre' was established in the ward in 1968. In spite of its title, however, the permanent health component of the Centre was a limited one, being confined to the attachment of mental health officers and health visitors, both being employees of the local authority. The welfare side was represented by child care officers, social workers and probation officers, as well as representatives of a variety of voluntary agencies, such as the Royal Scottish Society for Prevention of Cruelty to Children. Advice came from Marriage Guidance Councils of different denominations and the Citizens Advice Bureau. An official of the City Rents Department was also attached. The development of this multidisciplinary social casework centre took place before the Social Work (Scotland) Act came into force in 1968. Since then it has become the headquarters of an area team.

It is important to realise that such a Centre does not yet assemble all the possible agents of social welfare and social control. General practitioners and district nurses, officials of the Department of Health and Social Security, local teachers, the police, lawyers, clergy, town councillors and a local Member of Parliament are all involved in decisions affecting the health and happiness of families in the community. In addition, numerous voluntary associations play a significant part in the lives of the local inhabitants making, in some cases, a very determined effort to improve local conditions and change the community's image in the eyes of the rest of Edinburgh.

A psychiatrist who was temporarily attached to the Centre during the early months of its operation reviewed the characteristics of the clients at that time (Ebie 1971). He found that they were predominantly married women of child-bearing age, mainly belonging to Social Classes IV and V. Amongst clients whose personal and expressed concern was to obtain material help, social workers frequently discerned psychological problems and referred them to the psychiatrist for assessment. In fact, 73 per cent of their problems were seen by the clients themselves to be material ones. Ebie was puzzled by the disparity between the views of social workers and clients regarding the underlying nature of the latter's problems and he put forward some possible explanations. For example, material problems might be masking or producing psychological ones; the client's psychological problems might be receiving attention elsewhere; or, possibly, the client did not expect the Centre to handle her psychological problems. All these suggestions, however, implied the ability of clients to conceptualise and differentiate 'psychological problems', a matter relatively easy for a psychiatrist or social worker, but presenting considerable difficulties for women lacking the education and language thus to express their personal experiences. Moreover, material problems might well be burdensome in such a district.

THE SAMPLE SURVEY

From a number of counts it seemed as though the views of the community from which the clients came would be worth exploring, but it was not feasible, for practical reasons, to interview a random sample of the entire population. Consideration of the clientèle made it clear that women with family responsibilities were conscious of many problems, however defined. It was therefore decided to study a group of mothers who had recently entered a five-year-old child in school. These women formed a distinct and manageable group, identifiable from school records. Their responsibilities in relation to a young child would probably preclude them from employment outside the home, which would consequently absorb their main attention. Their views on the practical difficulties of raising a young family in a despised and deprived neighbourhood and their ideas about where or when they should seek help might be of more than passing interest, since the mothers' behaviour in the face of problems would form part of their own childrens' early experience, encouraging the perpetuation of local attitudes and norms.

Starting, therefore, from an informal enquiry into the characteristics of current attenders at the clinic, the investigation was to move out and concentrate upon a chosen group of women. Discussions with the social worker directing the area team suggested that, by early 1971, there had been little change in the nature of the problems with which the staff were confronted. The material dilemmas felt by their clients were certainly no less; the threat of evictions involved the team in vigorous and time-consuming exertions every week on behalf of families in immediate danger of homelessness; much time was spent, especially in the New Year, on dealing with people unable to pay their gas and electricity bills. It was estimated that at least three-quarters of the calls for help were still prompted by immediate material problems.

It is important to remember that those who did approach the centre for help constituted a self-selected group, whose experience need not be representative of the entire ward. Impressions formed from studying the sick should not prejudice one's picture of the healthy. Only the examination of those who are not presently seeking help can contribute to a comprehensive picture of community well-being.

But even the views of potential consumers of supportive social services, like busy mothers, will be partial and one-sided. As has been mentioned, however valuable their opinions and personal reactions, they may lack both depth and precision in the telling. So the opportunity ought to be taken to interview some of the providers of services, such as workers at the centre, general practitioners, police, local councillors and others. A further group of people whose views certainly could not be ignored were the local Festival Society. Begun for the limited purpose of organising an annual gala or summer fair, this voluntary organisation had gone on to concern itself with a multitude of pressing local issues, attracting public attention for its serious aims as well as funds for a system of community self-help through neighbourhood workers and aides.

In brief, the method of this enquiry entailed structured interviews with 141 mothers of five-year-olds (available out of the total of 165 drawn from school admission lists) and less formal discussions in depth with representatives of the other categories of helping agents who have been detailed. The interview material was supplemented by available literature, such as that produced by the Festival Society for regular distribution in the area and beyond. The content of the questionnaires will become clear in the course of the following account of some of the results which have been obtained.

Although a proportion of the families (14%) had left the district by the time the interviewers called, there was, on the other hand, a solid corps of respondents (25%) who had lived their whole lives in Craigmillar. This recalled one finding of the much earlier study, in 1952, which drew attention to the tendency for young couples at that time to seek their own accommodation near the parental home which had been their first married lodging.

Ninety-nine per cent of the mothers fell into the age group 20–44 and closely corresponded to those who visited the Centre for help and advice. Thirty-eight per cent had their own mother living less than a mile away, that is to say, in the same housing estate. Twenty-eight per cent belonged to social class V, a large proportion when compared with the figures for Edinburgh as a whole (16 %), but less than the proportion in social class V among Centre attenders (38%). Most of the women's husbands had experienced frequent periods of unemployment over the past five years; the majority of the mothers (67%) did not go out to work themselves and very few took part in any kind of organised social activities or clubs.

VIEWS OF MOTHERS

The results of the enquiries into the mothers' feelings about certain aspects of their environment have been summarised in respect of items upon which two-thirds or more of the women were in agreement. In respect of the physical environment, at least two-thirds of the respondents were agreed regarding:

The gross neglect of the neighbourhood by the local authority.

The unsuitability of the area for child-rearing.

The absence of safe play spaces nearby.

The preferability of the area to the city centre.

The fact that housing was not, for them, a matter of personal choice.

The primary and frequent complaints related to the state of the access roads and the common ground about the houses; strewn with rubbish and broken glass and with the pavements poorly maintained, they constituted a constant hazard to small children at play. If children roamed further afield they might be bullied or interfered with and, moreover, the adjacent railway line was inadequately fenced and no play equipment was ever kept in order or supervised. Even with all these disadvantages, however, most of the mothers would not wish to return to rented accommodation in the centre of town.

But the women felt strongly that they had been presented with no proper choice of accommodation, simply told, 'You go there . . . or nowhere'. Just over half remarked rather plaintively that, if it was possible, they would prefer to live in the country. In this respect their desires approximate to those of many members of the middle class, but they are realistic enough to realise that fate has determined otherwise.

The social environment, the behaviour of neighbours, the accessibility of relatives and the felt atmosphere of friendliness or rejection deeply affect people's estimates of their living conditions. Along these parameters, at least two-thirds of the mothers were agreed regarding:

The desirability of having their own mother nearby.

The likeableness of most neighbours.

Their opinion that it was only a few families which gave the neighbourhood a bad name.

The fact that neighbours greatly affected one's personal satisfaction
with housing.

They were explicit in their criticism of certain kinds of 'bad neighbours',
those who were interfering and would not mind their own business,
who constantly made complaints, who would not control their own
children. They also took exception to people who were noisy and swore,
they even complained of 'hippies', and they reiterated the feeling that
it was impossible to bring children up in a 'bad neighbourhood'.

The mothers were given an opportunity to respond to statements
about their own role. In respect of certain aspects of child-rearing and
mothers' roles there was agreement among at least two-thirds on the
following items:

The mother is central to her family's well-being.
The woman exercises the most effect on the home.
The ways their own mother brought up her family was best.
A mother should have a job outside the home.
Poverty provokes a feeling of general hopelessness and makes marital
discord more likely.

Few had managed, as we have seen, to get employment but, probably
for financial reasons in the main, they felt a keen desire for work. The
pressure of poverty was very real to them and they made repeated
complaints about the overall lack of job opportunity in the neighbourhood and their husbands' precarious employment prospects.

One of the statements put to the mothers was to the effect that no-one
felt ashamed of living there, it was no worse than any other part of
town. They tended to agree but, on the other hand, they accepted that
it did have a very bad name that was to the disadvantage of anyone
admitting to being a local resident. Blame for this state of affairs was
variously attributed, some accusing the few 'bad' families who contrasted with the general run of respectable neighbours, whilst others
were inclined to implicate supercilious outsiders. In summary, at least
two-thirds agreed that:

The area was no worse than other housing estates.
The area's bad name derived from a few families.
To live there was a bad social label.
Such a derogatory label is difficult to remove.

Finally, in relation to ideas on possible participation in decisions
affecting the neighbourhood, two-thirds were agreed that:

Local residents should have the right to be consulted.
There was an overriding need for more jobs locally.
Tenants should get together to make their influence felt.
There were some sources of help available to them locally.
Self-help and initiative were needed.

The women who held these views were, it will be recalled, mostly very far from having any part in decision-making at present, being neither workers nor members of active voluntary associations.

Another section of the enquiry focussed on chosen sources of help with specific family problems. They covered some situations which might have caused disquiet in middle-class households, such as shop-lifting by a schoolboy son. In this instance, 72 per cent regarded such behaviour as fairly common, although calling possibly for peremptory chastisement. Presented with several imaginary difficulties which might have prompted either social or medical help, the tendency was for the doctor to be the preferred source of advice. An incidental finding, of special interest, related to the mothers' experience of people who had resorted to an overdose of tablets in an attempt to deal with some emotional problem. The phenomenon of 'self-poisoning', or 'para-suicide' as it is sometimes termed, has been closely studied in Edin-burgh and the area of the present survey had been found to feature the highest rates for the city. When asked about their experience of this kind of behaviour, 22 per cent of the mothers had encountered it in an acquaintance and 16 per cent had experienced it in their own family.

VIEWS OF HELPERS

Apart from the mothers, who were potential recipients of help and advice, certain helpers, in the person of workers at the Advice Centre were questioned, utilising sections of the same questionnaire which the women had answered. As a result it was possible to find the matters upon which both groups were substantially in agreement and those where their views conflicted. The results of this section of the enquiry are summarised in the following tables.

It is clear that, whereas there was substantial agreement on all these points, on certain issues the Centre workers were more positive than the mothers (Table 1). For example, the Centre workers were more conscious of the area's bad image than were the residents. This attitude was confirmed by the response of 'helpers' to a question asking whether they personally would ever contemplate living there. With one excep-tion they all rejected such a suggestion. It is a little surprising that the proportion of helpers who agreed that 'everyone can improve their own situation if they try hard enough' was lower than that of the mothers. On the whole, the philosophy of social work encourages self-help and seeks to bolster the client's self-reliance. On the other hand, social workers may see themselves as vital intermediaries in this process.

The topics on which helpers and helped disagreed have been illus-trated in Table 2.

In some ways the disagreements are more revealing than the topics on which both agree. Perhaps it is not surprising that the helpers place more blame for children's derelictions upon parents than the latter are ready to assume. Again, the helpers' point of view on mothers working

TABLE 1. *Topics on which both helpers and helped were in broad agreement*

Topic	Mothers		Centre workers	
	% agreeing	% disagreeing	% agreeing	% disagreeing
Local Authority neglect of area	66	44	68	32
Lack of local job opportunities for men	92	8	94	6
Stigma consequent upon residence in area	78	22	100	0
If rents were lower most peoples' problems would disappear	36	64	24	76
Poverty increases likelihood of mental disorder	83	17	88	12
Children suffer more than adults from bad housing	75	25	61	39
Difficulty of bringing up children in a bad neighbourhood	61	39	82	18
Mothers prime influence on children's future character	67	33	77	23
Importance of self-help in trying to improve domestic situation	93	7	71	29
Importance of encouraging local participation in decision making	96	4	100	0

TABLE 2. *Topics on which helpers and helped disagreed*

Topic	Mothers		Helpers	
	% agreeing	% disagreeing	% agreeing	% disagreeing
Usually parents' fault if children get into trouble	41	59	62	38
Desirable for mother to have an outside job	71	29	50	50
Most wives know their husbands' earnings	61	39	44	56
Family happiness does not depend on earnings	54	46	88	12
No one ashamed of living in the area	67	33	23	87
A few families stigmatise the area	89	11	53	47
Housing department deliberately sends 'problem families' to the area	50	50	79	21
Once a district gets a bad name not much can be done about it	84	16	30	70

away from home can be interpreted in terms of the wide experience of child neglect which social workers in such districts are likely to have had. When it comes to the father's pay packet, the Centre workers seem to hold the popular stereotype of the working class. But, of course, wives who believe they know the state of their family finances may be deceived. The helpers and helped take different views on the relevance of money to family happiness; the Centre workers probably think more in terms of adjusting to difficult circumstances and learning to cope, whereas the mothers are less inclined to under-estimate the effects of material deprivation. Once more, the question on stigma reflects the revulsion from their working environment felt by the helpers. Residents tend to blame the few, helpers think in terms of the many 'problem families' they encounter daily. The same difference in experience may underlie the strong feeling of Centre workers about local authority housing policy. A survey of opinions such as the present one cannot uncover the true situation regarding placement of people on housing waiting lists, but it may well be the case that Centre workers have evidence for their acquiescence in a widely-held belief.

The mothers are more fatalistic than the helpers about the possibility of removing the stigma attaching to residence in this area. The helpers may be of the opinion that modifications in local authority housing policy would go some way towards this end; they may even go so far as to hope that their own work there is not merely therapeutic but also prevents 'social problems' and alters the image of the district in which they perform their missionary functions.

When asked about the difficulties attendant upon their own work in the vicinity, the Centre workers voiced many causes for dissatisfaction. They found little opportunity to develop casework relationships with clients and were continually reduced to providing desperate expedients for people in desperate financial straits. A small minority of the workers considered that it was an important part of their job to point out to clients the details of their welfare rights. But the main reaction was of dislike at having constantly to encounter 'demanding' clients, whose 'deeper' needs they felt unable properly to probe and treat.

VIEWS OF LOCAL FESTIVAL SOCIETY

Finally, there is the remaining major group of helpers, the members of the local Festival Society. How do they fit into the picture? They are a much more hopeful group than either the young mothers or the social workers. Local residents themselves, they resolutely refuse to subscribe to the outsiders' viewpoint on their home territory, and all their activities and public utterances are directed to stressing the positive aspects of the community's life. Although their function as festival organisers is limited to a summer season, they maintain the title and the aura of festivity, rejoicing in the human resources which they can command and organising a wide variety of social welfare activities. If they do feel any stigma attaching to residence in the area, it has only been sufficient to stimulate reactions designed to remove offending labels and replace them with new and creditable associations.

It should be pointed out in passing that the activities of a group such as this local Festival Society are by no means unique in Scotland. Ever since the depression of the 1930s, Gala Day Committees in many working-class communities have engaged in activities of a very similar sort, arranging for summer fêtes for children, Christmas parties for the elderly and other good works expressive of social concern for society's dependent members. However, in a community which is self-contained and predominantly working-class, the articulate and socially concerned minority do not feel themselves to be struggling against a stereotype imposed from outside their own group. The members of the Festival Society in this Edinburgh ward resent the persistent implication that their area is 'different' and 'worse' than others. Such considerations are a tiresome irrelevance, distracting attention from their necessary task of improving local conditions. However, they can never fully escape their situation in a status system or ranked order of desirable housing areas within the city and they are obliged to fight with constant determination to secure a better place in the sun. (The full implications of this kind of struggle cannot be discussed here, but it may be worth remarking that other 'underprivileged' housing estates in the city have lately been known to express resentment at the volume of social work effort, money and attention which has been lavished upon a rival area!)

CONCLUSIONS

It is not easy to summarise impressions at this stage of the work, for the study of the mothers has not yet been fully analysed and it may well demonstrate the existence of separate groups within the main sample. No attempt has been made here to represent the attitudes of the Centre workers in detail, nor have the idiosyncratic opinions of doctors, police and the rent collector been described. All that has been offered are vignettes of three views of a deprived area where different groups of people all have their own diagnosis of the cause of their personal dissatisfactions. It would be interesting but inappropriate at this stage to suggest whose diagnosis is the correct one, far less to prescribe treatment. There can, however, be little doubt that many mothers who have to live there are experiencing poverty, uncertainty and anxiety, and are faced with major obstacles to rearing children in any way fitted to compete with their contemporaries in more affluent surroundings.

REFERENCES

Craigmillar Festival Society (1971) *A Community on the Move*, Report of the Craigmillar Festival Society, 1970–1, Edinburgh.
Ebie, J. C. (1971) 'A multidisciplinary social casework centre with a staff psychiatrist', *The Health Services and Mental Health Administration Health Reports* 86, pp. 863–6.
Goffman, E. (1968) *Stigma*, Penguin Books Ltd, Harmondsworth.
Hope, K. (1969) 'A guide to social investment', *Applied Social Studies*, 1, pp. 21–8.
Pahl, R. E., ed. (1968) *Readings in Urban Sociology*, Commonwealth and International Library, Pergamon Press, Oxford.
Philip, A. E. and J. W. McCulloch (1966) 'Use of social indices in psychiatric epidemiology', *British Journal of Preventive and Social Medicine*, 23, pp. 111–15.
Scottish Housing Advisory Committee (1970), *Council House Communities: a Policy for Progress*, Scottish Development Department, Edinburgh.
Stein, L. and S. A. Sklaroff (1952) 'The health of an urban community', *British Journal of Preventive and Social Medicine*, 6, pp. 118–51.

CHAPTER 13

Practical aspects at local authority level

F. J. C. AMOS

It is customary, and normally useful, to attempt to define the topic which is to be explored. However, one of the principal difficulties encountered in this case is that 'environment' is an indefinite article. Any interpretation of the term will result from the individual's cultural experiences and psychological condition and there are always likely to be as many definitions of environment as there are persons involved in its discussion.

For a local authority this situation presents particular difficulties, for local government is supposedly a democratic institution, in which the good of society is achieved by carrying out the will of the majority. The majority (or at least the majority of the articulate) are now apparently concerned about the environment, but, since it cannot be defined, there is no possibility of achieving a consensus of opinion and acting accordingly. Yet, the pressure for action is great and local government cannot remain inactive.

Probably, as a consequence of the pragmatic character of local government, a way out of this dilemma has been found by fragmenting the environment and its treatment into a number of constituent parts. This solution has many pitfalls and shortcomings. The first and most important is that the whole environment is greater than the sum of its parts and, by subdivision, not only is the synoptic value lost, but the treatment of individual components may be positively harmful to other components. The second, and almost equally serious, effect of fragmentation by local government is that the subdivisions tend to be located in similar positions to the traditional divisions between departmental responsibilities and between professional specialisms. Consequently, aspects which are not the central concern of a department or well-established profession, tend to be neglected by local authorities.

The practice of subdivision presents particular problems and frustrations for the planner in local government. In the first place his training to make synoptic examinations of conditions makes him particularly sensitive to the need to protect, maintain and improve the environment. Yet, the terms of reference of his own and other departments deprive the planner of the opportunity to take or stimulate the necessary action. The second difficulty for the planner is that, in popular usage, the term 'planner' is applied in an all-embracing sense with the result that, in public participation exercises, he is held answerable for many things outside his control. His inability to deal with matters outside his terms of reference thereby reduces the utility of public participation and the credibility of local government.

These difficulties raise questions about the infrastructure of local government and the role of planners, which are not the subject of this chapter. However, it is not possible to discuss the practical aspects of environmental quality without referring to these matters.

THE USE OF STANDARDS

Notwithstanding the hazards of fragmentation, the establishment of universally accepted criteria is a great stimulus to action by public authorities. Public money is always scarce in relation to the opportunities and the pressures for its use, and decision makers are constantly seeking objective indicators of the greatest need and of the effectiveness of alternative courses of action.

The Roskill Commission is an elephantine illustration of the need to make comparative measurements which is felt by decision makers, and this is instanced more generally by the widespread adoption of new management techniques by local government. Amongst these comparative techniques one frequently finds what is sometimes called 'gap analysis', that is to say, an assessment of the difference between that which exists and that which is desirable. In such exercises the difficulty most commonly encountered is that there is no indicator of what may be regarded as socially acceptable minimum standards.

In some fields, standards have been established, such as: daylight and sunlight codes; stability of buildings in the event of fire; public health dwelling standards and, to a lesser degree, tolerable levels of atmospheric pollution and noise. However, in other fields it seems that no progress at all has been made in the establishment of standards, and it may be worth while considering where standards might have some value.

First there is the question of traffic safety. No standards exist for the tolerable levels of death or injury on residential, principal, trunk or motorway routes. Yet, setting aside all emotional considerations, it has already been shown to be reasonably straightforward to show the economic costs of death or injury and, by setting these against the costs of prevention, it should be possible to establish a minimum standard of prevention. Since all major highways already have to have an econmic justification, the extension of the practice would not appear to create substantially new precedents and it should bring some rationality into arguments about the cost of safety measures.

In an entirely different field one might seek to establish the tolerable incidence of deaths from hypothermia. Those concerned with the built environment may argue that this is a welfare problem, but it would be equally true to say that the incidence has been increased by housing those elderly who are also poor in dwellings which are too spacious, which are inadequately insulated against heat loss, and which have excessively expensive heating systems.

Similarly, what are tolerable levels of mental ill-health or vandalism? While not subscribing to theories of architectural determinism, there seems to be a *prima facie* case for contending that environment affects the incidence of these social malfunctions. Furthermore, if one sees the environment as a vehicle of human satisfaction then death, ill-health, stress and damage to property are likely to be the cause of greater public concern than the niceties of architectural design.

If the first use of standards is to indicate where action is needed, the second and consequential use is the identification of appropriate action. There is little value in knowing that something is seriously wrong if one does not know how it may be put right, and at what cost. The state of knowledge about preventive and remedial measures is uneven and there seems to be an implicit acceptance of the need to improve our knowledge. There seems, however, to be less awareness of the need to study the economic implications. But, when resources are limited, costs may play a crucial role.

The development of standards brings in its train another risk which should not be overlooked. There will always be a pressure for humanistic and prestigious reasons to steadily raise minimum standards and, if this pressure is unchecked, there is a real danger that situations or people will sink into a category which is without hope. Currently one sees this situation in relation to multiple deprivation. Certain families fall below the standard which qualifies them for public housing: they fall below the standard where social security benefits can make good their economic deficiencies, and they fall below the standard of education or ability which would ensure an earned income and so they are forced into a vicious and degrading downward spiral.

THE ADMINISTRATIVE PROBLEMS OF IMPROVEMENT

Even if the intrinsic problems of standards can be overcome, the problems of achievement by local government are formidable and vary according to the subject of control and the local conditions.

An example may be drawn from the author's own local authority in relation to air pollution. Liverpool City Council has adopted a clean air policy and has now converted fifty-nine per cent of its area to smokeless zones. But, just outside the local authority area, to the south-east, there is a group of chemical industries which emit large volumes of smoke and noxious fumes; to the east there is an oil refinery and to the north a man-made fibre factory, both of which affect extensive areas with offensive smells. In the case of the chemical industries, the responsible local authority is too small and too dependent on the industries to take rigorous action and, in the other cases, the smells, although thoroughly offensive, do not fall within any legislative definition.

Apart from problems of boundary and legal definition, there are also problems of responsibility and consistency. For example, conditions under which people work in factories are prescribed in the Factories Act and enforced by the central government, whereas other places of employment are covered by the Shops, Offices and Railway Premises Act, which is enforced by the local authorities. Consequently, any decisions to revise the standards or control of working conditions cannot be dealt with comprehensively.

The decision whether to adopt and work towards any or all of the many environmental standards now being established is left to the discretion of local authorities, and the arguments of pressure groups are well known in relation to smokeless zones, conservation orders and the provisions of community and recreational facilities. It is often the case that the authorities which are in greatest need of environmental improvement are those which are the most financially impoverished and which have the lowest level of aspiration. Thus, those in the greatest need have the least opportunity and the least will to effect improvements.

THE ACHIEVEMENT OF IMPROVEMENTS

The methods by which a local planning authority achieves its environmental improvements are manifold, and much will depend upon the influence which it can exercise outside its statutory powers, through good relationships with other departments and developers.

There are, however, certain matters over which it has mandatory powers and, although they are now commonplace, the importance of the right to control density, natural lighting and external appearance should not be underestimated. On the other hand, one must remember that an over-rigorous exercise of an authority's power can offend architects, discourage innovation, inhibit needed development and bring planning into disrepute. It is not always appreciated that most development is the product of the interaction between the interests of the individual (the developer) and society (the local authority) and a good product is only likely to be achieved if the two parties enter into constructive collaboration. To this end, a T.P.I./R.I.B.A. Joint Working Party on Local Plans issued some advice as to the most useful form which such documents might take.

Improvements which are effected through the authorities' statutory powers are mainly confined to areas where change (i.e., development) is proposed by a public or private agency and, in these cases, the initiative rests with the agency in the first instance. Local authorities can, however, effect improvements through direct action and by inducement.

The most obvious method of direct action on a large scale is by compulsory purchase and subsequent development, either by the authority or under the strict control of a lease. But the authority may also act directly in other ways. For instance, it may reclaim and restore derelict land, it may impose preservation orders on buildings and trees and, most importantly, it can influence the work of housing, highways, parks and other departments, so that the direct actions of these departments also bring about improvements or, at least, inhibit deterioration.

The local authority can also conserve the environment by inducement. Probably the most significant operation in this field will be in relation to General Improvement Areas, but, in addition, of course, grants may be made towards the preservation of buildings or places of character.

One of the great difficulties which is frequently encountered in the design of the built environment is the lack of suitable skills. It seems that architecture has tended to concentrate its attention on the individual building, while a substantial amount of planning effort has been turned away from three-dimensional planning and towards strategic issues and management. The result is that there are now few people who are both able and willing to give their undivided attention to a great number of minor projects which individually are of little consequence, but collectively create environmental chaos. Into this category fall accommodation, works for roads, the treatment of space about buildings, the design and installation of street furniture and the design of boundary walls.

But, even in this well-established case, local planning authorities encounter serious difficulties. Wind tunnel tests can only be secured on a fee basis which represents an abnormal (and therefore contentious) cost in processing applications. Additionally, in general terms wind tunnels are only capable of testing small groups of buildings on a trial-and-error basis; techniques and equipment have not yet developed to the point where aerodynamic design for urban areas can be derived from first principles.

At a larger scale also, there is much public interest in the character of a town or locality and to a large degree this depends on visual appearances. Many planners would very much like to establish a policy to maintain local character, but again the necessary skill does not seem to exist.

THE MAINTENANCE OF THE ENVIRONMENT

Very often the quality of the environment depends rather more upon the care which is given to maintenance than upon the quality of individual buildings. In an era in which maintenance costs of all types are rising, and in which we are likely to keep many old buildings of all qualities for a considerable period, this topic deserves serious consideration.

With regard to new development, the Civic Trust in its Award Scheme for 1971 had cause to remark very critically upon the unkempt appearance of many new projects; uncut grass, litter and graffiti detracted from the appearance of many projects. This criticism poses two alternative questions. First, are buildings and their environs being designed in a way which creates intolerable burdens in maintenance? The other question is whether new developments are so ill-matched to the needs of their users that there results a rapid deterioration in building and environment. So little work has been done in this field that there are no clear answers, yet these are questions which cannot be ignored.

CONCLUSION

These last remarks about maintenance bring the argument full circle to the question of synoptic appraisal and action. Local authorities have considerable statutory powers and administrative resources. Despite the plea for more information, much could be achieved by a more consistent and economic operation within local authorities. Professionalism and trade union demarcation have led to duplication and waste. A building surveyor checks that the building regulations have been complied with, while a planner does the same for a planning permission. A highways man cuts grass on the road verge, while a housing employee cuts grass in the adjoining estate. While resources are wasted in this way, opportunities are lost through failure to integrate operations. Schools are not designed for dual use because nobody has the job of identifying the non-school needs. Special buildings have to be provided for the handicapped because nobody has the responsibility of ensuring that all buildings contain those minor additional features which would make them suitable for able-bodied and handicapped alike.

Similarly, traditional local government organisational patterns tend to make expenditure on environmental issues the smallest and most 'Cinderella-like' items in large budgets containing major prestigious projects.

It must not be overlooked that, if authorities do become more effective and more influential, they will be able to do so only at the price of individual liberty and the public will submit to further restraints only if they are satisfied that the benefits are greater than the cost.

For the professional this means that he must be sure that the work he does is of the highest quality. But there is a further educational problem. At present, public awareness and understanding of environmental matters is very limited. If a more constructive public attitude is to be developed, considerable foundation work must be built into primary and secondary school curricula.

The problems are partly those of a new kind of planning which merges into environmental management. This planning extends beyond the physical environment to the social and economic objectives of the people in an area. It is not a task which is entirely the province of the planner. At present there is an administrative/organisational void in local government which can be partly filled by planners, but the achievement of an improved environment depends largely upon a recognition of the need for corporate action on the part of all concerned.

CHAPTER 14

Lies, damned lies and decision-making

E. BROOKS

The democratic ruler is inevitably Janus-faced. As a creature of conflict and political polarisation he is forced to encourage the clash of sectional interests. Yet, as a practical administrator burdened with office, he has to reconcile the warring factions, at least to the extent necessary for an effective implementation of his party's policies.

Such chronic schizophrenia naturally arouses bewilderment and even cynicism among the ruled. They see 'the public interest' being glibly identified with narrow class objectives. The more discerning recognise the semantic sleight-of-hand which conjures away the pork barrel. But such is the mystique of statistical gimmickry that few of the electorate have yet realised that so-called rational political decision-making is a contradiction in terms.

The present craze for rational decision-making is, of course, a comparatively recent phenomenon. In the good old days politicians were content to play with their matchsticks. They planned not, neither did they forecast. Instead they followed their hunches, clutched the Hidden Hand, and prayed. Not for them the rigours of cost-benefit analysis; instead that simple wisdom which defined economic development as going 'on and on and on, and up and up and up'. Perhaps, had Mr. Ramsay MacDonald been asked to distil his experience of the business cycle, he might have elegantly added that what goes up must come down and down and down.

In these quantitative days, such felicitous vagueness is disparaged. Decision-makers are now exhorted to make rational choices between explicitly defined and costed alternatives. Even when they obstinately refuse to dispense with subjective judgments, they are required to expose their hidden motives and implicit priorities and have them explicitly defined and weighted. Following such statistical deep therapy, executives are expected to behave in a manner befitting *homo sapiens*.

ATTEMPTS TO IMPROVE DECISION-MAKING

Such exorcism of the Id from the flanks of Whitehall is clearly a high priority in our scientific and technological age, and two major rituals have gradually been introduced for this purpose. First, there has been the institutional ritual to achieve better governmental and parliamentary surveillance of the decision-making process. Secondly, there has been the methodological ritual to improve the technical manipulation of the data or input handled by that same process. Both rituals, however, form part of the same order of service, which may be briefly titled Democratic Accountability. It is a demanding service, particularly in a society whose professional experts become increasingly *incommunicado* behind both their esoteric languages and their forbiddingly insulated hierarchies of power.

A simple illustration of these current dilemmas of communication and control can be seen in the history of the Concorde as written in successive volumes of the Reports of the Public Accounts Committee (P.A.C.) of the House of Commons. The P.A.C. is a Gladstonian survival which has for more than a century undertaken post-mortems of such financial extravagance and inefficient cost-control as have been revealed by the Comptroller and Auditor-General's Department. Although sometimes criticised as a public watch-dog which barks only years after the burglar has fled, the deterrent value of such inexorable—though belated—identification of guilty spending departments should not be under-estimated.

Yet it is exceptionally difficult for such a committee to discipline major long-term projects involving sophisticated technology. Such projects as a supersonic civil airliner or a uranium gas centrifuge are obviously complicated, perhaps even on the frontiers of knowledge, and the difficulties of scrutiny are compounded when (as in both cases mentioned) more than one government is involved in the research and development. The gestation period of the research and development (R. & D.) may be upwards of a decade, as in the case of Concorde, and this does not lend itself to the 'posthumous' annual review of internally audited and externally checked accounts of completed programmes. To put it crudely, some of the blemishes may have been carried forward or temporarily masked, and might not stand revealed, warts and all, until several more years of escalating expenditure have passed by.

In any case, even when the dimensions of the escalation have been revealed (Fig. 1), it is difficult to seek clarification of such increases and of the oddly inconsistent criteria on which they are based without straying into technical problems beyond the competence of a strictly financial committee. From such impotence has grown the demand for so-called efficiency auditing, in which quasi-judicial procedures of a gladiatorial character (as in planning enquiries) could be employed to set technical experts at each other's throats.

Apart from querying whether such adversary techniques produce more light than heat, there remains the problem for a lay audience of comprehending the incomprehensible. Even straightforward financial scrutiny in the old sense is becoming ever more complicated by the sophisticated accountancy procedures being adopted throughout industry and government. The Members of Parliament serving on the Public Expenditure Committee (P.E.C.), set up by the incoming

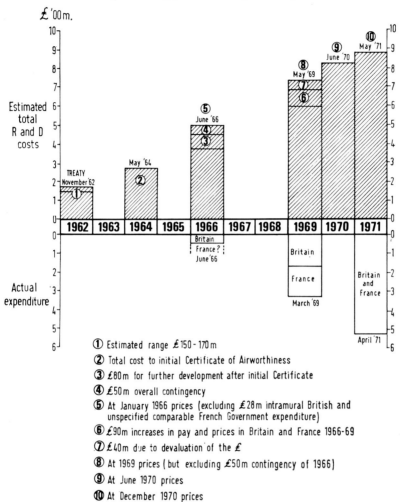

Fig. 1 Concorde: escalation of costs 1962–71
(Excluding production expenditure)

① Estimated range £150 - 170 m
② Total cost to initial Certificate of Airworthiness
③ £80 m for further development after initial Certificate
④ £50 m overall contingency
⑤ At January 1966 prices (excluding £28 m intramural British and
   unspecified comparable French Government expenditure)
⑥ £90 m increases in pay and prices in Britain and France 1966-69
⑦ £40 m due to devaluation of the £
⑧ At 1969 prices (but excluding £50 m contingency of 1966)
⑨ At June 1970 prices
⑩ At December 1970 prices

administration of 1970 to improve forward control of spending programmes, have to grapple with the language of discounted cash flow,
critical path analysis and input-output matrices. Yet even when
M.P.s, and perhaps local councillors, too, have attended crash courses
in statistical decision theory, or output budgeting, or the elementary
ideas of games theory, they are unlikely to be able to outwit the professional experts serving the lobbies and pressure groups.

Against this background, and confirmed by the most cursory glance
at the graph of expenditure on Concorde, it is not difficult to understand the urge towards rationality in decision-making. Concorde may
be justified as a disguised form of urban subsidy to Bristol, or as a sop to

French national pride; but it seems highly 'irrational' to spend a thousand million pounds developing a plane which cannot remotely hope to break even financially and will never recoup its R. & D. cost. Some experts, however, are prepared to give it the potential to wreck the atmosphere and destroy the human race, and in that case the billion pounds will have proven highly cost effective.

Given the disconcerting ability of the experts to differ, pressures have mounted to restrict their ability to mislead us, consciously or inadvertently. It is argued that if democracy is a system designed to safeguard society from the absolute corruption of absolute power, then it must devise appropriate checks and balances for professional élites.

At this point the institutional rituals being undertaken by the present

Fig. 2 Parliamentary accountability and the role of the Central Policy Review Staff.

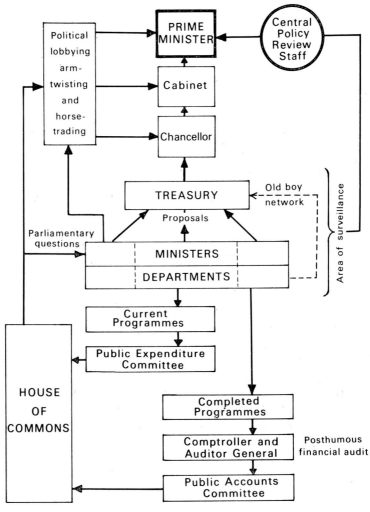

Conservative Government may be examined in more detail, and in particular to those outlined originally in the White Paper *Reorganisation of Central Government* (H.M.S.O., 1970) with its proposal for a Central Policy Review Staff (C.P.R.S.) to be attached to the Cabinet Office. The C.P.R.S. has two objects: first, as a central planning unit located at the apex of the constitutional hierarchy of responsibility. Second, it enables decisions on the allocation of public spending between departments to be taken in a much more rational way than hitherto (Shanks, 1970).

Perhaps this approach has some echoes of the P.A.C.'s role in setting an expert to catch an expert. As is shown in Figure 2, the Prime Minister can (in theory) outflank those linkages in the decision-making process which have traditionally given the Treasury such overwhelming importance in the government machine. The resilience of the Treasury was shown in the skilled euthanasia of the Department of Economic Affairs, which left the Chancellor alone on the commanding heights of economic management and resource allocation, and only time will tell if the new C.P.R.S. can breach the rampart of intellectual mandarins which presently looms over the spending departments. The intention, however, is clearly to subject sectional interests to the discipline of external scrutiny, and this, it is argued, should permit wiser allocations of scarce resources among conflicting priorities.

The C.P.R.S. is presumably a pilot venture, but it seems clear that it is not intended to conduct programme analysis. The P.A.C., as has been shown, was not competent to carry out any such efficiency audit, nor did the former Estimates Committee ever have the staff to perform such a role. The P.E.C. could perhaps shoulder such responsibilities in time, but only if adequate professional staff are provided.

AMERICAN EXPERIENCE

The scale of the task can be estimated by reference to American experience. The former Budget Bureau in the U.S.A., originally formed in 1921, was replaced in July 1970 by the Office of Management and Budget (O.M.B.). The Director of this office serves in effect as a counterpoise to the Cabinet Ministers who plead their special interests and, with a staff of 525, he can mount a formidable critique of any tendentious lobbying.

Figure 3 attempts to depict the threefold role of the O.M.B. (Thomas, 1970). First, it helps the Treasury and the Council of Economic Advisers to formulate over-all policy. Secondly, it is the 'filter' which checks on the proposals flowing from Congress and the executive branch of government to the White House. This filter is specific to the American system of divided powers, but it may have some resemblance to the British Government's innovations discussed above.

Finally, the O.M.B. has been instructed to place a greater emphasis on fiscal and programme analysis than had hitherto been done by the

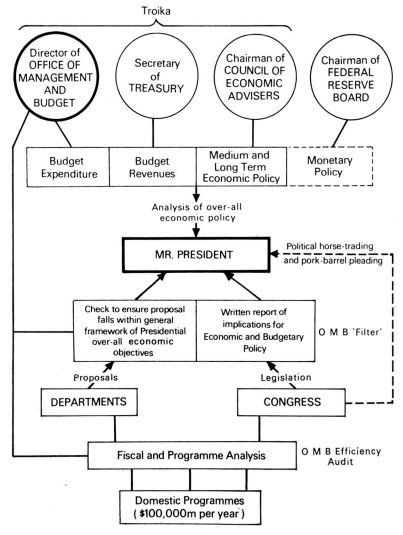

Fig. 3 The role of the Office of Management and Budget in the U.S.A.

Budget Bureau. This is no small task, given the well over one thousand domestic programmes which are currently being handled by some 57 Federal Departments and Agencies. As a precaution against special relationships developing with particular interest groups representing this multiplicity of activities, the O.M.B.'s professional staff is rotated regularly.

By so cutting the lobbies down to size, the O.M.B. enables the President to walk that much taller. This serves as a reminder that politics is about power, and that the White House is no ivory tower for scholars. Instead, it is the focus of acquisitive ambition and the fount of patronage, the hub of a capitalist society where morality is the fig-leaf of business ethics and the Mafia is reputed to be the biggest business of all.

In his democratic manipulation of contending forces, the President must be adept in the art of pressing the flesh, sometimes until it hurts. But if henceforth, in addition to rolling out the pork barrel, he can roll out the latest I.B.M. computations of the O.M.B., then he will be enabled not so much to divide and rule, as to blind with statistics and slide rule.

The relevance of this to the new methodological rituals is apparent. Both the British and American experiments in improving executive surveillance are rooted in the assumption that the old and crudely intuitive methods of political decision-making give scope for 'irrational' choices in terms both of means and of ends. Conversely, a scientific methodology is deemed to be attainable, which will, by charting the contracted cost-effectiveness of various potential policies, permit choice of the right goals and the best methods of attaining them.

ACCOUNTING AND COST BENEFIT

This is the conventional wisdom which has led to increasingly sophisticated cost-benefit analyses and which reached its apotheosis in the monumental Roskill study of the Third London Airport. To critics who are sceptical of such exercises, the stock reply is to argue the need for still more elaborate work to refine understanding and improve the models of reality. Since it seems academic treason to dissent from the plea for greater knowledge, the conventional wisdom has not seriously been challenged; but, since Roskill, a growing anxiety has begun to be expressed about the basic approach.

This anxiety is part of a wider unease throughout the accountancy profession, which has become focussed on the presentation and auditing of company accounts. In part, the criticism is of lack of consistency in the interpretation of such concepts as stocks, depreciation and profits; but increasingly this lack of consistency is being seen as a reflection of possibly fundamental ambiguities in the meaning of even the most apparently straightforward terms.

A characteristic example of the lack of consistency was shown in a recent study of the treatment of investment grants (Greener, 1969, p. 417). Of the twenty-five firms examined, seventeen admitted to receiving grants. Of these, nine deducted them from assets and depreciated on the basis of net cost, while eight credited them to reserve. Again, among the latter group, there were no less than four different methods of so crediting the grants. Moreover, it was found that at least four firms of auditors were prepared to endorse different methods when examining their various clients' books.

The more general, and perhaps inherent ambiguities involved, have been graphically suggested in *The Sunday Times* Business Supplement (Kellner and Searjeant, 1970). Figure 4 is based upon the hypothetical

Fig. 4 The alternative balance sheets of Twoface Corporation.

START OF YEAR ONE		
Assets £5m cash represented by £5m share capital		
ASSETS AT END OF YEAR ONE		
£	FIXED ASSETS	£
400,000	Freehold H.Q.	400,000
408,000	Depreciation of toy plant and machinery costing £510,000	459,000
	20% on reducing balance basis / 10% on straight line basis	
60,000	Depreciation of representatives' cars costing £90,000	75,000
	Over 3 years / Over 6 years	
800,000	Crash barriers. On rental at cost of £1m less 20% depreciation / 14 year rental agreement capitalised at 7 times annual rent and depreciated over 14 years	1,300,000
1,668,000	TOTAL FIXED ASSETS	2,234,000
	CURRENT ASSETS	
2,000,000	Work in progress on power station. At direct cost / At direct cost plus expected profit on work already completed	3,000,000
300,000	Material stocks for toy factory	300,000
500,000	Stocks of toys. At lower of cost or realisable value with possibility that product may be changed / At cost because product still being sold at profit	700,000
1,100,000	Debtors of toy business. After special bad debt provisions for boutiques / After normal bad debt provisions	1,200,000
200,000	Cash (from net rental income)	200.000
4,100,000	TOTAL GROSS CURRENT ASSETS	5,400,000
1,000,000	Less creditors of toy business	1,000,000
3,100,000	TOTAL NET CURRENT ASSETS	4,400,000
4,768,000	TOTAL NET ASSETS	6,634,000
5,000,000	Represented by share capital	5,000,000
PROFIT AND LOSS ACCOUNT		
232,000	DEFICIT SURPLUS	1,634,000

alternative balance-sheets which were drawn up for one and the same imaginary company, Twoface Corporation, which began operations with £5 million share capital in £1 shares. Having bought a freehold headquarters for £400,000, it used the remainder to start three businesses: a construction division to build a power station over three years; a toy division selling trendy adult amusements via boutiques; and a division which rented crash barriers to the Ministry of Transport. Although, as the authors accept, the resultant alternative balance sheets after the first year's operations involve a measure of oversimplification, it is argued that 'basically both results are legitimate. Indeed possible sources of even bigger differences, like research and development costs, overheads and inflation of stock values have been avoided.'

The enormous contrast in the results is evident. The left-hand balance-sheet would lead to a share price of perhaps $87\frac{1}{2}$p; the other result in a price of roughly £3. And the truly daunting fact is that neither balance-sheet is more 'rational' than the other. The implications of such a profound confusion over accounting concepts have long been recognised by academic critics, and it might be argued that, if their various proposals for, say, distinguishing between tangible cash flows and the more uncertain items which reflect more-or-less arbitrary expectations were to be implemented, then much of the present chaos would vanish.

Perhaps this would be the case but, until such (arbitrary?) rules of consistency have been adopted, the scope for misleading shareholders—and taxpayers too—remains serious. Indeed, the experience of take-over battles and bankruptcies in recent years favours a view of accountancy, like war, as nothing more than the continuation of politics by other means.

The more traditional political arena, meanwhile, continues to see the massacre of the innocents in such financial matters. Figures quoted in Parliament illustrate the point. Costs are frequently compared across time with little regard for constant prices, and discount rates to refine long-term expenditure programmes are applied (if at all) in a random fashion. The Concorde saga is rich in such inconsistencies—a simple example (see Fig. 1) being the £50 million 'overall contingency' which suddenly appeared in 1966 and equally mysteriously vanished in 1969.

The relevance of such apparent pedantry to the stuff of politics may seem remote to some M.P.s. Yet these accounting concepts are fundamental to the bread-and-butter issues of the costs of electricity, coal and gas, the calculation of the 'economic' rents of council houses, or the allocation of costs between socially justified railways as distinct from economically profitable ones.

Let it be conceded, then, that more consistency and greater semantic precision may be of value in exposing the special pleading and even trickery of the interest groups. There still remains the fundamental difficulty that even when assumptions are explicit and rigorously

defined, they may be little more than a best guess liable to be disproved
in the event. For example, how can anyone meaningfully calculate the
generating life (and therefore the depreciation charges) of an advanced
gas-cooled reactor nuclear power station?

In reality, of course, the spectrum of uncertainty within which the
attempt is made to quantify assumptions and plans for the future
widens exponentially down the years ahead. The variables (plus the
presently unknowable factors) multiply in an ever more complex mix
of possibilities. *Pace* the futurologists, nothing in social or political
development is inevitable, as is confirmed each time a President is
assassinated or yesterday's opinion polls confounded. Yet we cannot
entirely ignore the modern Oracles of Delphi, for the danger of their
seemingly harmless astrology is that their incantations, like those of
witchdoctors in more heathen societies, can induce a sense of fatalism
which then confirms their original reading of the entrails.

BENEFITS FOR WHOM?

Moreover, as is increasingly well understood, the prophet is himself
a creature of desire. Futurology is not just guesswork, it is an index of
the mores of its practitioners. Thus, to those who are willing victims of
the technological imperative ('You can't stop progress'), arguments
about the validity of such an ultimate social strategy tend to be dismissed as unquantifiable theology. It is not entirely unfair in this connection to recall the Roskill Commission, whose brief automatically
assumed that the benefits of having a Third London Airport automatically outweighed the dis-benefits.

Benefits, however, even in the restricted sense employed by Roskill,
are an elusive concept to quantify in a society possessing income contrasts. Figure 5, which is based upon the example given by E. J.
Mishan to show the relevance of income distribution to optimal positions, illustrates a conflict situation between A, who owns a house with
a pleasant view, and B, who owns land on which he is contemplating
seeking planning permission to build (Mishan, 1969, pp. 92–3). It will
be clear that the rich tend to get their own way and, moreover, can
make this happy outcome seem the optimal one in any conflict situation.

A similar point is made by J. Adams in his devastating critique of the
Roskill Commission (Adams, 1970). Indeed, if the business man's
journey time is to be so highly valued, whereas Westminster Abbey,
to use the Commission's criterion, is worth no more than its insured
value of £1·5 million, it can convincingly be argued that the best site
for the airport would be Hyde Park.

In other words, it is not simply a problem of intruding a scale of
value judgments into weighting of objectives, which means trying to
quantify the unquantifiable. There is the additional problem of deciding
which particular scale of value judgments, relating to individuals'
differing capacities to translate their desires into monetary terms, is to

Fig. 5 Alternative optimal outcome of conflict situation.

ALTERNATIVE OPTIMAL OUTCOMES OF CONFLICT SITUATION
(After E.J.Mishan)

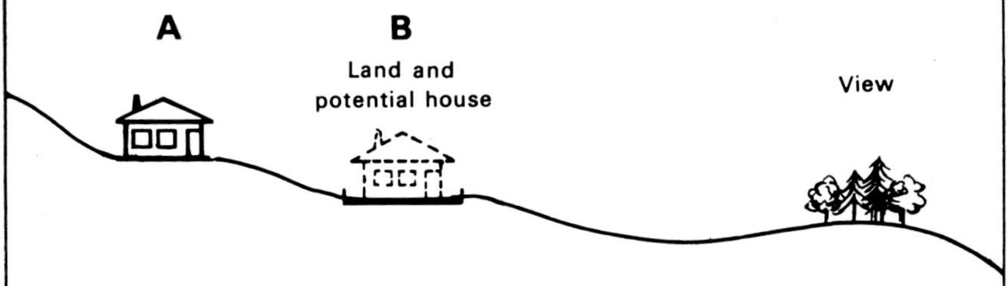

A richer than **B**	**B** richer than **A**
A's valuation of view £2,000	**B**'s valuation of successful planning application to build £1,500
B's 'bribery' price for building elsewhere £1,500	**A**'s 'bribery' price for withdrawing objections £1,000
A compensates **B** to maintain status quo £1,750	**B** compensates **A** to alter status quo £1,250
Both gain by maintaining status quo.	Both gain by altering status quo
Present situation optimal	Present situation sub-optimal

be used in the weighting procedure. As Adams puts it: '. . . the values which the Commission attaches to non-material benefits reveal a very strong bias which is not only materialistic and philistine, but also discriminatory against low income groups.'

To which, of course, one can respond, 'So what?' Is there any logical or rational reason why the Commission should endorse the Sermon on the Mount? Can the virtues, if such they be, of poverty, humility and chastity be weighted? And, even if they could, should such weighting be used?

Even to pose the question is to reveal the absurdity of seeking 'rationality' in political decision-making. Political choices may indeed be clarified, in at least some of their future implications, by rigorous and scientific analysis using mathematical models. But to assume that sophisticated statistics will obviate the ultimately ethical and moral beliefs which are central to the political drama is to confuse means with ends and perhaps fatally blur the distinction between them.

PLANNING MODELS AND SUBJECTIVE JUDGMENT

Perhaps the most appropriate way to summarise the argument of this chapter is to show how outwardly imposing mathematical planning models are simply the distillation in symbolic form of fundamentally subjective judgments. This can be illustrated by a formula developed by G. A. McBride in his account of the methodology for formulating investment plans, using the Appalachian Development Highway system as an example (McBride, 1970, p. 245):

$$\text{Max} \sum_{j=1}^{m} \sum_{i=1}^{n} \left[\frac{(w_{iji}\bar{B} - \bar{M}_{ji})(1 - (1/(1+r)^{T}))}{r} \right] - K_{j}$$

$$\text{Subject to} \sum_{j=1}^{m} K_{j} \leqslant K^{*}.$$

This formulation represents a situation where there are m projects and n objectives. McBride's framework simultaneously treats multiple objectives, specifically economic efficiency (net contribution to national income) and income redistribution (net contribution to regional income in Appalachia). Either can be maximised without undue concern about the other. Alternatively, the relative importance of each distinct objective might be explicitly specified by weighting the net contributions which each project makes to each objective within the over-all programme. Having so weighted these values (e.g., a benefit $ accruing to Appalachia is 'worth' maybe two, three or four times more than a $ benefit accruing elsewhere), the projects would be selected which maximise the weighted sum.

Thus $w_{i}B_{ji}$, which represents the weighted benefits to objective i attributable to development project j, represents an essentially political decision about the relative values of Appalachia and other regions of the U.S.A.

Next, M_{ji} represents the current costs of operation, maintenance and replacement associated with generating the benefits or contributions to objective i from project j. Clearly this is at best an educated guess, particularly vulnerable to error over, say, a fifty year life.

K_{j} is the capital costs, including the opportunity costs of resources. Again, this is very much an estimate, with opportunity costs notoriously difficult to calculate except on the basis of a host of hypothetical scenarios.

r is the interest rate chosen for the discount operator, an arbitrary figure also notoriously difficult to calculate in public investment decision-making.

T is the expected life period of the investment and, as with the A.G.R. stations discussed earlier, it is hard to see how any precise figure can be fed into the calculations.

Nevertheless, however arbitrary both r and T are, they are used to calculate the single present value discount operator which, for simplicity, has been applied by McBride to the mean annual benefits and operating costs.

Finally, it is all subject to the budgetary constraint which states that the sum of the capital costs of the individual projects ($j = 1 \ldots m$) cannot exceed the total amount K^* authorised for the entire system. K^* is a political decision, in effect the pork barrel, and might even become K^{**} if the barrel is enlarged to accommodate deficit financing.

As McBride neatly summarises the argument: 'It is shown that the outcome depends largely on the policy makers' statement of objectives, the relative values assigned to contributions to these objectives generated by the investment, and the selection of a rate of interest and economic life of the project' (ibid., p. 241). Another way of putting it is to recall the jest about the computer: 'Garbage in, Garbage out!' Which is not, of course, to say that political judgments are garbage.

REFERENCES

Adams, J. (1970) 'Westminster: the Fourth London Airport?', *Area*, 2, pp. 1–9.
Greener, M. (1969) 'Inconsistencies in auditing and accounting methods', *The Accountant*, 4th October, pp. 416–19.
Cabinet Office (1970) *Reorganisation of Central Government*, Cmd. 4506, H.M.S.O., London.
Kellner, P. and G. Searjeant (1970) 'How to give or take £5 m.', *The Sunday Times*, 6th September.
McBride, G. A., 'Policy matters in investment decision-making', *Regional Studies*, 4 (2), pp. 241–53.
Mishan, E. J. (1969) *The Costs of Economic Growth*, Penguin Books, Harmondsworth.
Shanks, M. (1970) 'A better machine for policy', *The Times*, 16th October.
Thomas, A. (1970) 'How Washington handles the budget machine', *The Times*, 16th October.